SPITFIRE ACE

SPITFIRE ACE

MARTIN DAVIDSON
&
JAMES TAYLOR

First published by Channel 4 Books
an imprint of Macmillan Publishers Ltd
20 New Wharf Road, London N1 9RR
Basingstoke and Oxford
Associated companies throughout the world
www.panmacmillan.com

ISBN 07522 2511 1

Text Copyright © Martin Davidson and James Taylor

Extract from 'Lie in the Dark and Listen' © The Estate
of Noël Coward, taken from his Collected Verse,
published by Methuen Publishing Limited.

9 8 7 6 5 4 3 2 1

A CIP catalogue record for this book is available from
the British Library.

Designed by Perfect Bound Ltd
Colour Reproduction by Aylesbury Studios Ltd
Printed by Butler and Tanner Ltd, Frome, Somerset

This book accompanies the major television
series *Spitfire Ace*, made by RDF Media for
Channel 4.

Lie in the dark and listen
It's clear tonight so they're flying high
Hundreds of them, thousands perhaps
Riding the icy, moonlit sky
Men, machinery, bombs and maps
Altimeters and guns and charts
Coffee, sandwiches, fleece-lined boots
Bones and muscles and minds and hearts
English saplings with English roots
Deep in the earth they've left below
Lie in the dark and let them go
Lie in the dark and listen.

Noël Coward

This book is dedicated to Julian Lowe, 1920-2003,
Spitfire Photo-Reconnaisance Pilot, 1942-1945.

CONTENTS

INTRODUCTION

One fine summer's day, I took my six-year-old son to

Duxford to see an air-show. I hadn't been to one since I was in my early teens, when I used to go every year to Leuchars in Scotland, armed with a camera and very wide eyes, ready to devour every plane on offer, on the ground or in the air, most of which were dangling in tiny plastic kit form from my bedroom ceiling. It was a passion, though, that fell an early and total victim to later adolescence – all-consuming one moment, a distant and embarrassing memory the next, airbrushed out of my life. Down came the posters and the Airfix models, as though they had never existed. Yet, three decades later, I was back. Not for me, of course, but for a small boy who was going through stage one of the same infatuation I had experienced all those years ago.

Nothing had changed. The ground shook as formation jets flew low and fast overhead, the tannoy bleated its hearty list of planes, manoeuvres and pilots' names. The stalls were still selling the pilots' jackets, the old aircraft magazines, and mountains of models, replicas and insignia. It was as if the whole world of historic aircraft had been simply shrink-wrapped, put in cold storage, and reanimated. My son was transfixed.

Then came the roar that shook me out of my musings, a throaty growl that had this irresistible effect on my neck. I craned round, peered up, and there it was, a splash of silhouette: the Spitfire. I wasn't the only one. Everyone was gaping upwards. I was as rooted to the spot as my son. What a wonderful thing to see and hear! It all flooded back, the same

Previous page: the two-seater
Spitfire at Duxford

Above: Nick Grace in the plane
he restored himself

encyclopediac collection of minutiae that only children have, and which you never quite lose: the fiercely partisan discrimination that absolutely thinks the Mark V is better than the Mark I; the fetish of top speeds and performance attributes. But the Spitfire did something more; it punched right through the artifice of the air-show, one of those strange events that somehow seem to exist outside time altogether. The whole of Duxford was transformed, too, from a showcase aircraft theme-park to a place that breathed real history. It was the sound of the past, and I found it simply impossible to look at the Spitfire whipping through its manoeuvres without, once again, thinking about the Battle of Britain.

There is a Spitfire on a plinth outside Edinburgh airport. It used to live by the gates opposite the old airport at Turnhouse, which had also been a fighter base during the war. Even to this day, when I pass it, I look at it and have exactly the same sequence of thoughts. Could I have flown it? Could I have been one of 'the Few'? And here I was thinking the same, all over again.

The Duxford Spitfire had returned for one last, low-level pass, and then I noticed something. This wasn't like any Spitfire I had ever seen. It had two cockpits! It was like a breach of natural law. Everyone knew Second World War Spitfires only had one cockpit.

I checked my programme. Oh, I see; it was a specially adapted Mark IX, used after the war by the Irish Air Force, before retiring to a museum. It had been bought and lovingly restored by a Spitfire enthusiast called Nick Grace, and was now being flown by his widow, Carolyn Grace. It had D-Day stripes, because it saw action over Normandy, so while not strictly speaking a Battle of Britain aircraft it was as near as dammit.

Two seats, dual control. That means *somebody could sit in the back.* And that person didn't necessarily have to be a professional pilot. It could be anyone. And that person, with a real Spitfire control column between their knees, would have what must simply be the best front-row seat on history. It would be possible for them to find out what it was like to fly a Spitfire. And then I realised. I would give anything to find out what it was like to fly a Spitfire. But more than that, I would give anything to find out what it was like to fly a Spitfire in 1940. I suspected I wasn't alone.

Another snippet of historical detail had long since lodged in my mind. It's the scene in *Battle of Britain*, the slightly flat-footed big-screen film made in 1969, when two new recruits arrive and proudly tell their commanding officer, played by Robert Shaw, they've had less than ten hours in a Spitfire. I put the two together. Things in the Battle of Britain were so bad they were actually sending up nineteen- and twenty-year-olds with barely ten hours' practice. The same question: what *must* that have been like? At nineteen, I didn't even have a driving licence. I wouldn't have lasted an afternoon, before being riddled with cannon fire and shrouded in flames.

So we wrote to Carolyn and asked her if she would be willing to participate in a television experiment. Would she let us put two young men, of the same kind of age and background as those who formed the backbone of Fighter Command in the summer of 1940, in her Spitfire, and see just what ten hours of training got you? And would she let us film it, giving us all a tantalising glimpse of what remains one of the seminal historical experiences of the twentieth century?

Remarkably, Carolyn said yes, and so many months later, on a blazing hot day, we found ourselves back at Duxford, with Carolyn's Spitfire parked on the grass waiting for her to fly it. We had chosen four young volunteers, and given them each a number of sorties in the kind of Tiger Moth their Battle of Britain predecessors would actually have used for their preliminary training. From that we narrowed our class of 2003 down to just two. And from that pair, we would then pick one, who would be given nine hours of advanced flying training on the Spitfire, not just savouring the thrill of flying this wonderful plane, but being tutored by Pete Kynsey, a close friend and associate of Carolyn

Carolyn Grace with John Sweet (left) and Dave Mallon (right), two of our twenty-first century class of Spitfire pilots

and a world-class aerobatics pilot with special interest in, and expertise with, Second World War aircraft. He had taught Carolyn to fly her Spitfire, now he would do the same with our twenty-first century pilot.

By this point, we had all realised that while the Spitfire was interesting as a machine, it was the events that it took part in that make it truly fascinating. Just seeing people at the controls of a Spitfire wasn't enough. The Spitfire was important not just because of what it could do, but because of what it did. It fought, alongside the Hurricanes and other assorted planes of Fighter Command in the Battle of Britain. It's why, finally, the Spitfire is so compelling a piece of machinery in a way that its precursors, the Schneider Trophy-winning sea-planes, just aren't. The Spitfire saw service throughout the Second World War, and beyond. Indeed, of the twenty-two types made, only the first two featured in the Battle of Britain. But it's the association of the Spitfire with the 'Few' of 1940 that makes it historically significant.

It's still the most famous air battle in the history of warfare. Other air battles may have lasted longer, or involved more aircraft, or more sophisticated technology – but none of them competes with the Battle of Britain for drama and immediacy. You, and three thousand like you, are all that stand between the British homeland and the German armada of bombers and fighters, many of whom are veterans with hundreds more hours logged than you. Apparently outnumbered, outgunned, but never outflown, the RAF seemed to come close to defeat, but hung on long enough to defy the odds and save Britain from invasion.

Carolyn Grace's Mark IX dual-
seater Spitfire, ML407

At the heart of the story is one particular figure, a legend ever since. The RAF fighter pilot. And one particular plane, resting in a position of almost mythic historical glamour. The Supermarine Spitfire. They still stir the blood, more than sixty years later. Together they fought the classic dogfights of the imagination, not aircraft firing missiles at each other from miles apart, but close up and personal, combat flying at its most visceral: weaving, diving, banking, closing in on enemy aircraft, and shooting fourteen seconds' worth of ammunition with all their heart.

Of course, it was undoubtedly more complicated than that. History always is. So alongside the powerful question, the 'What if it had been me?' that has inspired generations of people since, came a much more straightforward one. I just wanted to be reminded of what exactly the Battle of Britain actually was. Why it was fought; how it was fought; and what is now the consensus about the significance of its outcome.

Above all, I wanted to meet some of those pilots, the ones who still survive, the few of the 'Few' now in their eighties. I wanted to know more about them, who they were, where they came from, and what fighting the Battle of Britain had meant for them.

I had always known the Battle of Britain was an exciting story, but could I have done it? Would I have been able to fly the Spitfire, and how long would I have lasted in the dogfight-infested skies above Kent that blazing hot summer?

Martin Davidson
January 2004

CHAPTER ONE

THE FEW

'All of our hearts go out to the fighter pilots, whose brilliant actions we see with our own eyes day after day. Never in the field of human conflict was so much owed by so many to so few.'

Winston Churchill to the House of Commons

20 August 1940

July 1940:

Britain's fate is hanging in the balance. Across the Channel lies the greatest threat that Britain and its empire have ever faced: the belligerent might of Nazi Germany. An enemy already flushed with a run of staggeringly quick and efficient victories. Suddenly, Britain is alone, its Continental allies ruthlessly crushed, America still on the sidelines in 'international isolation'. One country left to fight the malign power of Nazism, to save a continent from a new world order of barbarity, a descent into a new dark age. Britain can no longer depend on its traditional defence, the English Channel, guarded always by the supreme strength of the Royal Navy. Aerial warfare marks the modern age, and German bomber planes can fly across the Channel in just a few minutes to launch an attack. So the fight will be in the air against the formidable Luftwaffe, fresh from its recent intensive experience in mainland Europe where the tactical brilliance of Blitzkrieg has overrun one country after another. Facing up to the threat are the pilots of the RAF, in many cases so young that they are barely out of boyhood. Keen to fly, keen to fight, but relatively untested and numbering a mere three

thousand or so, negligible on the scale of worldwide war. Churchill's famous tribute couldn't be more apposite: 'Never in the field of human conflict was so much owed by so many to so few.'

By the time he said these words, on 20 August, the battle had been raging for over a month. It was to be almost another month before British victory was assured; by 15 September the tide was flowing Britain's way. It was a close-run thing, a tremendously hard-fought battle – with everything at stake. On the shoulders of those few young men rested the fate not only of their own country but the whole of Western Europe and, ultimately, the world. Their war would be different from everybody else's, though just as dangerous. It wouldn't be the duelling of chivalry-minded single opponents, aristocrats spared the humiliations of lumpen carnage on the ground – whatever some of the German pilots would later claim. It would be conflict that depended, absolutely and ruthlessly, on personal talent, on reflexes, speed, mental agility, instinct. And on a cast-iron confidence in the technology of their planes: an assortment of aircraft but primarily the Hurricane and the plane that was to become synonymous with the battle and achieve iconic status – the Spitfire. Crucially, underpinning this confidence was an effective structure of control and command, planning and deploying an entire early warning system that surrounded them.

Whatever the merits of technology and the efficiency of systems, though, the man himself is the key, and the RAF fighter pilots of the Battle of Britain – many practically joined at the hip with their beloved Spitfires – have a unique reputation and an indelible hold on the public imagination: a byword for courage, charisma and sheer glamour. All these years later the surviving veterans can make their experiences sound like one big *Boy's Own* adventure, but in 1940 these were young men who unexpectedly found themselves thrust onto the front line. Boys who had followed every new development in the rapidly changing world of aviation technology became men who turned the tide of war.

'The mere sight of them and the pilots climbing into them, they were my heroes and I wanted to fly from that day on.'

Geoff Wellum

Most of the fighter boys had still been at school when Hitler came to power in 1933, and it was in those innocent days that a passion for flying had first been ignited. Aeroplanes were at the cutting edge of technology, each year bringing exciting new innovations, with the latest models able to achieve ever greater feats and ever higher speeds. Battle of Britain veteran Bob Doe took a great interest in flying from an early age.

'To me aeroplanes were very romantic things when I was young. I used to have to cycle six miles each way a day to school. And it was a long way downhill one way and uphill the other way. And one afternoon I was coming home and an RAF biplane fighter, one of the early ones, had to force-land in a field close to where my road was. I stopped and got out and I walked around this thing, and I think that was where the fascination of flying started for me. From that moment onwards I used to keep a big cuttings book – I cut out pictures of any

aeroplane I could find, and stuck them in there.'

Geoff Wellum was another early convert, for whom pilots were heroes.

'As a young boy, knee high to a grasshopper, I lived near North Weald airfield and my dad used to take me over to look at the aeroplanes. In those days – I'm talking now about the late twenties, early thirties – it was a fighter airfield and they were gaily painted in squadron colours, reds, whites, blues, huge roundels on them. Knights of old, as it were. And the mere sight of them and the pilots climbing into them, they were my heroes and I wanted to fly from that day on. And I never looked back from that.'

Alan Cobham arrives back in London in October 1926 after his first flight to Australia, welcomed by a large crowd gathered on Westminster Bridge

Like many boys of the period, Wellum was an enthusiastic model-maker, producing miniature versions of his dream machines: 'I used to buy Skybird models and make them. I had about thirty-five. You made them out of little bits of wood.' Little did Wellum know that this childhood interest would take him to the Battle of Britain.

One prominent showcase for the technological developments in aviation was the Schneider Trophy. First launched in 1911, it became a regular race with rival nations competing to win the prize. It was Supermarine, the company that would later develop the Spitfire, that won the trophy for a third successive time in 1931, thereby securing the trophy for Britain permanently. Nigel Rose, another future pilot, was captivated by the Schneider Trophy races: 'The races were pushing the boundaries of aviation into the future. I mean, these planes were flying at speeds which hadn't been thought of before. I think practically every young person who had read Biggles and so on, will understand that this was romantic stuff altogether.'

Looking at planes was one thing, but it would be the experience of flying in them that would really capture these boys' imaginations, as Bob Doe explains.

'There's a feel to flying which is unique. You're in control of a large lump of machinery which is doing what you want it to do. And you can do things that no one else on Earth can do, unless they're flying an aeroplane. And to be able to sit up above a place and look down at it and see what's happening below, it's all a lovely mystery. I just love it.'

In the early 1930s, some boys were fortunate enough to get the opportunity to actually fly in an aeroplane, as Billy Drake recalls.

'I think the whole of our pre-war generation were mad keen on flying, and I think you will find that practically all of us had our first experience with a chap called Alan Cobham and his Flying Circus. He used to wander around England over weekends and for five shillings we went up for a ten-minute flip in one of his aeroplanes. As a result of that we got more and more interested in flying, as it was a brand-new sport really.'

> *'I think you will find that practically all of us had our first experience with a chap called Alan Cobham and his Flying Circus.'*
>
> Billy Drake

Born in 1894 into an English farming family, Cobham was a member of the Royal Flying Corps during the First World War, but he didn't particularly distinguish himself. In the 1920s, though, he was to become one of the most celebrated pilots of the decade, flying from London to Cape Town in November 1925, and then from London to Melbourne and back in the summer of 1926, covering an astonishing 27,000 miles. Landing his sea-plane on the Thames, next to the Houses of Parliament in a theatrical finale, Cobham was met by cheering crowds. Although neither of the flights was the first of its kind, Cobham was crucial in demonstrating the reliability of aeroplanes as a means of transport, and his achievements were in any case still remarkable for the time. He was the first pilot to convince governments, and the wider public, that air transport was a feasible option for long distances – even though he had been shot at by Bedouins over Iraq, forcing an emergency landing, after which his co-pilot died in hospital in Basra. Cobham then surveyed the coast of Africa from the air, before touring Britain with his famous National Aviation Day exhibitions, which informed and entertained the public. It was when his so-called 'Flying Circus' came to town that Basil Gerald Stapleton became airborne for the first time.

'In 1936, Alan Cobham's Air Circus came to our school and landed on the football pitch. We took down the football gateposts, and I went up for a five shilling trip. My brother, who finished up as an air vice marshal, had already joined the Air Force, and I'd always been in competition with him, at individual sports, like fives and the gym and shooting and that sort of thing. So I thought, "Well, I'm going to join the Air Force, too." That was in 1936, and I joined in 1939.'

Seeing his school from the air was quite a novelty for Stapleton as a schoolboy.

'It was extraordinary, absolutely extraordinary. You never had any idea what the Earth looked like from way above it. And the pilot took us over the school, because the playing fields

Peter Brothers with his wife (far right) and a friend on a day out just before the Battle of Britain

of the school were a couple of miles away from the school buildings. To see what we lived in from the air, and worked in and played in, we had a big playground, we used to kick a tennis ball about, and we had five courts there, and that was where you saw part of your life going through. You didn't realise it at the time but when you reflect on it, it's beyond belief, at that age, because it was extraordinary. Alan Cobham had about six aeroplanes in his air circus, at our place – at our playing field! And I remember the noise of the aeroplanes and that sort of thing, and the pilots were all laid-back characters. You automatically thought, "Well, I'd like to be one of them", because they were all heroes to us, flying aeroplanes. That's how it all started.'

Cobham's Flying Circus would typically visit each location for two days, bringing exhilaration and drama, a thrilling display for the large crowds who'd come to watch. Archie Winskill was also impressed when he saw one of Cobham's displays.

> *'The pilots were all laid-back characters. You automatically thought, "Well, I'd like to be one of them", because they were all heroes to us, flying aeroplanes.'*
>
> Gerald Stapleton

'I had a five shilling flight with Sir Alan Cobham, who used to come round to cities and towns in the United Kingdom. Now this was the early thirties – I think my flight was in 1932. So I must have been fifteen at the time. And they used to hire fields from farmers, or land in our case, on the banks of the

River Eden in Carlisle, and that was the first introduction to flying, because you never saw aeroplanes in the air in those days, it was a rare thing.'

A rare thing indeed, long before the days of mass travel and cheap flights. The aeroplanes themselves were 'stringbags', little developed from those in use in the First World War. 'They were made of canvas,' recalls Winskill, 'and they were held together by bits of wire, I expect.' His flight was in a little two-seater cabin, just in front of the pilot, one of the Gipsy Moth series. 'I think it lasted about five minutes,' he says. 'But there you are, in the air for the first time.'

It wasn't the last time that Winskill came across Cobham. Nearly twenty years after the end of the war, in 1964, Winskill (by now an air commodore) was posted to the air attaché in Paris. In preparation, he was visiting aircraft factories and had taken a train from Paddington to Yeovil.

'There, in the compartment, was an old boy and, of course, Englishmen would rarely, in those days, talk to each other. As you leave Paddington the main road follows the railway. This old chap was looking through the window and he said, "Just look at that, there's a Mini Minor which is keeping up with us." And I said, "Goodness me, the tyres must be getting hot," and he said, "Yes, they must be." Then I said, "I suppose the motor car industry has benefited from the spin-off from the aircraft industry, in this." He said, "Yes. Are you in the aircraft industry?" I said, "Not really." So he then extracted what I was, we talked, and then developed quite an intense aviation discussion. I said, "Hang on a minute, aren't you Sir Alan Cobham?" He said, "Yes." I said, "Well, you started me off wanting to be a pilot." "Oh," he said, "I started thousands of you chaps off." And so he had, and I think my story about the five bob flight from the banks of the River Eden in 1932 must be very similar to many, many of my colleagues who joined the Volunteer Reserve later on.'

> *'I was never interested in toy trains, and so on, after all they were stuck to rails. I was interested as a small boy in aeroplanes, and I used to have model aeroplanes, these oil silk skin jobs, powered by an elastic band.'*
>
> Peter Brothers

For those inspired by Cobham as boys, the arrival of adulthood provided opportunities to learn to fly for themselves. Peter Brothers didn't wait any longer than necessary to take up the challenge.

'I was never interested in toy trains, and so on, after all they were stuck to rails. I was interested as a small boy in aeroplanes, and I used to have model aeroplanes, these oil silk skin jobs, powered by an elastic band. You wound the propeller up and launched them, and I used to fly those. And my whole enthusiasm was for aviation, which was why, when I was sixteen, my father said, "It's time you got this bug out of your system, and for your birthday present you're going to learn to fly, and then you'll get bored with it and think it's like riding a bicycle uphill against the wind and you'll settle down and come into the family business." And so I learned to fly at the Lancashire Aero Club, and that was it. So I didn't settle down and go into the business. As soon as I was seventeen and a half – the minimum age – I applied for the Air Force.'

So Brothers joined No 32 Squadron in 1936, and his passion for flying would lead to him becoming one of the most successful pilots in the Battle of Britain. By the end of July 1940, he'd already destroyed four enemy fighters, both in France and Britain, and in August he destroyed four more. After being posted to No 257 Squadron in September, he destroyed two Dornier Do 17s, and received numerous honours, being appointed an Air Commodore during the latter part of the war.

Tom Dalton-Morgan also wasted little time before pursuing his dream of flying.

'When I was about eighteen, I'd been away at school and I learnt about short-service commissions in the Officer Training Corps. They came around and so next holiday I saw my father and he said, "Well, I want you to go into the Navy." We discussed things for a long while and in the end he said, "All right, I agree, you may go into the Air Force." So that was it – I always wanted to fly. The Air Force told me I'd been accepted, I was interviewed, and cleared the medical, but they wrote to me and said, you know, you won't be called forward for about seven months, I think. We were living just outside Penarth in South Wales, and I borrowed my brother's bike and went to Cardiff Aeroplane Club and saw the Chief Ground Engineer. I asked him if I could come into the hangar and familiarise myself, but I wasn't expecting to be paid. He had one licensed aircraft maintenance engineer, a very good chap, and that's where I started, and I learnt to hand-start one of the Gipsy Moths or Tiger Moths. Flying Officer Pope took me up, showed me the effects of controls, and over a few flights he showed me how to approach the land, and takeoff, and so anyhow I could fly before I joined the Air Force.'

There were essentially three routes for converting this early enthusiasm into actual training. The most formal was to join the RAF and attend their officer training college at Cranwell, opened in 1920. For Allan Wright, flying was in the family, and Cranwell was the first step in joining the RAF for a permanent career.

> *'My dad and my uncles had been in the RAF, or the Royal Flying Corps before that. So I hadn't really been in contact with any other business except aeroplanes.'*
>
> Allan Wright

'My dad and my uncles had been in the RAF, or the Royal Flying Corps before that. So I hadn't really been in contact with any other business except aeroplanes. When it came to choosing a career, I shrugged my shoulders and said, "Why not? I don't know anything else." My dad was fairly keen, anyway, and sent my brother and myself to Cranwell, which is the Royal Air Force college for those who want to make the RAF their permanent career. If you imagine the RAF as a tier, everybody joins at the bottom, but only a few will get to the top. So, of many people that joined, not many can make a permanent career, because there's no room for them. So that's why they had short-service commissions, which is up to five years, and permanent commissions – well, you went to RAF College first, and then you would have a permanent career in the Royal Air Force.'

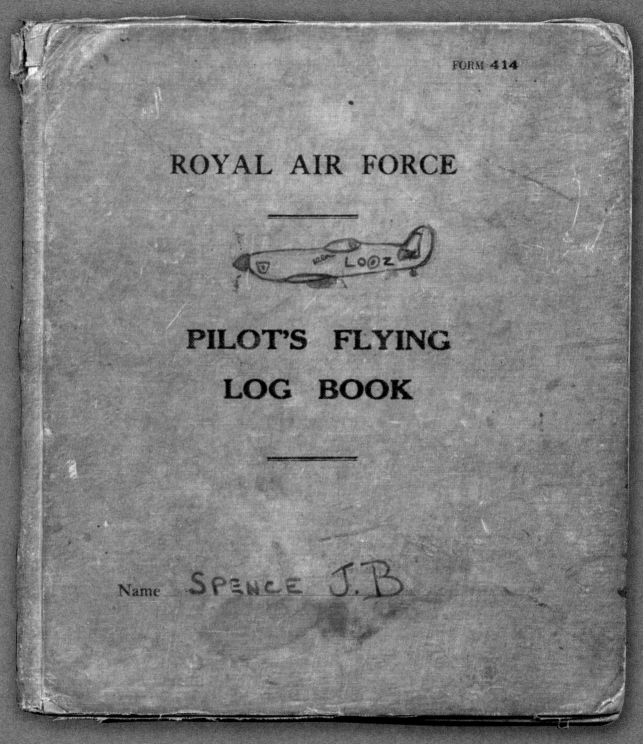

FORM 414

ROYAL AIR FORCE

PILOT'S FLYING

LOG BOOK

Name SPENCE J.B

A pilot's log book. This one belonge to Jim Spence who flew with Bomber
Command during the Battle of Britain

Wright was nearly eighteen when he went to Cranwell. He describes the initial training.

'It was a sort of university career, where the flying was only part of it. And we did quite deep thinking in history, and mechanics and mathematics, particularly the physics and mathematics side. I should add one other thing, and that is that we spent quite a lot of time pulling aeroplanes to pieces and putting them together again – not that we were going to have to do that, but just so that we'd have some idea of what the airmen were doing to our aeroplanes. You'd be able to understand what they were doing and they always appreciate that.'

This training would stand Wright in very good stead, but the emphasis was on a firmly theoretical approach.

'In a way, flying was almost secondary. We obviously had to go solo, in an aeroplane of some kind or another, but we didn't have operational aircraft at all. So the aeroplanes we flew were trainers, that was a tutor, basic trainer. One aeroplane was a Hawker Hart and Hawker also made the Fury, also a biplane, and that was a front-line aeroplane, at that time. So it was just at the change from biplanes to a single-wing monoplane.'

However, despite the theoretical nature of much of the training, tactics were not something that future Battle of Britain pilots were able to pick up at Cranwell.

> 'About 1937, I wrote to the Air Ministry saying I was going to leave school within a few months, very much wanted to fly an aeroplane and could they give me a job?'
>
> Geoff Wellum

'They couldn't have really talked about tactics. I mean, tactics only developed from meeting the enemy. What they did teach us was the range, actually what we saw on the practice sight, how to gauge the distance the enemy was in front of you in order that you shouldn't fire too soon and be out of range, which everybody tended to do. When there's nothing to gauge anything by, just two items in the sky, it's very difficult to judge how near or far you are.'

Geoff Wellum also went to Cranwell.

'About 1937, I wrote to the Air Ministry saying I was going to leave school within a few months, very much wanted to fly an aeroplane and could they give me a job? I was keen to join with a short-service commission. Being academically thick, I thought Cranwell was a bit beyond me. So they wrote back and a huge form came back, which I filled in with the help of three other people in my study, friends of mine at school. We held a meeting and discussed each question and worked out some really superb answers and sent it back to the Air Ministry, and it went on from there. They wrote to the headmaster, who said that the Air Ministry had asked him to perjure himself by saying that I was academically brilliant enough to get into the Air Force. I said, "Well, you know, perjure yourself, it can't be the first time." They also wrote to my dad – said if he wanted to get rid of me that badly, would he sign because I was under twenty-one. He complied, I gather, by return of post and then I went for an interview.'

Wellum found the interview 'a little bit daunting'.

'One chap bullied me about the maths question. I got a little bit bloody-minded, which I'm afraid I do, and took it to them, which is what they wanted. I think I was one of five to

Thousands of New Pilots Get Ready

pass out of twenty. The interview was in the morning, and then that same afternoon you went to see the doctors, who pushed and pulled and shoved and checked that you'd got two of everything and they both worked, you know, that sort of thing. And about three or four months later – they didn't hurry themselves, in those days – they told me I'd been accepted. So I had a last term of school, captaining the cricket team, and I enjoyed life to the full and left school and within fourteen days I went to join the Air Force. It's probably worth considering that within ten months of leaving school, raising my hat to the headmaster, I was in a Spitfire squadron.'

Trainee pilots looking at models of German aircraft, photographed for The War Weekly

Wellum's experience points up the most poignant fact about the Battle of Britain pilots: their youth. These defenders of democracy were in many cases too young to vote.

A second route into the RAF was to join the Auxiliary Air Force, a kind of Territorial Army for the air established in 1925. It soon gained a reputation as a club for the country's wealthier individuals, and by 1936 it was clear that these two entry routes would not provide enough pilots for Fighter Command. So the Volunteer Reserve was set up to train eight hundred young men a year. For those who joined the Reserve, like Archie Winskill, it was an opportunity to pursue flying as a hobby. He joined as soon as it started in 1937: 'I became a weekend pilot. We flew at weekends, in my case at Perth, which was a training school, and then we usually had a lecture once a week at the town centre, where we were lectured on navigation, aerodynamics, engineering, maintenance and all that sort of thing associated with an aeroplane.'

Nigel Rose gave due consideration to other branches of the armed services.

'I didn't care for the thought very much of joining the Army, because I'd been to ATC at school and didn't enjoy that very much. The Navy seemed rather remote to a sort of landlubbing chap who'd never really been to sea at all. And, so, oh yes, the RAF, now that's a modern service and there were things like the Schneider Cup results, which were very good indeed. And somebody flying from Edinburgh to London in under an hour was quite incredible. Somehow that seemed to be the service to join. So I went along to the town centre in Southampton and signed up for five years in the Volunteer Reserve Service. I was only twenty years old, then, in 1938. At the town centre, one had lectures on airframe engines, navigation, hygiene, for some reason, and how to tell a marshal of the Royal Air Force from an air marshal, very important things like this.'

Tom Neil joined the Volunteer Reserve in 1938.

'I first tried to join the Auxiliary Air Force when I was still at school. In those days, you could join when you were seventeen and three-quarters. So I tried to join No 611 Squadron, which was my local squadron in Liverpool. In the meantime, my parents had moved to Manchester, so they deemed I was too far away from Liverpool and, of course, they were a squadron rather than a training establishment, so they turned me down, which absolutely flattened me. But they did recommend that I tried to join the Volunteer Reserve up in Manchester, which I did. So, until I joined the Volunteer Reserve, on my birthday in 1938, I'd never been near an aeroplane.'

> *'I first tried to join the Auxiliary Air Force when I was still at school. In those days, you could join when you were seventeen and three-quarters.'*
>
> Tom Neil

Iain Hutchinson had been in aeroplanes several times before he joined the Volunteer Reserve.

'I had a friend who started flying at the Scottish Flying Club, at the airport, and he took me up once or twice, and the bug bit at that time, and I felt I really wanted to fly. And so I took a flying course there, and I started flying in May 1938. I realised that His Majesty provided a much better flying club, with more powerful aircraft, and so I applied to join the Royal Air Force Volunteer Reserve, which I did. We flew at Prestwick about every second or third weekend, where we flew, initially, Tiger Moths, and then graduated to Hawker Harts and Hinds, which was the first biplane operational aircraft that I flew, and I got my wings there.'

Hutchinson found that there was more than flying involved in being a member of the Reserve: 'We went through the standard wings course that the RAF administered in all their

SEQUENCE OF INSTRUCTION.

```
 1.    Air experience.
 1A.   Familiarity with cockpit layout.
 2.    Effect of controls.
 3.    Taxying.
 4.    Straight and level flight.
 5.    Climbing, gliding and stalling.
 6.    Medium turns.
 7.    Taking off into wind.
 8.    Powered approach and landing.
 9.    Gliding approach and landing.
10.    Spinning.
11.    First Solo.
12.    Sideslipping.
13.    Precautionary landing.
14.    Low flying (with instructor only).
15.    Steep turns.
16.    Climbing turns.
17.    Forced landing.
18.    Action in the event of fire (with Instructor only).
18A.   Abandoning an aircraft.
19.    Instrument flying.
20.    Taking off and landing out of wind.
21.    Re-starting the engine in flight ( with instructor only).
22.    Acrobatics.
Nav.   Air Navigation.
X-Country      Cross Country.
```

units. We had to do all the ground subjects, navigation, gunnery and all the rest of it, and then we had to pass the flying test. When that was done, we got wings, which were as good a qualification as those who were going through a regular course in the Air Force.'

A page from Jim Spence's logbook showing the order of training that pilots underwent

For Hutchinson, though, joining the Volunteer Reserve was still second best.

'There was an expectation that you'd be called up when you were needed, but I did want to fly the whole time, and I made a tactical error in going into the Volunteer Reserve. If I'd applied for a short-service commission, I would probably have been able to get that. But I didn't, and so after I'd flown for a while in the Volunteer Reserve, I applied for a short-service commission and, not surprisingly, I was rejected because they already had me as a pilot, a trained pilot, so why should they pay more money to me to do the same thing? So I then applied for a commission in the Navy. On the 31st August, 1939, I got a letter saying, "You have been accepted for a short-service commission in the Fleet Air Arm, joining instructions will be sent," but that was a bit late, because the next day we were called up. I got a notice from the Air Ministry saying I was now embodied in the Air Force, report to headquarters in full uniform, and be ready to move at a day's notice. So that was the end of my short-service commission in the Navy.'

Fighter Command also recruited pilots from the Royal Navy, such as John Sykes.

'I was up in London and I went past the Admiralty, and I saw a large gentleman in a frock coat and a top hat. I said, "Excuse me, sir, where do I join the Navy?" He said, "Go round there and get some papers." Eventually, having filled in some papers, I was asked to report for various interviews, and a medical.'

Sykes was accepted into the Navy, but by 1940 was serving as an RAF Spitfire pilot with No 64 Squadron. 'When the war was on, there was an Admiralty Fleet Order that concerned pilots volunteering to go on loan to the Royal Air Force because they were short of pilots. Quite a few of us went, seventy-five or so naval pilots, which included a couple of squadrons.'

Flying was proving to have a very wide-ranging appeal, attracting men from a variety of backgrounds, brought together not by social class, but simply a love of flying. A war artist who accompanied the men of Fighter Command in 1940 observed that 'the most striking thing about the fighter pilots is their ordinariness. Just you, I, us and co; ordinary sons of ordinary parents from ordinary homes.' Bob Doe certainly didn't come from the kind of background that the Auxiliary Air Force would recognise. In the early 1930s, he'd thought that his early fascination with flight would have to give way to financial necessity.

> *'I left school when I was fourteen, and in the 1930s, jobs did not exist in Britain at all. It was the time of the Jarrow hunger march and all those things.'*
>
> Bob Doe

'I left school when I was fourteen, and in the 1930s jobs did not exist in Britain at all. It was the time of the Jarrow hunger march and all those things, and my dad was a gardener who worked for a man who owned a business in London. So he went up to his boss and said could he possibly find a job for me? This bloke got me a job as an office boy in the *News of the World*, which he owned. Whilst I was at the *News of the World*, the government introduced the Volunteer Reserve Scheme where, provided you were fit and had the time, they would teach you to fly and pay for it. I leapt at this.'

It wasn't just pilots who were being recruited at this time. Fred Roberts, later an armourer, was also looking for a new opportunity when he applied to join the RAF.

'I worked in the tin works, the tinplate industry, rolling tin plates, for eighteen and threepence a week. There was no future, not in those days, anyway, none at all. I was having to support my two sisters and brother, because my father was unemployed and he was on means-tested benefit, and I got fed up with all this, with no future for me. I decided I wanted a trade as well, and the only way to get it was join the RAF so that's what I did.'

At the age of eighteen, Roberts went to his local recruiting agency in Swansea.

'They gave me an examination there and said, "Yes," they would accept me, providing I passed my medical exam. A couple of days later, I was sent up to Cardiff, past the doctor and they sent me home, saying, "You'll hear in a few days' time", which I did. And I went up to Cardiff again, joined a party of seven others, and we were taken by train to West Drayton, where we were sworn in.'

He had the option, when he joined at Cardiff, to sign for six years and choose a trade there and then, or sign for seven years and select a trade when he made his mind up. 'I signed for seven years and went to West Drayton, and from there I went to Uxbridge and during the first two weeks at Uxbridge they gave us a list of trades, and I selected to be an armourer. And that was it.'

George Unwin was also driven to the RAF by necessity.

'The flying was a dream. I didn't join the Air Force to fly, I joined the Air Force in desperation. In the 1920s was the deepest depression this country's ever known, due mainly to reparations with Germany. Particularly in my area, the South Yorkshire coalmining area, because German coal was so cheap that British coal was priced out of the market. My father was a coalminer and they were restricted to working three days a week, which barred them from any dole, and our total income was thirty shillings a week to keep a family of four. Luckily I'd passed the eleven-plus or

> *'The flying was a dream. I didn't join the Air Force to fly, I joined the Air Force in desperation. In the 1920s was the deepest depression this country's ever known, due mainly to reparations with Germany.'*
>
> George Unwin

whatever they call it and I'd gone to grammar school. I matriculated and I was sixteen but I couldn't find a job anywhere, other than going down the coalmine. Well, my younger brother had gone down the coalmine and the sight of him coming home at two o'clock in the afternoon, black in the face, was not for me. My headmaster produced this pamphlet for an apprenticeship which was limited to people who had matriculated – they needed people with a bit of education – and so I joined it literally as the last resort.'

Unwin went in as an apprentice clerk.

'I had the choice of apprentice clerk or a fitter and the fitter had three years' apprenticeship, the apprentice clerk two, so I took the lesser of the two evils and after that, when you passed out and became a man at eighteen, if you felt like it you could apply to be a pilot every six months, but only apprentices with the education, that was the point, were allowed to volunteer and only one per cent were accepted every six months. You kept on applying and you went through every routine until eventually you were accepted. I was getting a bit desperate because I'd every other qualification – you had to be good at sport, you were good at everything, this, that and the other, I had all that and I couldn't understand why I wasn't being accepted. The one question I always got stuck on, in the interviews, was, "What is your hobby?" Well, I was so busy doing sport and everything else – and going to dances and chasing the local talent – I didn't have time for a hobby and I must have failed on that every time.'

Eventually, Unwin was driven to desperation by several rejections and 'thought I'd do a bit of research' ahead of his next opportunity.

'The Air Vice Marshal was the final step and I'd got to that stage by then – because I started volunteering in 1931 and this is now 1935 – and so I found out that he was a millionaire and very keen on polo. So when I got up to him and the dreaded question, "What is your hobby?" came, I said, "Oh, riding, sir." "Oh," he said, "really? Where do you ride?" I said, "On my pay I obviously can't afford to ride locally, but I ride when I go on leave. The local farmer, local friends of ours." It was all bullshit, of course. "Oh," he said, "what do you ride?" I said, "Only a pony." He said, "How big is it?" I'd done my homework and said, "Fourteen and a half hands, sir." I was on the next course.'

Unwin laughs at the memory. 'So that's how I became a pilot.'

Like any future pilot, Unwin had to go through considerable training.

'By this time the expansion of the Air Force was on – this was 1935 and several civilian flying clubs were all bankrupt at the time, and luckily they saved them and the Air Force took over these and I went to the one at Woodley near Reading. I was on the first course there to have a monoplane, because they had the little Miles Hawk as it was called then. We had a couple of months there, then I went on to Wittering, which was the service school, and then practice camp and I was selected for fighters, luckily, and flying the old Furies, that beautiful little aeroplane – a biplane of course.'

Nigel Rose also did most of his training on biplanes.

'After these lectures in the town centre, the call-up paper came to go to Hamble, where there was a flying school. And for a fortnight in April 1939, it meant flying Avro Cadets. I think I went solo in about ten or twelve hours, fairly average. After about forty hours of varied solo and dual flights, you graduated to Hawker Harts and Hinds. Now, these had been first-line bombers in the early 1920s, after the First World War, but were being pushed off to flying training schools when the Gloster Gauntlets and ultimately Hurricanes and Spitfires were being issued to the squadrons. The Hawker Harts and Hinds were beautiful aircraft, biplanes, of course, but you could hear the humming in the wires and struts and things, it was wonderful flying, particularly over cloudy skies around Southampton.'

George Unwin remembers that a lot of the basic training concentrated not so much on flying as landing.

'Forced landings were the thing you really did concentrate on. Engine failures were a kind of regular feature – once a quarter you could expect an engine failure, you know, they weren't reliable. But you were expected to put it down in a field and you did an awful lot of practice on that, and it worked because I had something like four or five engine failures throughout my life, we got them all down.'

While flying skills were taught, Unwin remembers that combat skills were strikingly absent from the training he received, just as they were for the officers trained at Cranwell.

'We were taught nothing about combat at all and nothing about shooting. You just went

to the practice camp and did a bit of shooting, but nobody told you about deflection. You had a hundred mile an hour ring – it was electrically lit and it gave a crossing speed of a target flying at a hundred miles an hour. You started shooting when it entered the ring.

Refuelling a Tiger Moth, the plane in which many Battle of Britain pilots first learnt to fly

That was as near as you got to being able to shoot. Well, luckily I went to No 19 Squadron where the great Harry Broadhurst was my Flight Commander, and he was the top shooting man of the RAF and he taught you his principles. There were no kinds of experts to teach you shooting in those days, but his principle was quite the old-fashioned one. Wait until you see the whites of their eyes then you can't miss – and it worked. There was never any technical training until the middle of the war when they started the Central Gunnery School up at Sutton Ridge. I went on the first course there and later on, after I'd done my final tour in 1944, I went there as a Squadron Commander and Instructor. We did teach how to shoot then properly, but before that every summer you went to practice camp. Three weeks and you fired at a drogue being pulled by some idiot risking his life at a hundred miles an hour. You fired your guns and you had three coloured bullets, red, blue and plain, and there were chaps on the ground used to mark them. Whether you got the right score I never did know, but nobody

Hawker Harts, another of the RAF's training aircraft, in flight

bothered whether you hit it or missed it, I mean you came home, you'd done your three weeks' shooting and that was it and it was very much neglected, shooting was really neglected.'

For many future Battle of Britain pilots, the first plane they flew was the Tiger Moth. Evolved from the Gipsy Moth, it was flown for the first time in 1931, but developed after that as a military trainer. Gerald Stapleton was among those who trained on the Tiger Moth, and he has fond memories of the plane.

'I soloed in seven hours, twenty minutes. That's one thing you'll always remember, your first solo. We had three ex-Imperial Airways pilots as instructors, and they were absolutely first class.'

Gerald Stapleton

'I soloed in seven hours, twenty minutes. That's one thing you'll always remember, your first solo. We had three ex-Imperial Airways pilots as instructors, and they were absolutely first class. If you made a mistake, they didn't damn you down, they said, "Well, try this again, do it this way." We trained at the De Havilland School of Air Training, and we hadn't officially joined the Air Force. I got a bit annoyed, because we were being paid sixteen and six a day. When we joined the Air Force at Uxbridge, and you became an acting pilot officer, you only got eleven and six a day. But the Tiger Moth was a fabulous aeroplane. To land it, it didn't drop a wing, it just went down straight. So if you were three or four feet up in the air when you thought you were on the ground, it would just drop on to the ground. If you asked me what aeroplane I'd like to fly in, I'd say a Tiger Moth. You've got the wind in your hair and you really feel you're flying something, you're not in a cocoon. It really was a magic aeroplane to fly.'

Geoff Wellum rates the Tiger Moth highly as an all-round trainer aircraft.

'The Tiger Moth was ideal as an initial trainer. It had to be flown the whole time. You couldn't really take your hands and feet off it. Landing it, we were taught in those days to three-point it. Tail dragging they call it now, the modern idiom. But you had to get it right. And I think because of that and because you had to fly it, it was probably a very good *ab initio* trainer. They teach you to do everything, aerobatics, looping, rolling, spinning, stall, everything. By the time you've finished that, you could do everything with the aeroplane that the RAF wanted you to do in the advanced training. But I never looked upon it as being easy to fly. Pleasant, yes, but you had to keep your mind on the job, no matter what aeroplane you were in.'

The problem, though, with flying Tiger Moths, as Gerald Stapleton recalls, is that they provided inadequate experience for future fighter pilots, and the opportunity to learn key skills simply wasn't available.

'Flying a Tiger Moth can't teach you to be a fighter pilot. But you go up in stages. We went from Tiger Moths – this is in 1939 – to Hawker Harts and Audaxes, they're biplanes. From there we went to AT-6s, which were Harvards, from there you're going up step by step by step, into a Hurricane or a Spitfire, depending which operational training unit you went to. That was at 11 Group Pool at St Athan. After you've done a month on Harvards and Hurricanes, you get posted to an operational squadron. I was posted to No 32 Squadron at Biggin Hill, where Peter Brothers was, and I was not there for very long. None of our training trained us for combat flying, apart from shooting at a drogue towed by an aeroplane. That's the only training we had. And when we went down to the Battle of Britain we learned very quickly from the Germans how they flew.'

> '*I enjoyed doing rolls off the top, that's over the top of the loop. You could do anything in the Tiger Moth.*'
>
> Gerald Stapleton

Tiger Moths did, though, allow pilots to learn to fly manoeuvres.

'I enjoyed doing rolling, I enjoyed doing looping the loop, and I enjoyed doing rolls off the top, that's over the top of the loop. You could do anything in the Tiger Moth, it was fully aerobatic, and you could do anything as soon as you got confidence in what you were about, you could go up and hide away somewhere and do all sorts of things where they couldn't see you from the aerodrome you were on. And it was surprising the number of chaps who got lost. We had to do a cross-country, from Maidenhead to Hamble, which is down near Southampton. The number of chaps who got lost there and landed in fields and things, was extraordinary, because we hadn't been given much navigation in the schoolroom, let me put it that way, because we'd had lectures on all sorts of things other than flying and navigation, like how to look after your aeroplane and that sort of thing.'

Navigational problems aside, Stapleton recalls that it was relatively easy to fly off-course in a Tiger Moth.

'One disadvantage of the Tiger, if you had a crosswind, it would blow you miles off your course, because the first thing you did if you were going from A to B was draw a line, a pencil line, on the map, and you would pick up ground, bits like churches and railway lines and rivers and that sort of thing, and then you knew where you were. But if you didn't do that, you were a damn fool, because that's what we were taught to do. And we had a system of getting the weather report, getting the wind speed and direction, and then you could work out what – you couldn't fly down this line you made, because the wind would blow you off. You could work out that your compass bearing wouldn't be down that line, you needed to compensate for your drive. That was one thing with the Tiger, any wind would blow it miles off course, because it was such a light aeroplane, and it had those biplane wings and the fuselage for the drift to take you off. But it was a lovely aeroplane to fly, it really was, before we went onto the bigger ones.'

Tom Neil flew a variety of aircraft types during his training.

'When I got to No17 Elementary and Reserve Flying Training School, we had Gipsy I Moths, which were the aeroplane that Amy Johnson flew to Australia in 1930, and our aircraft was just about as old as that. In fact, I remember the first aeroplane that I flew was K1900, and I remember thinking at the time, my God, this is when it was made. Then we re-equipped with Tiger Moths, about nine months later, which came as a great thrill, being a new aircraft. So they were the only aircraft that I flew until war started, when I was just about to go on to the bigger types, which were Hawker Harts and Hawker Audaxes and Hawker Furies, which I didn't succeed in doing until I went to flying training school.'

> *'One thing with the Tiger, any wind would blow it miles off course, because it was such a light aeroplane … but it was a lovely aeroplane to fly.'*
>
> Gerald Stapleton

The Tiger Moth holds fond memories for him.

'The Tiger Moth was a hot ship, you know, all of 140 horsepower engine. It was a lovely aeroplane, it really was. Of course, it was the trainer right throughout the war, principally, and it was absolutely vice-free. So, once you'd gone solo, which took me quite a time, because only turning up at the weekend, particularly, and over the wintertime, sometimes you didn't fly for two months, and you went on doing the same errors you'd done two months before. So it took me sixteen hours to go solo. Thereafter, my instructors left me alone, and I didn't get any more instruction after that. And my idea of aerobatics was what I'd read in books and I'd taught myself, virtually, and they weren't very good. And even when war broke out, I still was half taught, although I'd done sixty hours total, I didn't know much about flying. I mean, the engine was just a black mass up front which operated when you pushed this lever backwards and forwards, but I didn't know very much about the aeroplane, nor did any of us, I don't think. When you're nineteen, as I was then, it's rather like a car, you don't really know very

much about the car, it just goes or doesn't go, according to whether it's unserviceable or not, and the same with our Tiger Moths, except they were new and they kept going. They were a good aeroplane, splendid aeroplane.'

Peter Brothers and his squadron prepare to board their planes during a training exercise before the war

Despite the enthusiasm that still exists among many Battle of Britain veterans for the Tiger Moth, Iain Hutchinson remembers it as being a good solid training aircraft, but no more than that.

'It was all that an elementary trainer should be. I didn't like its looks, it looked much clumsier in the air than the ordinary Gipsy Moth that I used to fly before then, that had straight wings instead of swept-back wings. Swept-back wings looked a bit incongruous on such a slow aircraft, and it didn't look quite so pretty, but it was a nice aircraft to fly and aerobatic and easy to land. Hard to fly well, in the sense that because the lift–weight ratio was so high, they bounced about the sky so that if you're doing formation flying, it was much harder to keep position in a formation. Landing was also difficult, the slightest puff of air and you're up in the air again. I think for normal use they were safe aircraft to fly, and rather more difficult to fly properly. Overall, I'd give it eight out of ten, I'd say.'

Training meant that young men like Nigel Rose could finally fulfil their boyhood dreams and get to fly a plane.

'I just think that having got safely off the ground, you felt the sky was your own. Of course in those days, there wasn't an awful lot flying around, and the restrictions were practically nil, so we hardly had to confine ourselves to anything. One flew up and down Southampton Water and there was even a nudist camp there, I think, where the instructors used to take us low flying, if I remember right. Oh, those were the days.'

As well as a new perspective on the world below, Rose enjoyed aerobatic flying.

> *'I just think that having got safely off the ground, you felt the sky was your own. Of course in those days, there wasn't an awful lot flying around, and the restrictions were practically nil.'*
>
> Nigel Rose

'You started off fairly early with spinning and then where an aircraft is stalled and you kick rudder on and you go into an uncontrolled spin, uncontrolled until you apply corrective action, which is putting the stick forward and full opposite rudder, after which a good aircraft, like a Hawker Hart or a Tiger Moth, would come out just so easily, no bother at all. Spinning was important because if you did fail at any height to maintain control for some reason, you would go into a spin, perhaps if the aircraft stalled. And so you had to know how to get out of it. So with an instructor to start with, and later on your own, you used to induce a spin and having spun a few times, you'd take it out of it and start flying again. You did ordinary aerobatics too with the loops and rolls.'

While these pilots enjoyed carefree flying, Hitler's Germany was adopting a more aggressive foreign policy that threatened European peace. Many pilots, for all their training, gave little thought to where it might lead, paying little attention to the developing international situation. Allan Wright puts it simply: 'I didn't join the RAF to fight, I joined the RAF to fly aeroplanes.'

Iain Hutchinson was of like mind.

'I don't think I consciously thought about the fact that war was pretty inevitable really. You were aware on two levels. On the one level you were aware of the fact that things were getting pretty tense in Europe. On the other hand, you were a young man, enjoying yourself flying, and having a day job as well. And although the threat was obviously there, it never struck home until I actually got called up and then realised that this was serious.'

Similarly, he gave little thought to the Luftwaffe.

'Never thought very much about the Luftwaffe, really. I didn't think very much about the opposition, and I never thought very much about being invaded or attacked. Because we'd been living in a peacetime situation, we flew aircraft and saw other aircraft in peacetime conditions, and the sky was peaceful. Although, when I was at Kirton-in-Linsey in 1940 we had one or two sorties to look for bandits coming in, we didn't really run into the Germans until the end of August, when we were sent down to relieve No 264 Squadron at Hornchurch. And then we took off the next day and then you were right into a war, which really you hadn't been in before, everything was peaceful up north. The countryside was just the same, going about your normal business. But down there it was quite different. That was when things struck home, you saw these people who are actually invading your skies.'

The prospect of war was also far from the mind of Geoff Wellum.

'I was too busy being happy to think much about war. You didn't go straight into the Air Force, you went to a civilian flying school to do your initial training, and that took you up to about fifty hours. We did it on Tiger Moths and I was up at Desford, and war was declared when we were half-way through our initial training. And even then it didn't register. Nothing happened. You know, England was a peaceful place. We were learning to fly. Full of *joie de vivre* and the rest of it. Flying as God meant us to. With helmets, goggles, string bracing wires quivering. Lovely. Different world. War? What war?'

> *'Nobody told me we were going to have a war, it was all going to be pleasant, happy weekend flying.'*
>
> Christopher Foxley-Norris

Young men may have been inspired to fly, but they weren't signing up for war. Christopher Foxley-Norris had joined the Oxford University Air Squadron in 1935, but fighting the Nazis was the last thing on his mind. He was more concerned with buying a car.

'My friends had motor cars with bench seats, which were admirable for sex. And I hadn't got any money. But I went and saw my older brother, sought his advice, as always, and he said, "Go and join the Oxford University Air Squadron, they pay you £25 down for joining." So I joined. Nobody told me we were going to have a war, it was all going to be pleasant, happy weekend flying. I don't know whether I would have still have joined had I known they were going to have a war, I think not. We decided war wasn't really for us. And, of course, in those days, one was thinking in terms of trench warfare and the unacceptable hardship. My idea of warfare was something avoided at all costs, particularly after people started getting burned. What people were frightened of in the war was not being killed, it was getting burned, at least I was, extremely frightened of getting burned.'

In Germany there were also thousands of young men training to fly fighter planes. Young men who like their British counterparts had been fascinated by the latest technological developments in the exciting world of aircraft. Ernie Wedding was one young German who joined the Luftwaffe. As for many of his English counterparts, Wedding found flying a liberating experience.

'The appeal of flying is you are free from the Earth, you're not Earth bound. Your horizon is unlimited. On a clear day you can see so far as ninety, a hundred, a hundred and ten miles. Today you're tied by radar. Well, we weren't. Once the wireless operator had signed off from the airfield then you were on your own. Nobody looked in your pocket. And it was a terrific feeling to be free of everything.'

Soon, though, these happy days of flying would come to an end for both British and German pilots. The pace and progress of Germany's expansionist foreign policy after Hitler came to power in 1933 had been staggering. Rearmament, an unashamed violation of the Versailles Treaty, began in 1935; the Rhineland was invaded in 1936; Austria annexed in 1938; Czechoslovakia claimed by 1939. By August 1939, any threat from Russia had been neutralised, at least temporarily, thanks to the Nazi–Soviet Pact.

Tom Neil was one of many Britons who had visited Germany in the 1930s and he recalls being impressed with what he saw on his frequent visits.

'If you go back to 1936, 1937, I used to go to Germany, as a boy. I loved them, I really did. I was tremendously impressed by the Germans. They were, it seemed to me, all in this lederhosen, long legs and fair hair, awfully charming people. I was very friendly with people in the Hitler Youth, and I used to play races with them. I was tremendously impressed with Germany. You used to go through on the train, you usually went by sea to Ostend, and you go through Belgium. And Belgium was crummy. As soon as you got to Aachen, you went into Germany, and the place transformed. These chaps in long coats and tall hats and everything was spick and span. And there were lovely girls in peasant uniforms and so on. Most impressive. And then Germany itself – marching troops, lots of aeroplanes in the sky – tremendously impressive to a chap aged sixteen, seventeen. So that was my impression of Germany before the war. I didn't know about books being burned in the streets or anything like that. I didn't even know what was happening to the Jews, we never heard about these things. The atrocities and all the other things came later, one simply didn't know about them then. You saw what you saw through the eyes of a seventeen-year-old, and I liked what I saw.'

> 'I used to go to Germany, as a boy. I loved them, I really did. I was tremendously impressed by the Germans.'
>
> Tom Neil

Neil would find it difficult in 1940 to see the same people he'd known as friends just a few years before as enemies once the war began.

'When I fought the chaps in fighters and bombers, they were the same chaps that I met on the ground in Germany. I had no animosity. And the ones we shot down and met, as captives, very charming fellows, very charming. How does one treat an enemy who's a good-looking guy very much like yourself and – it's difficult to beat them. On 31st October, thirty 109s attacked North Weald, and No 249 Squadron shot down three. They landed just south of Colchester, Langanhoe, in fact. One of the chaps was a real dyed-in-the-wool Nazi, who as an oberleutnant was so proud and so much a Hitler person, that he wouldn't be attended to by our doctors and he died, horribly injured, but he died. There was that sort of person. And there were all the other people who were so much like us that it was difficult to really view them with any animosity. And if you're shot down across the other side, which happened later in the war, usually you were very well treated by the Air Force. It's only when they handed you over to the Gestapo that things got a bit nasty. But I think, on the whole, I found the Germans excellent soldiers, excellent airmen, decent people.'

One future RAF pilot who did have forebodings about the situation in Germany was Nigel Rose, who visited the country three times before the war, in 1935, 1936 and 1937.

'I stayed with a family and saw quite a bit of how the Nazi grip was taking hold of the country. Most extraordinary, it really was. The family I stayed with were very anti-Nazi, which was fairly rare and rather dangerous for them, in fact. I'm not sure how much I noticed that, because I was very smitten by the daughter of the house, who was about my age.' He adds, 'Incidentally, that girl and I still write to each other now, after nearly seventy years.'

Rose remembers the militarisation, the Stormtroopers marching along the Volksgartenstrasse, swinging their arms and singing the Horst Wessel song, and found it 'a fine sight'. Yet, even at a young age, he had misgivings about the regime he witnessed at first hand in Nazi Germany.

'It was rather a shock, from the militarisation of everything to the way the Jews were being treated, and it seemed all wrong, especially as some of the family's friends were Jews and were disappearing, I think with a knock on the door at night, even in 1938. You could see glorification of the Nazi regime, with the firework displays in Cologne. It was very much based on marching and singing and the military side of things. I joined a tennis club there and one wonderful day, we were all gathered around the radio in the tennis club when Perry beat Baron von Cramm in the final at Wimbledon, and I think that's one of the finest days I can remember in my life.'

While Tom Neil and Nigel Rose saw developments in Germany for themselves, the British public was shielded from the real truth about what was happening at the centre of the continent. Stuck in the depths of the Depression, and still feeling the effects of that great conflict whose long-awaited Armistice Day was just twenty years before, appeasement had seemed like a rational approach to dealing with the international situation. To our contemporary minds, the sight of Neville Chamberlain waving his slip of paper after the Munich Agreement in 1938, heralding 'peace in our time', standing proudly on the balcony of Buckingham Palace, appears to be a weak figure, a man riddled with naivety. This, though, was a man in touch with his people, a Prime Minister fighting to keep the peace, surrounded by dense, cheering crowds. That slip of paper was reassurance, though for many, including Gerald Stapleton, it was the moment when an air war suddenly felt imminent.

'You didn't know for certain that there was going to be an air war, but you had a damn good idea, after Chamberlain and Hitler signed a piece of paper called "Peace in our Time". And my mother nearly went off her head when she said, "Chamberlain, putting his name on the same piece of paper as Hitler," she said, "this is it."'

At this stage, though, Stapleton didn't yet envisage being on the front line of a war himself.

'It didn't occur to me that I would find myself at war in an aeroplane. You never thought about it, never. You were carried along with it, all the impetus. Even when the war started. I

> *'It was rather a shock, from the militarisation of everything to the way the Jews were being treated, and it seemed all wrong, especially as some of the family's friends were Jews and were disappearing, I think with a knock on the door at night, even in 1938.'*
>
> Nigel Rose

think I'd just got my wings, then, at Drem, in Scotland, and that's when I was going, from there, to get on to the Harvard and the Hurricane. Everything is so exciting, and exhilarating, you're posted to a squadron, and there are so many things going on at the time that you don't have time to sort of think deeply, it's all on the surface. And that's all the time. The people I felt sorry for were the people who had wives and children.'

While the life of a fighter pilot was still far off from the mind of Gerald Stapleton in 1938, Nigel Rose had been increasingly aware of the growing threat to European peace.

'When we came back to England from our last visit to Germany in 1937, the war drums were sort of faintly being heard, I think. This was softened, to some extent, by Chamberlain coming back from Munich and waving his piece of paper. And one thought, "Well, perhaps there's nothing much to worry about," but within a week or two, Hitler had started taking hold of other countries around Germany and I think there was a general feeling that horrid things were about to happen and there was no escaping it.'

> *'It didn't occur to me that I would find myself at war in an aeroplane. You never thought about it, never. You were carried along with it, all the impetus.'*
>
> Gerald Stapleton

Yet for many of the young men drawn to join the RAF, the prospect of fighting would not automatically make them think of the horrors of trench warfare seen in the First World War. Growing up in Britain in the 1930s, they may well have been more impressed by glamorous stories of the flying aces, taking part in heroic dogfights, flying in the very best biplanes available. Tom Neil was one of those gripped by these stories.

'I knew all about the First World War, in fact, my bedroom was covered in photographs of Sopwith Camels and Bristol Fighters and all sorts of things. I was an expert on that sort of thing. And, of course, this stood me in good stead, indeed it stood most of us in good stead during the Battle of Britain, because we knew all about the First World War, which was only twenty years before. Now of course, we're talking about the Battle of Britain, which is over sixty years ago, but the First World War then was very much part of our recent history. And our station commander, indeed, some of our flight commanders and squadron commanders, had been in the First World War – Victor Beamish, for example, was in the Air Force at the time, and the AOCs, Leigh-Mallory and all those, had been majors in the First World War, so they knew all about it. But they were in their forties, you see, and we were kids, aged nineteen or thereabouts.'

There was no denying the other side of the Great War, though. The experience of trench warfare at Ypres, Amiens and the Somme had left deep scars on a whole generation. No wonder the British public was reluctant to embrace the reality of a forthcoming pan-European conflict. No wonder the cheering crowds greeted Chamberlain as a hero. When he had returned from his meeting to discuss the Czechoslovakia crisis with Hitler at Berchtesgaden, Munich, on 30 September 1938, he had been driven straight from Heston aerodrome to the Palace, before Parliament could debate or vote on the agreement. It was by royal invitation that he made his balcony appearance, standing next to the King and Queen to acknowledge the people's clearly overwhelming support. *The Times* produced Christmas cards in December featuring an exclusive souvenir photo of the scene.

The prospect of another major European war was increasingly dominant on the political and diplomatic agenda, though. Indeed, Chamberlain's apparent naivety hides a more assiduous political agenda, as Allan Wright, who would go to fight as a flight commander in No 92 Squadron, recalls.

'One could see that Chamberlain in 1938 was playing for time. He couldn't possibly have gone to war. He had an impossible mission, to go and talk to Hitler. So, all he could do was to try and pacify him and make him think that we're not going to bother to fight him, just to gain time. Chamberlain did a very good job, under very difficult circumstances.'

George Unwin was also aware that the Munich Agreement was far more likely to signal another war than the promised peace.

'I don't think we ever thought it would happen, I never did, but on the other hand Hitler had to be stopped. I suppose it was inevitable, but I never took it seriously. I'll never forget the 1938 emergency with poor old Neville Chamberlain. By this time we had three Spitfires and nine Gauntlets and we were put at readiness and dispersed – there we were sitting in the cockpit of our Spitfires. We never did take off, of course but if we'd ever have, I've often wondered what would happen. We sat there solemnly waiting for the word to go but it never happened, but that shows how stupid it was.'

> *'I don't think we ever thought it would happen, I never did, but on the other hand Hitler had to be stopped. I suppose it was inevitable, but I never took it seriously.'*
>
> George Unwin

Chamberlain, though, could only buy so much time. The fervour surrounding the Munich Agreement passed, and just under a year later, on 1 September 1939, Poland was invaded. Later that day, members of the RAF Reserve and the RAF Volunteer Reserve were called up for permanent service. Allan Wright, still training at Cranwell, found that 'our course was contracted a little bit, by a term and a half, in order to get us into the front line as quick as possible'. On 2 September, two squadrons of Fairey Battle bombers and two of Hurricanes of the Advanced Air Striking Force were deployed to bases in France.

At 10 a.m. on Sunday 3 September, the BBC told its listeners to stand by for an announcement of national importance. While the nation waited, entertained by music and a programme instructing listeners on 'how to make the most of tinned foods', Britain declared war on Germany at 11 a.m. Chamberlain delivered his famous radio broadcast at 11.15.

'I am speaking to you from the Cabinet Room at 10 Downing Street. This morning the British Ambassador in Berlin handed the German Government a final note stating that, unless we heard from them by 11 o'clock that they were prepared at once to withdraw their troops from Poland, a state of war would exist between us. I have to tell you now that no such undertaking has been received and that consequently this country is at war with Germany.

Now may God bless you all. May He defend the right. It is the evil things that we shall be fighting against, brute force, bad faith, injustice, oppression and persecution, and against them I am certain that the right will prevail.'

Tom Neil recalls vividly the moment war broke out. Though his father had insisted that he go to work in a bank, he had continued as a member of the Volunteer Reserve.

'I used to go over there two nights, three nights a week, learning how to do navigation and various things like that. And on the 3rd of September we all appeared at our headquarters in Manchester, and somebody said, "We're now at war, chaps", and they had a radio which gave the Prime Minister's speech, and I remember it virtually word-for-word.'

> *'This morning the British Ambassador in Berlin handed the German Government a final note stating that, unless we heard from them by 11 o'clock that they were prepared at once to withdraw their troops from Poland, a state of war would exist between us. I have to tell you now that no such undertaking has been received and that consequently this country is at war with Germany.'*
>
> Neville Chamberlain
> 3 September 1939

Just after Chamberlain's broadcast, the first air raid of the war sounded when an unidentified aircraft was spotted passing over Maidstone. But it turned out to be a French plane that hadn't filed a flight plan, and the all-clear was sounded at 11.50 a.m. By the end of the day on 3 September, France, Australia and New Zealand had joined Britain in declaring war on Germany, and the RAF had carried out the first operational sortie of the war, when a Bristol Blenheim went on a photographic reconnaissance of the German naval base of Wilhelmshaven. During the night, bombers from two RAF squadrons carried out the first raid over Germany, dropping six million leaflets over Hamburg, Bremen and the Ruhr. But despite the drama of the day, little happened in the weeks that followed. As Europe entered into the so-called 'Phoney War', the autumn witnessed occasional episodes of conflict, but it was hardly sustained warfare. The RAF recorded its first losses of the war on 4 September when five Wellingtons were shot down during a raid on German warships in the Elbe estuary but, apart from occasional bombing missions from both sides, most of the action remained in Eastern Europe.

Tom Neil remembers the feeling of anti-climax after the declaration of war: 'We all waited to be thrown in at the breach expecting to be bombed out of existence almost immediately, instead of which nothing happened – we were all sent home. And we wandered around for a few weeks at home, drawing the princely sum of £12 every fortnight – the like of which I'd never received in my life.'

Nigel Rose also recalls waiting for something to happen.

'I'd done a total of about eighty-seven hours' flying before 3rd September, I think, when we were called up. And then we were sent away on sort of indefinite leave, reporting to the town centre about every week, I think, "not wanted yet". We thought we were going into the front line, at that stage, we really thought we were quite important. It was a bit *infra dig* to find ourselves posted to, in my case, Cambridge, to the initial training wing there. I went to Clare College where this initial training wing had been put in, and I shared a room with Geoffrey Verdon-Roe, who was the son of Alliot Verdon-Roe, the pioneer aviator who founded Avro and did remarkable things during the war, both the First World War and the Second World War in fact. We went back to lectures, we did PT and route marches in the snow, it was a bitter winter that winter of 1939, if I remember right. And we waited and waited for our postings to come to flying training school where, really, we'd got to start more or less at the same stage as when we had moved over from Cadets to Hawker Harts and Hinds. And we then started flying North American Harvards. This was a wonderful training aircraft, the American one. Very stoutly built and with quite a lot of sophistications that we hadn't got in British aircraft, especially training aircraft. One I most remember is the fact that it had a urinal clipped underneath the seat and so if you got caught short in the middle of a flight, you weren't entirely at a loss. And the only thing was that if you did a slow roll and this thing came unclipped, it used to waggle in front of your nose like a mad python or something, you know, it was very odd.'

> 'We all waited to be thrown in at the breach expecting to be bombed out of existence almost immediately, instead of which nothing happened – we were all sent home.'
>
> Tom Neil

The action in September 1939 was restricted to Poland, which finally surrendered on 27 September, following an intense struggle between German and Soviet forces. Ludvik Martel was a Polish reservist who was called up immediately on the German invasion to defend his homeland, collecting aircraft coming from France to Romania. During the campaign in Poland he spent his time travelling to Romania: 'The beginning of the war in Poland was very sudden. I was called in and reported in my unit in Poznan on the first day of September. And the first bomb came down as I left the train. From then onwards, we were just more or less running away from the bombers – we were extensively bombed all the time.'

By 17 September, the unit was more or less disbanded, and Martel was one of many who moved to France. It was a moment of realisation for him and his countrymen.

'It was a very unpleasant time because we realised that everything is gone, it's finished and we have to look ahead by joining the fighting in the West. All we wanted was to get back to the operation and be able to fly and fight the Germans. And fight them to the very end. That was our feeling. There was no sympathy because they were just bombing every possible target with people running away from homes. All the convoys with people trying to get away were bombed. It looked like they chose the people as a target.'

Martel would go on to fight not only for France, but for Fighter Command in the RAF where he joined No 603 Squadron, based in Hornchurch, flying on numerous Spitfire missions. Like many other Europeans whose countries had been invaded by Hitler's forces, Martel fought with conviction during the Battle of Britain as part of Fighter Command, angry at the loss of Poland's liberty, hungry for a return to peace in his homeland.

Polish airmen taking part in a physical training exercise with an RAF instructor

By the spring of 1940, the Phoney War was coming to an end, and the theatre of war began to move towards Western Europe. The offensive began in Norway. Several large concentrations of enemy warships had been reported at naval bases in the seas of Northern Europe during the first week of the month, but bad weather had prevented the RAF from engaging and German warships were able to enter the Trondheim fjord. Allied fears of an invasion were confirmed when the Germans arrived in Norway on 9 April. Denmark was next, but its forces didn't even resist the enemy. RAF bombers had a prominent role in the weeks following the invasion of Norway, carrying out bombing missions against enemy shipping and minelaying operations, but despite their work, the British Expeditionary Force was forced to evacuate Norway in early June. The cost was considerable: the carrier HMS *Glorious*, charged with carrying members of the BEF and Hurricane pilots to safety, was intercepted and sunk by two German battleships, the *Scharnhorst* and the *Gneisenau*, with just two RAF officers surviving the sinking. On 10 May, Germany followed up its success in Norway with invasions of Holland, Belgium and Luxembourg, and began to attack Western France. There was no doubt as to the alarming rapidity of the German offensive across Europe. For Tom

Neil, sat on the sidelines during the Phoney War, it was time to move from endless training to full combat alert. As a member of the Volunteer Reserve, he'd been sent to flying training school in 1939.

'I'd hoped to go to Sealand, which is not too far away from where I live, but I was sent up to the north of Scotland, to Montrose. There we were introduced to Hawker Harts and Hawker Furies and Hawker Audaxes. It was a wonderful period, and I was there until early May 1940, by which time I'd done a hundred and fifty-six hours and fifteen minutes flying, and I was posted straight to a squadron, there being very few operational training units in those days. I got posted to a newly forming squadron at Church Fenton. I had no idea where Church Fenton was. I had to look at my school atlas to find out where it was, in Yorkshire. I turned up there by train, because it was the only way of travelling around, by train, in those days, cars were pretty thin on the ground and nobody had any petrol, anyway. It just so happened that I was the first officer to arrive in No 249 Squadron. So I had a rather spurious element of seniority, being the first to arrive, Acting Pilot Officer T.F. Neil. I found that we had no aeroplanes and that we were designated as a Hurricane squadron, because it said so on my posting notice. So it was no surprise to us when eighteen Spitfires turned up!'

Getting Church Fenton, along with dozens of other squadron bases, ready for warfare had to be a speedy operation in May 1940, with little time for the training that might have been considered necessary to prepare pilots to go into combat with these new planes.

'We flew Spitfires straight from biplanes, none of us had ever flown monoplanes before, and suddenly we were faced with these fearsome aeroplanes called Spitfires. And the bloke said to me, "This is a Spitfire, get in it and fly it." All the training you had was to sit in the hangar with the blindfold round your eyes and the Spitfire was on trestles, and you felt round the cockpit trying to identify all the bits, pulling the wheels up and you put the flaps down, etcetera. Half a day. Then you were introduced to your aeroplane and told to get on with it, and that was that. We flew incessantly, because we were told we'd been given five weeks to become operational, that is, operational meant fit to take on the enemy. So, on 15th May, I started flying Spitfires, and I did a hundred hours in four weeks, about five hours a day, because you had to do other duties in those days, being a pilot was only part of your life in the Royal Air Force, you had to do the duty pilot, you had to do orderly officer, you had to do all sorts of things as well. So, sometimes you couldn't fly during the day. The squadron did more flying on Spitfires than anybody else had achieved ever before, one thousand and ten hours, in four weeks, which is a lot of flying. Then, suddenly, one day, we were told that our Spitfires were going to be taken away from us and we were going to be given Hurricanes. The Hurricanes turned up the next day, we climbed out of one aircraft into another and flew Hurricanes, just as hard as we'd flown Spitfires.'

The military crisis that Neil was preparing to deal with in Church Fenton was matched by a political crisis in Britain. With France about to fall to the Germans, it was clear that Britain faced a peril without parallel. The politicians were failing, and confidence in the government was dangerously low. When members of the Labour and Liberal parties refused to serve in Chamberlain's proposed National Government, he was forced to resign. Who, though, would be able to provide the decisive leadership the country needed? Lord Halifax, the Foreign Secretary, was one option, but he was reluctant to take office. So Chamberlain, who according to party rules had the responsibility as the outgoing Conservative Party leader of nominating his successor, turned to his First Lord of the Admiralty. The one politician alive to the fact Hitler wasn't just another Bismarck, or Metternich, or Charlemagne even.

> *'All those bands of sturdy Teutonic youths, marching through the streets and roads of Germany, with the light of desire in their eyes to suffer for their Fatherland, are not looking for status. They are looking for weapons...'*
>
> Churchill, November 1932

Someone who knew that the price for defeat wouldn't just be strategic disadvantage – but the extinction of everything Britain thought it stood for.

Winston Leonard Spencer Churchill. It was he more than anyone who blew apart the German bluff. Who saw what a German future of Europe would entail. Who went beyond routine demonisation of the dastardly Hun. Who had a sobering conviction – entirely borne out by events – that Hitler's Europe wouldn't even just be a fascist and anti-democratic one. It would be far worse. Not just the death of liberal democracy, but of freedom. Hitler meant slavery – the entire Continent not just controlled by Germany but utterly subjugated to it. Not some kind of Nazi Raj. Churchill may have told the Commons that 'I have nothing to offer but blood, toil, tears and sweat', but he could offer so much more. He understood the nature of the crisis that Britain was facing. That is why, finally, the Battle of Britain 'belongs' to Churchill in the same way that the invasion of the Soviet Union belongs to Hitler; they both tell you all you need to know about what sort of military leaders they were. It wasn't Churchill who *won* the Battle of Britain; but it was Churchill who ensured Britain fought it at all.

It was Churchill who had, from the political backbenches, warned continually of the Nazi threat throughout the previous decade. As early as November 1932, two months before Adolf Hitler even took office, he had delivered his first warning to the House of Commons.

'Do not delude yourselves. Do not let His Majesty's Government believe... that all that Germany is asking for is equal status... All those bands of sturdy Teutonic youths, marching through the streets and roads of Germany, with the light of desire in their eyes to suffer for their Fatherland, are not looking for status. They are looking for weapons, and, when they have the weapons, believe me, they will then ask for the return of lost territories and lost colonies.'

A year later, in October 1933, Churchill warned the House of Commons once again about the possible threat emerging from the Continent when he stated that Germany was well on its way to becoming the most heavily armed nation in the world. This was a striking speech at a time when Germany was still bound by the Treaty of Versailles that had banned the country from rearming itself. Churchill went on throughout the decade in speeches and articles attempting to alert the British Establishment of the threat that Germany was representing, describing the Munich Agreement as a 'total and unmitigated defeat'. Churchill was an isolated voice for much of this time. Stanley Baldwin, then Prime Minister, certainly seemed unconcerned by Churchill's prophetic warnings. In March 1934, he confidently assured the Commons that should the Geneva Disarmament Conference fail, Britain would take the lead and organise an Air Disarmament Conference itself. Should even that fail, in all unlikelihood of course, the RAF would be strengthened so that it could match the strongest air force within striking distance of the UK.

Baldwin's calm authority would continue to be the consensus for some time, while Churchill's warnings would be ridiculed. A 1934 cartoon jests 'suppose we took Winston seriously', depicting him as a misguided warmonger against an international background of pledges of peaceful intentions pouring in from various world powers. Even as the tide of events turned towards the end of the decade, and Churchill's views began to garner some sympathy, he remained an outsider. At a Buckingham Palace dinner party in 1939, Chamberlain was seated between the Queen and the Duchess of Kent, both of whom spent the evening urging the Premier in no uncertain terms not to bring Churchill into the government. The Queen was one of the many powerful figures who loathed Churchill, and she was appalled when he took charge in May 1940. She wrote a handwritten condolence note to Chamberlain, revealing her political leanings. 'How deeply I regretted your ceasing to be our Prime Minister. I can never tell you in words how much we owe you. We felt so safe with the knowledge that your wisdom and high purpose were there at our hand.' The Queen continued to back the policies that Chamberlain had pursued in the years preceding the outbreak of war, adding, 'You did all in your power to stave off such agony and you were right.'

> 'How deeply I regretted your ceasing to be our Prime Minister. I can never tell you in words how much we owe you. We felt so safe with the knowledge that your wisdom and high purpose were there at our hand.'
>
> The Queen to Chamberlain, 1940

By May 1940, though, such views were outdated, and out of touch with the reality that France was on the brink of collapse. Most former appeasers were now agreed that this was not a contest that Britain could afford to stand back from. The cost of going to Berlin and asking for a compromise peace would be too great. So, this was Churchill's moment. And in June 1940, it was Churchill alone who was able to stir the will of the British people, still suffering from the shock of Dunkirk, into putting every energy into continuing the war. Who can forget the stirring words delivered to the House of Commons on 4 June? '…We shall defend our island, whatever the cost may be, we shall fight on the beaches, we shall fight on the landing grounds, we shall fight in the fields and in the streets, we shall fight in the hills; we shall never surrender.'

Christopher Foxley-Norris was one of many inspired by Churchill's rousing speeches: 'I think he was an enormously inspirational figure. I'm quite genuine in thinking we'd have lost under Chamberlain, or anybody else. You trusted him, though I'm not quite sure why. He had an inspirational quality.'

George Unwin remembers hearing Churchill's stirring orations on the radio, and the sense of relief that he was now going to be in charge.

> *'I think he was an enormously inspirational figure. I'm quite genuine in thinking we'd have lost under Chamberlain, or anybody else. You trusted him, though I'm not quite sure why. He had an inspirational quality.'*
>
> Christopher Foxley-Norris

'We never missed one of his speeches. I can tell you, when Churchill was made Prime Minister we were sitting out dispersal, nothing to do, we were getting very bored because the Phoney War was the most boring thing of everything, nothing to do, and Chamberlain was still Prime Minister and we had a little kind of portable out there when they announced that Churchill was Prime Minister. You should have heard the roar that went up. And I remember Peter Brothers saying, "That's it, we're all right now" and that's the way we felt. We can't lose now and of course we didn't. Churchill was fantastic. He made a lot of mistakes but as a morale booster and a leader he was outstanding.'

Listening to Churchill's speeches with Unwin was Brian 'Sandy' Lane.

'Sandy Lane was out of this world, he really was. He was one of the nicest fellows, completely unflappable. His nickname was "Dopey" because he looked half asleep all the time, but he was far from it. He was a first-class bloke, we got on famously. He was on my junior course at flying school, then became my Flight Commander and finished up my COE, and when Churchill made his famous speech in which among other things he said, "Never in the world of human conflict has so much been owed by so many to so few", Lane said immediately "You know what he's talking about, unpaid mess bills."'

Lane was responsible for shooting down six enemy aircraft during the Battle of Britain, but died in 1941. He wasn't alone in parodying Churchill's most famous lines. Gerald Stapleton remembers the Fighter Boys coming up with 'Never were so few messed about by so many'. But he admits this was just the 'Brylcreem Boys', as the fighter pilots became known, trying to be clever, and most RAF men saw Churchill as the right man at the right time, as Allan Wright recalls.

'Churchill was a wonderful man, and I continue to think so. I don't think any other politician could have led us into war the way that he did. He had made his mistakes, I assume, but he was a leader. So it was great to have somebody in charge of the nation and of ourselves that you could follow and trust to do the best. It would have been hopeless if somebody hadn't taken over from Chamberlain. Some people said, "Of course we'll win" and they thought that would improve our morale. But I didn't think that at all. I just said, "We must not lose," rather than, "We're going to win." So that meant you did your best, and you would give it your

As featured in *The War Weekly*, Winston Churchill visits Ramsgate to see the extent of the air-raid damage, August 1940

all – there wasn't any question of holding back. Whenever you were likely to be, or actually in the presence of the enemy, there's only ever one thought in one's mind, and that was, "Get into the buggers and get them down".'

Some pilots, like Nigel Rose, would say that it didn't need Churchill's great oratory to show the line of duty.

'I remember reading about his speeches in Parliament in the papers, but I don't remember hearing Churchill speak on the radio. He made some remarkable speeches in those days, but I don't think they were noticed as being especially memorable until after the Battle of Britain. He was, of course, a wonderful speechmaker. I've got all his books, too, he was a wonderful author, really terrific. He was the right chap in the right place, you know, which everybody would admit, I think. But I don't think we needed Churchill's speeches to get us flying or fighting. One had joined up with the service to do one's best and so one went on doing one's best. I don't think there was much more to it than that. I don't think one was aware of fighting to save civilisation, at all. I think it was a rather rough and knockabout period in the war, which one couldn't see the end of in any way, and that one wanted to do one's best to keep the Germans out of it.'

Transport ships return to Britain from Dunkirk with members of the British Expeditionary Force, June 1940

Whatever the impact of Churchill's rhetoric on individual pilots, it was in any case only going to get Britain so far. Hitler ordered the invasion of France on 12 May, two days after Churchill had succeeded Chamberlain in Downing Street. Given the strengths of the opposing sides, it would be understandable to expect a long drawn-out struggle for supremacy over France. The French, supported by the Belgian and British armies, had a total of 125 divisions and 3600 tanks. The German army could boast 136 divisions and 2500 tanks. It was only in the air that the Germans could claim a real dominance, with 3000 aircraft as opposed to the Allies' 1400. Yet the Germans made significant progress with breathtaking rapidity. By 13 May, the French government was forced to abandon Paris. By 14 May, German tanks led by General Heinz Guderian had already crossed the Meuse and opened up a fifty-mile gap in the Allies' front. By 20 May, they had reached the English Channel.

It was at this point that Churchill ordered the implementation of Operation Dynamo, the emergency plan to evacuate British, and Allied, troops and equipment from the French port of Dunkirk. On 26 May, the British Expeditionary Force began its retreat. At this crucial moment, the Germans made a serious tactical error. General Gerd von Rundstedt, already doubting Guderian's aggressive war plan, persuaded Hitler that his tanks should halt until infantry divisions could catch up, so that a full military assault could be made on the Allied forces. This decision stopped Guderian from cutting off Dunkirk as an escape route for the Allies. By 4 June, the bulk of the evacuation had been completed: 338,226 troops, including 140,000 members of the French Army, had been brought back to the temporary respite of Britain. There were 693 vessels in that rescue fleet, including not only destroyers and minesweepers but also an array of fishing boats, yachts, barges, tugs from the Thames and lifeboats from liners in the London docks – just about anything that could sail the English Channel was called into service. Further troops left the French coast in the two weeks that followed, with the last departing on the 17th. It was on the same day that the French government asked Germany for surrender terms, and the Armistice was formally signed on 22 June. As well as the humiliation of the astonishingly rapid withdrawal, the Allies had also lost considerable amounts of heavy equipment as there had been no alternative to abandoning it in France.

The Battle of France was the first opportunity many British pilots had of fighting the Germans. For Billy Drake, it was an experience he wasn't going to forget in a hurry.

'I'd been shot down on the second day of the Battle of France and I was in the hospital being gradually moved away from the front line by the time France fell. What happened was that I was flying in a formation of four aeroplanes and suddenly realised that it wasn't my particular aeroplane. That was unserviceable so I got into this one and it was apparent that they hadn't put in any new oxygen, so when I got up to about fifteen thousand feet I realised that I hadn't got any oxygen so I called up my leader and said I have no oxygen and I'm going home. On the way home I looked around and I saw some Dornier 17s, three or four of them, and decided to have a go at them, they were quite low at about ten thousand feet, and I got behind one of them and shot at him and then realised I had inflicted damage on that one, so changed my sights onto another one and then there was an almighty bang and a Messerschmitt 110, twin-engined fighter, had got behind me and was doing the same damage to me that I'd been doing to his chum. He was a good shot because I was in flames and I decided the best thing was to get out. But being inexperienced in getting out of a burning aeroplane I undid everything, but forgot to release the hood, so I didn't get out that way, which probably saved me from a very nasty burn because all the flames were going upwards, but by the time I'd released the hood I was upside-down and all the flames were going in the right direction and not towards me. So I popped out and landed in a field.'

Baling out of aircraft in this manner would soon become a routine occurrence for RAF pilots. Few pilots who fought in the Battle of Britain for more than a few weeks didn't bale out at some point, and many did so several times, but during the France campaign it was a new experience, and few pilots had been taught how to do so. Those who did, like Drake, often found themselves in hostile territory.

'When I landed I'd been wounded and I thought my leg had been shot off because it was hurting like hell and my back was hurting and the French peasants, farmers, thought I was German because I was very blond in those days and so they walked gently towards me with scythes and pitchforks and things but fortunately I was able to talk French and I was able to persuade them that I was not a German but an Allied airman and when they realised that and I was able to show them my wings, they couldn't have been nicer. And they took me to the local field hospital, which was being evacuated at the time and so when I arrived there was no doctor but some nurses and they just said, "Oh, we've got to get all this stuff out of your back, but we have no anaesthetic." So I said, "Thank you very much, what are you going do?" They said, "Oh we'll give you some morphine" and anyway, it was a very unpleasant ten minutes while they took all the cloth and stuff out of my back and made certain that my leg was still all right, that it hadn't disappeared. And eventually they got me to the local hospital. From there I went back to Paris through the French system of evacuation, and ended up in the American Hospital where I knew some of the American doctors, and eventually joined up with No 1 Squadron who were at Le Mans and got a trip in an RAF aeroplane back to England.'

> *'I thought my leg had been shot off because it was hurting like hell and my back was hurting and the French peasants, farmers, thought I was German because I was very blond in those days and so they walked gently towards me with scythes and pitchforks...'*
>
> Billy Drake

By this stage, Drake was out of touch with the political situation, and recalls that he'd lost interest in the fact that France had fallen.

'We were not politically minded in those days so we didn't know, but we were surprised at how rapidly the Germans invaded France and how apparently the French just gave up without much of a fight. It was all rather sad, and as far as we were concerned, when I rejoined the mainstream of ourselves trying to get out of France, we realised that France had lost. But we weren't really aware of the terrible occurrence that was going on around us and it took us years really, reading history, to find out what the hell did happen.'

The experiences of Dunkirk would have their advantages for the British. Important lessons, like the value of teamwork, were learnt by pilots who would finish up in positions of command in the Battle of Britain. Allan Wright's first experience of real live enemy planes was at Dunkirk, and he found himself, like so many of the other pilots in these first weeks of real warfare, on a steep learning curve.

'It's rather amusing, really. Not having been to war at all, not having had an enemy to be nasty to, when we went up the first time to fly around Dunkirk, our briefing was very poor, I don't know why they didn't give us a proper briefing, telling us that we were retreating and

that we had to try and hold the enemy back from attacking our ground troops. All we were told, was that our ground troops were at Dunkirk, and that we'd recognise Dunkirk because there was a great plume of smoke coming up from it, because they'd pretty well burned the place down. So it was very easy to find, so we just were told to

Burning oil tanks spread black smoke across Dunkirk after the town was bombed during the evacuation

go there, patrol up and down, you'll doubtless see some Me 109s, and when you see them, shoot them down. As simple as that. And that's how it happened. In fact, the first ones I saw, I was with a squadron in formation, and when I looked over my right, I saw some aeroplanes with swastikas on, or crosses, they were, from that position, flying below there. And

I called up and I said, "Oh, I can see some aircraft down there with crosses on." And my leader said, "That's the bloody enemy, you fool." And then he said, "Down we go."'

Wright had suddenly found himself in the middle of a dogfight.

'It was a most extraordinary experience. We saw the aircraft over in the distance, and there was obviously something going on, just a few aircraft, and the closer you got to them, you saw that there was just a whole beehive of aeroplanes, there were just aeroplanes going in all directions, all over the place. And at first you think, "Well, I'll attack that one," but you couldn't because he was going past you, so you'd try another one. And you'd just keep trying, but I couldn't keep the sights on it. And you'd turn round, thinking we'll have to look at it in a different way, and pick one out when they're a good distance away from us, and then get yourself in a position and then, without being shot down yourself, manage to shoot it. It was, learning as you went along, and quickly.'

> 'I called up and I said, "Oh, I can see some aircraft down there with crosses on." And my leader said, "That's the bloody enemy, you fool."'
>
> Allan Wright

Dunkirk was also the first time that George Unwin, a member of No 19 Squadron, met the Germans in combat.

'We had thirteen pilots when we moved to Dunkirk. We moved to Hornchurch some twenty-four hours after it had started. It took the place of Stanford Tuck's squadron who had been literally semi-destroyed. There were thirteen pilots and they only wanted twelve and so they drew out of the hat who was going to be the unlucky one and it was me. So I missed the first sortie with No 19 Squadron which was luck. I've always been extremely lucky, this was the first time, because off went No 19 Squadron with Squadron Leader Stevenson and they ran straight into a horde of Stukas and they methodically followed Fighter Command attack number one and went in at a very slow overtaking speed at the target, and they were very slow Stukas, and these boys were creeping in, ready, when of course down came the Messerschmitts and shot down the first three straight away. The CO and the other pilot officer were killed. And that was it. Of the remainder, two or three others were missing and so on. In the meantime I was taking part an hour later because No 74 Squadron were down to nine which they weren't allowed to go with, so I was sent over with my aircraft to make the numbers up. So I actually went off after them and we never saw a thing the first trip, not a thing. But the second time we did.'

After the experiences of France, Unwin recalls that fighter pilots threw out the RAF rule books.

'We decided there and then that there was only one way in. Go in fast and go out fast. It's the only way. I mean, you were a sitting duck going in at about ten miles an hour overtaking speed, and we paid the penalty, but that day they were doing it as per training. The RAF didn't change their tactics. The squadrons themselves did. I mean we were flying in vics [V-formations] of three. Well, a vic of three is all right, looks very pretty at Hendon for displays and all that kind of thing, but if you try to do a sudden turn, left or right, you're going to run into whoever is left or right of you. The Germans flew in twos. In fours but two twos, so whichever way you turn, the other man with you could slip immediately behind you and you weren't turning into him at all. And we adopted that, it became known as the finger four. But it was the squadrons that did this entirely themselves.'

The evacuation of Dunkirk had been a startling event, a massive wake-up call for Britain. Six weeks was it all it had taken for France to fall. Six short weeks. That had been the great shock for all who were watching the rapidly unfolding events in Europe. The war that dominated living memory was the Great War, and that had lasted four endless years, most of them spent in utter deadlock. This time, it didn't look as if the conflict was going to be so drawn out. The German army had dispatched the old enemy in just over a month and a half. The Phoney War couldn't have been more dramatically – or traumatically – brought to a shuddering conclusion. This new Continental war seemed to have broken all the rules that had dominated nine centuries of conflict on mainland Europe. Wars had lasted years, decades, even centuries – this one would be lucky to last longer than a university vacation. Truly, it appeared, a war that would be over by Christmas.

> 'We decided there and then that there was only one way in. Go in fast and go out fast. It's the only way. I mean, you were a sitting duck going in at about ten miles an hour overtaking speed, and we paid the penalty.'
>
> George Unwin

Never mind the long-term consequences for Britain, and her Empire. The Fall of France had been simply unimaginable – its denouement in the evacuation of the remnants of the British army at Dunkirk, a chastening taste of things to come. Hitler had called this land war his 'big risk' – and it had paid off, so resoundingly that not even the Germans were quite sure what to do next, though nobody was in any doubt that Britain would have to be dealt with, one way or another. There was no comfort for the British in hoping that what had applied to France would be spared them. The French had had one of the largest, best-equipped armies in Europe – with tanks, men and munitions supposedly the equal of the Wehrmacht ranged against them. Certainly their Air Force was inferior to Germany's (though it had still been able to inflict serious damage on the Luftwaffe), but their capitulation had no consoling explanation. They had simply been out-thought, out-manoeuvred – and out-fought. Their comprehensive defeat had not only been near instantaneous, but it had been a fully military one. They had taken on the Germans – and lost.

So, suddenly Britain found herself on her own. America was still basking in a period of international isolation that had lasted since Versailles. The United States hadn't kept completely out of European affairs since then, and they were supplying significant quantities of military equipment to the Allied cause. The first RAF machine to engage in aerial combat with the Luftwaffe was an American-built Lockheed Hudson maritime patrol plane.

Nigel Rose in front of a Hawker Hart

Nigel Rose's squadron just before the Battle of Britain. Back row (left to right): Dochilly, Rose, MacDowell, Hart, Brazebrook, Proctor, Douglas, Phillips, Lyall, Whipps, Gage, Barthropp, Taylor, Niven. Front row: Mount, Boyd, S/L Johnstone, Urle, Jack

Throughout the Battle of Britain, not only would many of the planes and engines used by Fighter Command come from America, but so would the 100-octane fuel that did much to improve the performance of both Spitfires and Hurricanes. A number of American pilots added a personal contribution, too. The USA, though, had never joined the League of Nations and in 1940 was still not ready to fully engage in European politics, despite an increasingly fierce debate raging between the isolationists clinging onto the established foreign policy of a generation, and the internationalists who believed that now was the time to re-engage in world affairs.

All across the Low Countries and France now lay a military force of unprecedented threat. This was no Armada of sailing ships that a Channel gale could scatter. It wasn't even ships at all – it was aircraft, the most modern, and most intimidating, fleet of war planes the world had ever seen. Britain faced a devastating choice. Go the way of France and hope for the best – evacuate the VIPs and the royals to Canada, prepare for a war of rearguard attrition – or accommodate the enemy in an uneasy, Vichy-like entente cordiale. No wonder that across the country morale was low and resolve was hesitant. Some kind of armistice or accommodation was surely the only way forward – even those who had had little sympathy with earlier appeasement were coming to the view that this was Britain's only choice. 'Britain is not our natural enemy' was the message coming out of Germany – and it struck a chord. Of course Hitler was a duplicitous opportunist, but for those looking to clutch at straws, this seemed a good one. Let Germany have their Continental empire, its precious 'Lebensraum'. Maybe this time Hitler could be believed – after all, he claimed to respect the achievements of the British Empire.

With the benefit of hindsight, it is hard to sympathise with those who were ambivalent in their opposition to Nazi power, but this was 1940 and no one could predict the horrors that would unfold over the following years. This is why Churchill was so important. What he made abundantly clear was that this was a war Britain must not lose. The summer of 1940 wasn't going to be about whether or not Britain could fight the war, but what would happen if it didn't. It didn't matter if Hitler's real ambitions lay in the East and that he might be prepared to agree a peace. Churchill's message to Hitler was that while we may not be your natural enemies, you are ours. What was at stake was the future of civilisation. This was an ideological conflict, not just a question of power, a decisive struggle between two very different value systems. Churchill was more than anything else clear that not only was this a battle that the British were to engage in, but that it was a battle that it could win, and he told the British people that the only acceptable resolution to the conflict was Allied victory.

The evacuation from Dunkirk is, hardly surprisingly, viewed as a disaster for Britain, France and the Allies, but it was seen by the Germans as no less a disaster for them as well. The man with most to worry about in June 1940 was Hermann Goering, a former First World War German flying ace who won the Iron Cross before joining the National Socialist German Workers' Party soon after its formation in 1923, inspired by a speech delivered by its leader,

Adolf Hitler. Goering soon rose to prominence in the Nazi hierarchy, taking charge of the SA, and during the 1930s overseeing the establishment of Nazi concentration camps. By 1938 he was in charge of Germany's armed forces and, a year later, he officially became Hitler's deputy and legal heir. With the outbreak of war, Goering's continuing authority would depend on the performance of the Luftwaffe. Initially, Goering's leadership tactics paid off – the Luftwaffe performed brilliantly in Poland and in France. But Dunkirk was a disaster: the Luftwaffe had failed to deliver on its promise to wipe out the British Army on the beaches of northern France, and the British Army got away, albeit in a makeshift fleet including not only destroyers and minesweepers, but also an array of fishing boats, yachts, barges, tugs from the Thames and lifeboats from liners in the London docks – just about anything that could sail the English Channel was called into service. So the Germans were left with a problem in June 1940: Britain, and what to do about this island on the edge of Europe that remained outside the growing German grip of power.

> '*Once we lost the Army at Dunkirk we realised how serious it was, because actually, to be honest, if Hitler had only had the plan to invade immediately after Dunkirk nothing in the world could have stopped him, nothing.*'
>
> George Unwin

Exactly what Hitler had in mind for Britain has never been clear. His real ambition lay to the east of Germany, the chance to conquer the so-called 'Lebensraum'. It was not originally part of his plan to fight or defeat the British, or to occupy, conquer or carve up the British Empire. Indeed, the lack of a coherent German plan for the Battle of Britain suggests it wasn't even a battle that Hitler had expected to fight. It's possible that Hitler simply believed that the British would lack the spine to fight, that softened up with a short bombing campaign, and with the rest of Europe already dominated by Germany, Britain would have little option but to agree to peace. It is also possible that he believed he would simply be able to defeat the British and French forces, without having thought through what would happen afterwards. The events of the spring of 1940 forced Hitler to think through these issues once again, with Dunkirk providing a new opportunity. Suddenly the possibility of defeating Britain became a real one, and it wouldn't even necessarily involve a full-scale invasion. Against a Nazi-dominated Continent, surely Britain couldn't stand alone. Would now be the moment when the British would come to the negotiating table? If they did, it would be on Germany's terms. Hitler could agree a peace to suit Germany, and turn his attention to his real goals in the East.

George Unwin believes that the opportunity was there for Hitler to take:

'Once we lost the army at Dunkirk we realised how serious it was, because actually, to be honest, if Hitler had only had the plan to invade immediately after Dunkirk nothing in the world could have stopped him, nothing. We had no army here at all, and we'd shuffled a hell of a lot of casualties in. If he'd dropped ten thousand parachutists in, there was nothing to stop him. Luckily, he didn't have the plan.'

With Hitler's confusion came one saving grace – time. A lull in the conflict offered the British a lifeline they seized with both hands. Britain now faced an enemy she couldn't get at, that she was clearly unable to defeat on land, and with no serious allies left to help. If Britain was to choose to stand and fight, what with? The Royal Navy, scattered round the globe was in no position to play a decisive role in a Continental land war, even if it was still theoretically a power to be reckoned with. The Army was in tatters after Dunkirk, its equipment rusting around the French countryside and on the beaches of Dunkirk. That just left the RAF – barely a generation old, and untested in modern aerial warfare. And not just the RAF, but one small part of it – Hugh Dowding's Fighter Command.

Hitler poses with paratroopers he has just decorated with the Iron Cross, June 1940

Over those vital next few weeks, the RAF went into full mobilisation, not just the squadrons, but the aircraft factories and pilot training schools. A month would turn out to make a huge difference. If Hitler had launched an immediate invasion, he might have been able to establish a foothold on the south-east coast. Instead, he held back, knowing that he would need to have put an immense naval force at considerable risk in order to protect an invasion fleet. He was also preoccupied in showing off his recent victories to the world, staging an elaborate armistice ritual at Compiègne. There were during this period a few preliminary bombing missions. On 18 June, the Luftwaffe made its first large-scale raids, with a hundred bombers attacking targets between Yorkshire and Kent. The following night, another hundred bombers returned, targeting locations in southern, eastern and northern England, and South Wales. Seven more night raids followed in June, and the Channel Islands were bombed on 28 June. Raids continued in early July, including the first daylight raid on 1 July in Hull in Yorkshire and Wick in Scotland. The objective during these initial raids was to carry out strategic bombing of key targets that would be essential if any invasion was to be launched. So the attacks were focused on shipping, ports and aerodromes. The Germans weren't going to stop now.

Following the initial raids, the Battle of Britain itself is deemed – at least by British historians – to have begun on 10 July. Between that day and the end of October, it would be fought out, with these raids typical of daily activity. Even on a relatively good day, the British would usually lose a few planes, with a few pilots killed or wounded. Although the Blitz itself wouldn't start until September, there were regular civilian casualties. The Luftwaffe had embarked on their campaign to knock the RAF out of the sky and, in so doing, remove Britain from the war. The RAF was holding on, churning out replacement aircraft as quickly as it could, and training up new pilots even if, as time went by, that training time was forcibly cut again and again, from years to months and from months to weeks.

The Battle of Britain would be a new kind of conflict. Air combat was still a novel means of warfare, a battle on this scale unprecedented. Fighter Command was about to deploy a system that had never been used before, in a situation in which nobody really knew what was going to happen, and where the historical precursors were not really of any use. Even looking at what had happened across Europe was of little help – the 'lightning war' of the Blitzkrieg system developed by General Guderian certainly made use of bombers, but it was still essentially a land-based military offensive strategy, based on the speed and surprise of a military force of light armoured tank units supported by planes and infantry. Its devastating effect had certainly shaken the French, who had spent years, and 7000 million francs, developing the Maginot Line, a chain of concrete and steel defences that stretched from Luxembourg to Switzerland, supposedly offering an impregnable defence along the German border. The French had invested their confidence in this modern-day Hadrian's Wall, but, in the event, it was utterly useless – Hitler's Western Offensive bypassed it altogether, the German armed forces invading in the heavily wooded and semi-mountainous area of the Ardennes, north of the Maginot Line that the French had believed to be impassable to tanks, and therefore invulnerable to attack.

Britain had never needed to build an equivalent to the Maginot Line. Throughout history, it had been protected by the natural version of a defensive wall – the English Channel. But unlike the Maginot Line, the Channel couldn't simply be bypassed; the only way in was over or across it. At least that meant Britain's first taste of war wouldn't be the devastating and irresistible formations of tanks and infantry – and thanks to the power of the Royal Navy, it wouldn't be a sea-borne invasion either. The only way into Britain was in the air. And Hitler knew it too. The problem for Britain was that by 1940 even this offered only scant comfort. The Channel might offer temporary respite, but for the first time the threat of air power was just pretty terrifying in itself, a national fear that had crystallised and grown all through the 1930s. It was a fear of not just the Germans on the rampage, determined to reverse and revenge the humiliation of 1918, but a fear of aircraft. It had become a truism that the next time war came, death and destruction would come from the air. Just as the H-bomb was to be the fear in the 1950s and 1960s,the pre-war terror was the bomber. The development of fighter bombers would mean that, for the first time, the great defensive moat that had offered protection to Britain for centuries was going to have its value annulled. Planes could cross it in minutes.

If Britain was going to survive the new age of aerial conflict, it was going to need to stop the bomber. The systems that had been developed to detect the incoming bombers – radar and the Observer Corps – were about to be put to the ultimate test, as were the planes that had been developed to destroy the bombers once they'd been identified. Britain was about to find out if the predictions made in the 1920s and 1930s on the devastation that could be wreaked by bombing campaigns would be borne out.

The first offensive military use of an aircraft in war had been in November 1911 during the Italo-Turkish war, when several small spherical bombs were dropped on Turkish troops at Ain Zaia, a town in Libya then under Turkish control, by the Italian airman Guilio Gevotti. A glimpse of what could be expected had been seen in the First World War when German Zeppelin airships, followed by Gotha and Giant bombers, had begun a bombing campaign on British cities and coastal towns in January 1915. The campaign was only intermittent and haphazard, but the 103 raids had succeeded in killing 1413 people – all but a mere 300 of them civilians, as well as leaving between 3400 and 3500 wounded. One daylight raid in 1917 had reached the centre of London, the eighteen children killed in a school in Poplar just some of the victims of fourteen Gothas each loaded with a 500-kilogram bomb. These first air raids created real fear in the population, and offered a very real insight into what might come with another twenty years of development in the cutting-edge world of aeroplane technology. By 1925 the Air Staff were forecasting the possible consequences of prolonged aerial warfare, with their shocking prediction that a raid on London would produce 1700 dead and 3300 injured – and that was just in the first 20-hour period of conflict.

> *'The day may not be far off when aerial operations with their devastation of enemy lands and destruction of industrial and populous centres on a vast scale may become the principal operations of war, to which the older forms of military and naval operations may become secondary and subordinate.'*
> Lieutenant-General J. C. Smuts, 1917

The effects of bombing beyond civilian bombing were also envisaged. A report for the Cabinet on air organisation by Lieutenant-General J. C. Smuts following the German air raids on London in 1917 predicted the supremacy of air warfare: 'The day may not be far off when aerial operations with their devastation of enemy lands and destruction of industrial and populous centres on a vast scale may become the principal operations of war, to which the older forms of military and naval operations may become secondary and subordinate.'

Between the two world wars, there had been opportunities to witness at first hand the growing power of bombing campaigns. There was the Japanese bombing of Shanghai in 1932, when Japanese aircraft carriers had been in action for the first time with horrifying results. Europe itself had the experience of the recent Spanish Civil War as a forecast of what might be to come. Most famously, the German Condor Legion had destroyed Guernica, a small town of seven thousand inhabitants in the Basque province of Vizcaya in April 1937. In a three-hour raid, explosive bombs and incendiaries destroyed the town, one afternoon of sustained bomb attacks that shocked the world, and an event that has resonated in the decades since, thanks to Picasso's haunting depiction that was revealed at the Paris Exposition in May of the same year. These events made horribly vivid the predictions of Neil Bell's 1931 novel *Valiant Clay* that portrayed a large proportion of the urban population being wiped out in just a few days after the outbreak of war, the cities burning, and the inhabitants 'blown to rags'.

So in 1940, Britain knew the price it could find itself paying for Churchill's obstinacy might still be national annihilation, precisely the type of Armageddon the prophets of air power had been predicting. There was no doubt that Germany, like Britain, had been rapidly developing aerial warfare weapons. The modern German Air Force had become *the* political fetish of the 1930s – the most visible and trumpeted symbol of rising fascist power. It had been Hitler's conscious intention to show the world he meant business, that Germany was on the move. And he did it by giving birth to his Luftwaffe – and it always was *his* Luftwaffe, in a way neither the Kriegsmarine nor the Werhrmacht was. Only the SS was more closely intertwined with his dreams of personal world conquest. All through that decade, air power had become the international measure of threat and counter-threat, just as it had been naval strength before the First World War. Instead of Dreadnoughts, this time it was bombers. The role played by those fighters and bombers in Hitler's spoliation of Europe seemed to confirm all those fears. Blitzkrieg had battered Poland, the Low Countries, and now France, into submission. And Blitzkrieg was spear-headed from the air, by the dive-bombing Stukas, and the twin-engined bombers, escorted by the Messerschmitts.

Fresh from its brilliant performances in Poland and in France, Goering's Luftwaffe was now charged with the offensive. Battering England into submission would restore Goering's prestige and authority after the damage yielded by the German failure at Dunkirk, something Hitler was not going to let Goering forget quickly. There may not have been any particularly well-developed plan but, in broad outline, it was pretty clear what the Luftwaffe would have to do. The idea, which isn't a complete fallacy, was to establish air superiority over southern England. That would mean the Luftwaffe could fly more or less unmolested and at will over Britain, as they now did over most of Europe. That would clear the path for a full-scale invasion.

Alternatively, the Luftwaffe could expose London to the worst of Churchill and Baldwin's fears: destruction by round-the-clock-bombing. If the Spanish Civil War had shown the damage that could be done to individual civilian populations by bombing campaigns, the precedents from the early stages of the current war had shown how a single, carefully orchestrated campaign could bring a country to collapse. When the Germans bombed Warsaw, Poland surrendered. When they bombed Rotterdam, Holland surrendered. So it looked as if when London was bombed, the British would, if not surrender, at least come to the negotiating table. At which point the voices that had been drowned out by Churchill's belligerence would again come to the fore. Political figures like Lord Halifax and Lloyd-George would be forced to concede. They could rationalise it of course, as Realpolitik, that Britain had no fundamental conflict of interest with Germany, and anyway, even if it did, there was nothing it could do about it. Either way, Hitler would have got what he wanted – Britain out of the war, and a free hand for what he really wanted, a chance to smash the Soviet Union.

So now all Churchill had to do was make sure the Germans never got their air superiority. Everything now hinged on Fighter Command to relieve Britain from what was effectively a siege. Everyone on the island was a defender, whether soldier or civilian, but the outcome would be in the hands of just a few – the Few. Hugh Dowding, Commander-in-Chief of Fighter Command, had seen the conflict coming. He had famously written a strongly worded two-page memorandum as France was falling, urging Churchill not to commit additional British aircraft to fight across the Channel. On 16 May, under intense pressure for help from the French, Churchill agreed to send ten squadrons, more than had been agreed with his chiefs of staff, writing that 'it would not look good historically' if France was to fall when Britain still had the capacity to send additional help. Deeply disturbed by the large commitment being made to the French effort, Dowding then wrote his ten-point memorandum, addressed to Harold Balfour, Under Secretary of State for Air. While acknowledging that victory might still be possible in France, Dowding urged the Air Ministry to consider what Britain would need to fight on alone.

The Air Ministry had already agreed that fifty-two squadrons would be needed to defend Britain, and yet only thirty-six were currently available. With ten squadrons already in France, the RAF's home defences were already depleted. Dowding urged for a clarification 'as to the limit on which the Air Council and the Cabinet are prepared to stake the existence of the country' and that this limit, once agreed, should be rigidly adhered to. Dowding sent an uncompromising message to the Air Ministry on the gravity of the situation.

I believe that if an adequate fighter force is kept in this country, and if the Fleet remains in being, and if the home forces are suitably organised to resist invasion, we should be able to carry on the war single-handed for some time, if not indefinitely. But if the home defence force is drained away in desperate attempts to remedy the situation in France, defeat in France will involve the final, complete and irremediable defeat of this country.

Dowding received a reply to his memorandum a week later from the Air Council, although they declined to answer his questions. But the memorandum's importance is undeniable; its arguments were adopted by the Air Council, and Churchill ordered that no more squadrons should leave Britain, regardless of the worsening state of France. The RAF was now to concentrate on preparing to provide air cover in the event of an evacuation. History has only reinforced the fact that Dowding's line was absolutely right. Additional fighters would have made little difference to the situation in France. Moreover, it emerged after the war that the French had plenty of their own aircraft, mostly held in storage units. General Vuillemin, Commander of the French Air Force, eventually admitted that at the end of hostilities he had more aircraft available than at the beginning.

'One was going for what one saw in the sky. I don't think one differentiated between an aircraft and the people flying it. I know that a lot of people that I met and knew, people who I would regard as the aces, went to dispose of the pilot best of all, and if they got the aircraft, jolly good, too. But I don't remember having any sort of bloodlust at all.'

Nigel Rose

Dowding's refusal to allow more squadrons to be sent to France certainly boosted Britain's chances, but the numbers involved were still far from representing a decisive lead. There were three thousand or so pilots, and a force of Hurricanes, Spitfires and miscellaneous other planes. British history is littered with examples of how numbers alone don't always prevail. But three thousand is nevertheless a tiny number. In a war that would later be decided on the battlefields of the Soviet Union, and the Pacific islands, where casualties ran from the hundreds of thousands into the millions, three thousand represents about a morning's worth of fighting. And yet everything that followed would hinge on this negligible group, 'the Few' of Churchill's legendary phrase. The eyes of the world were squarely focused on men like Nigel Rose who were now being posted up ready to defend Britain.

'The posting came through and I went up to Kinloss on the Moray Forth, right up in the north of Scotland, to this flying training school at Kinloss. They had Oxfords for multi-engined pupils and Harvards for single-engine, and I was posted to single-engine. We went through all the stages of aerobatics and height climbs and cross countries, although they were rather a farce because being up on the Moray Forth, all they could do, really, was to send you round the coast, and so there wasn't much tuition in navigation, which probably accounts for the fact that if one was sent cross-country later on in life, one tried to find a suitable railway line, which was fine until it went into a tunnel, you know. But the main memory of the time in Scotland was mostly of cold. We lived in Nissen huts, and the bigger and earlier chaps to get on site pinched the beds which were nearest the tortoise stove, I think it was called, a fearsome, poisonous thing filled with coke, it used to burn absolutely white hot. At nights, how we weren't asphyxiated, I mean, the smell of fumes from this thing and carbon monoxide, presumably, was really quite something. We somehow survived. And so our flying days went on. The whole camp moved

down, just when the Battle of France started, to Cranwell, and we saw our month or two out there getting our wings. And then, when we got our wings, came the postings.'

Nigel Rose in front of his first Spitfire, shortly before an early training flight

Front-line RAF pilots were now getting their first real taste of what they were up against. The Germans were coming in force, flying a combination of fighters and bombers. With no other theatre of war active in Europe, no other battle for the Germans to fight, they could throw their full military strength at Britain. Not quite what those who'd expected the Germans to be forced to fight both Britain and France simultaneously had anticipated.

It was clear from the start that the Luftwaffe were not going to be an easy enemy either. They had the advantage of many years' experience, in Spain, and Poland and France. True, they'd never fought against an evenly matched opposition, but it was solid operational experience. They were cocky, and gorged on success. They had superb aircraft, particularly the Messerschmitt 109. In the hands of a good pilot, it could knock anything out of the sky. The Luftwaffe pilots would already have been well aware of what the men of Fighter Command would soon find out. It was clear that staying alive involved a lot more than just being able to fly. A pilot and a fighter pilot are very different creatures. Anything less than flying to the very limits of human and technological abilities would be fatal. Why? The power of these machines was immense. Admittedly, this is a world away from the guided missiles of the jet fighters seen in action in more recent conflicts, but they still packed a formidable punch. A plane flying straight and level was easy meat. Three or four seconds of machine gun fire was all it took. Sometimes just a handful of shells, especially cannon shells, could be enough. Hit the coolant, or kill the pilot.

On the front line were the young men of Britain. Eighteen, nineteen, twenty years old, charged with flying missions to shoot down enemy aircraft, surely a daunting prospect. The grim truth: Britain's young men were going out to shoot down the young men of another country, not so far away. Each fighter pilot had his own way of dealing with the job they were faced with in the summer of 1940. Nigel Rose recalls that he didn't think of it in bloodthirsty terms.

> *'If you'd seen London being bombed from the air by Germans, you had no sympathy with them when you shot them down. I mean it was all part of the game, wasn't it? I mean you couldn't feel sympathy for them.'*
>
> George Unwin

'One was going for what one saw in the sky. I don't think one differentiated between an aircraft and the people flying it. I know that a lot of people that I met and knew, people who I would regard as the aces, went to dispose of the pilot best of all, and if they got the aircraft, jolly good, too. But I don't remember having any sort of bloodlust at all. I would just dearly like to have knocked all the aircraft I could see out of the sky.'

George Unwin also remembers distinguishing between destroying enemy aircraft, and destroying enemy fighter pilots.

'If you'd seen London being bombed from the air by Germans, you had no sympathy with them when you shot them down. I mean it was all part of the game, wasn't it? I mean you couldn't feel sympathy for them. You didn't try and kill them, you just tried to disable the aeroplane, that was the main thing, but with a 109 you hadn't got much choice. With a twin engine you always aimed at the engines first, but there was no need to kill the bloke, just destroy his aeroplane.'

Over the following four months, it would be the ability of the fighter pilots on both sides that would determine the battle. For the British, just under 3,000 of them – 2,353 from Great Britain, and 574, like Ludvik Martel, from overseas. That's all that lay between capitulation and freedom. The whole nation knew it too. No wonder the reward for their eventual success would be nearly instantaneous mythologising. In 1805, it had been Nelson alone thus turned into legend. In 1940, it would be the pilots, many and nameless often, not the general or the admiral, who would be raised aloft. The future of Europe – who knows, maybe even the world – depended on less than the crew of an aircraft carrier.

Victory in the Battle of Britain did not, of course, end the conflict, but defeat would have meant the end of the war in Western Europe. Of the men who flew at least one operational mission in the Battle of Britain, 544 were killed. It's easy to forget that for those lucky enough to emerge from the Battle of Britain unscathed, the war still had years to run, eating even more deeply into their numbers and those of their replacements. A further 791 Battle of Briton pilots were killed in action or died in the course of their duties before the war ended. Today there are just a few still alive in Britain.

It's over sixty years since they turned up at bases like Duxford, and Tangmere, Biggin Hill and Kenley, up and down the country, either with years of flying experience behind them or just weeks. For them all, it represented the culmination of a process in which they had been trained to fly high-performance fighters, and use them to kill the enemy. As the summer months progressed, it became even clearer that this was a battle that hinged not on aircraft but on pilots. Planes could be built, but pilots were a different story. Pilots who took Britain one very crucial step closer to victory, against the odds.

Hawker Hurricanes photographed for *Flight* magazine, May 1940

In a speech to the Canadian Parliament in 1941, Churchill recalled that the French generals had warned the British Prime Minister and his Cabinet at the outbreak of the battle, 'In three weeks, England will have her neck wrung like a chicken.' Thanks to the pilots of the Spitfires and Hurricanes who flew on the missions of the Battle of Britain, Churchill was able to triumphantly declare: 'Some chicken! Some neck!'

Spitfire School *Tiger Moth Takeoff*

I t's a bright June day. Four young trainee pilots have arrived at Headcorn Aerodrome in Kent, eager to test their skills in a Spitfire. In just a few hours, they'll be flying over the countryside of south-east England, learning the key manoeuvres necessary to grasp this most iconic of aircraft.

This, though, is not 1940. This is a summer's day in the twenty-first century, and these pilots have come to Headcorn to recreate the spirit of Spitfire flying that is the enduring memory of the Battle of Britain.

They'll be competing for the opportunity to experience nine hours of advanced training in a Spitfire. All four have some flying experience, but none of them have ever flown a Second World War plane before. John Sweet, twenty, is a trainee pilot in the RAF; Christian Baker, twenty-one, sells performance cars; Dave Mallon, twenty-two, is a graduate in aeronautical engineering; and Ben Westoby-Brooks, twenty, is a student and flies with Bristol University Air Squadron.

Veteran Bob Doe believes that if they had to, young men of any generation could do what the pilots of 1940 did: 'Some people say that modern youth could never do it. I don't believe that. I don't accept that. I think that modern youth would do the same job if they had to. Whatever you say about them, if necessary, they'll come good. I'm absolutely certain of it.'

The modern-day pilots will be competing for the chance to fly a Spitfire, thanks to Carolyn Grace. Carolyn owns the only dual-seater Spitfire still operational in Britain. The plane was a single-seat fighter during the latter part of the war, and what saved it from subsequently being scrapped

Main picture: Carolyn Grace's
Spitfire in flight over the
White Cliffs of Dover
Above left: the Sptfire at
Duxford Aerodrome
Above right: Carolyn at the
controls

was its conversion by Supermarine at Southampton for the Irish Air Corps, who used it as an advanced trainer.

Being a two-seater makes Carolyn's Spitfire ideal for allowing young pilots of today to get as close as possible to discovering what it was like to be a Battle of Britain pilot. With the fully dual control configuration, you can fly it completely from the back or the front, so Carolyn can hand over control to another pilot but take over should she need to.

For Christian, it's an important opportunity to understand the Battle of Britain better. 'In twenty to thirty years' time, you won't be able to listen to first-hand experience, or have the ideas of what they really went through. But it is absolutely phenomenal what those lads did, young lads like myself.'

For Ben, there's a personal reason for wanting the opportunity to fly in a Spitfire. 'My grandad flew Spitfires. There's a picture of him standing next to his Spitfire in all the gear, and it looks such an amazing aircraft. He was lucky to fly it, and I'd just love to do the same.'

Although some RAF pilots in the Battle of Britain had several years' experience of flying, many others went through all too brief training periods. By the height of the battle, it was far from

unusual for Fighter Command to be sending up pilots with ten hours or less experience of flying Spitfires.

As Caroline explains, 'The successful pupil who gets the nine hours in the Spitfire, by the end of that period of time, he will be able to handle the Spitfire in the air flying straight and level, flying on a navigational exercise. He will be able to do the very steep turns, he'll be able to do basic aerobatics with it, very sharp turns, combat turns. He will have flown in formation, so apart from the actual takeoffs and landings, he will be very close to, hopefully, what a similarly houred Battle of Britain pilot may have had.'

Before John, Christian, Dave and Ben can go near a Spitfire, though, they must undergo some basic training. So at Headcorn Aerodrome they meet up with flying instructor Brendan O'Brien who puts them through their paces. At the start of his four-day basic training course, Brendan gives all the pilots a briefing before taking them out in a Tiger Moth, the same trainer plane that many of the 1940 pilots learnt to fly in.

Ben is the first of the pilots to go up in the Tiger Moth, and he loves the experience. 'It feels really good. It flies so differently to the aircraft that I've been used to flying. It's very sensitive on the controls, especially on the elevator. It's amazing with the wind in your face, compared to a closed cockpit. Brilliant, absolutely brilliant.'

Brendan is impressed with Ben. He explains that he is looking for the pilots who can handle the Tiger Moth's control most sensitively. 'Well, I think we're trying to do quite a lot in a very short period of time. So I'm just trying to see and get a feel for whether they have what we call "hands".'

Dave is next to go up in the Tiger Moth and, as he steps into the plane, he immediately gets a sense of history. 'When you first get into the aircraft, you really get this feeling of the smell. It's just like being back in 1940.'

He's hesitant at first, and surprised to find that he has complete control of the plane, even though the instructor pilot can assist him if necessary. But he soon gets used to it, learning quickly how to manoeuvre it.

'That's much better,' assures his instructor. 'You're starting to get your feet working now.'

At the end of the flight, Brendan congratulates Dave on a good flight: 'Mission accomplished!' He's impressed with Dave's first attempt on the Tiger Moth.

'Dave did well. He was thinking, he was moving well. When the pressure was going up, he started to get a little rougher round the edges, but his look-out was good, his attitude was good, and he had a nice pair of hands.'

Dave knows he still has a lot to learn, but is beginning to gain confidence.

'Well, I've definitely not proved my case yet for having a seat in the Spitfire, but hopefully on the next flight, I should get to grips with it.'

Back in the briefing room, Brendan takes the four pilots through some important points for becoming accomplished fighter pilots. Like many of the Battle of Britain veterans, he emphasises the importance of pilots being aware of what's happening around them.

'If you're going to be a fighter pilot, you need to have your head on a swivel. You have got to have eyes in your bottom. Even in the days of fast jets, of radar, and of all the other modern aids that you have, when it comes to the crunch, the best thing that you have available to help you is the all-singing Mark I eyeball.'

Having seen all four pilots' first attempts in the Tiger Moth, Brendan is impressed and, like Bob Doe, believes that they could fight a Battle of Britain if they had to.

'I can imagine all these people in the seat of a Spitfire during the Battle of Britain, and it is an extraordinary thing that ordinary young people were doing extraordinary things. I think that people of the modern generation do have the right stuff. I think every generation has its people with the right stuff. I think there's just as much go, and just as much bottle, in the modern generation as there was in previous generations.'

Impressed though he is, after four days of training on the Tiger Moth Brendan has to make a decision, as only two of the pilots will go on to fly in Carolyn Grace's Spitfire. Four days may not sound like very much training but, as Brendan points out, 'In the Second World War, many of the pilots that went from planes like the Tiger Moth through to planes like the Hurricane and the Spitfire really didn't have a lot of hours.'

He considers carefully the achievements of the four.

'Ben, I know how much you wanted it. You flew extremely well, and I can say that you'd be a credit to Her Majesty's forces, and if it were the Battle of Britain all those years ago, I'd very much want you as one of my pilots. Christian, a great effort, you're a great sport, and a great character. You did extremely well.'

Two of the pilots stand out, though.

'John, your professional training as an Air Force pilot obviously came through, as well as a great deal of aptitude. Dave, you actually made the greatest improvement over the period of time. Great job, well done.'

So, reluctantly, Brendan chooses John and Dave to go through to the next stage. They will get the opportunity to fulfil the dreams of just about every young boy since the summer of 1940: to fly a Supermarine Spitfire.

CHAPTER TWO

ACHTUNG, SCHPITFEUER!

'You're not flying an aeroplane, you've got wings on your back. You are just flying. It's a dream. It's the most wonderful sensation I have ever known. That is the Spitfire. It's the only airplane I know where you don't climb into it, you strap it on.'

Bob Doe

Perhaps no other battle in modern history has become so identified with one particular weapon. Not just the fighter plane but, very specifically, the Supermarine Spitfire. A plane that captured the spirit of every pilot who flew it, and a plane that captured the imagination of the British public. The Spitfire was by no means the only British plane fighting in the Battle of Britain – indeed, more Hurricanes saw combat than Spitfires – but it's the Supermarine Spitfire that lives on in the popular memory, and even during the battle was the plane most identified with Fighter Command. It's also the plane that the pilots of Fighter Command talk about with the most enthusiasm. Nigel Rose remembers vividly, more than sixty years later, just what a Spitfire meant to a young pilot in 1940.

'It's the most beautiful aeroplane you'd ever seen, a powerful thing but a wonderful-looking aircraft. It behaved like a lady all through, a beautiful plane. It answered to the controls so well. Got a bit frozen up in a steep dive but then most aircraft did. The first time I climbed into a Spitfire, there was certainly a feeling of pride and also a little bit of worry, that one had to perform, the hope that everything would go all right. In the event, it did, but with such

Previous page: Six
Supermarine Mark I Spitfires
lined up in a starboard
echelon formation

a powerful thing under your hand for the first time, it was quite something. It behaves so well the whole time. You could be quite fierce with it, putting on a lot of G, pulling out of a dive and so on, and you could turn very hard and fast without spinning. You could feel it beginning to shudder but you could ease off a little bit so that it didn't spin. It had the most wonderful characteristics, and I think everybody who's flown Spitfires would agree with that.'

Gerald Stapleton recalls a very similar enthusiasm for flying Spitfires in 1940.

'It was like a marriage. You get to know it so well that you know what all its foibles are. Every Spitfire's not the same, and you become attached to one, because, for some reason or another, you feel more comfortable in it. It seems the better you get to know it, the better you like it. A Spitfire had no real points to prove to you. Some aircraft, when you land them, drop a wing if you land them too high, but not the Spitfire. So you could make mistakes in a Spitfire and it would forgive you, and it's things like that which made you appreciate a Spitfire. You could get so used to it that you didn't have to think about flying it. It was such an easy aeroplane to fly.'

> '*The first time I climbed into a Spitfire, there was certainly a feeling of pride and also a little bit of worry, that one had to perform, the hope that everything would go all right.*'
>
> Nigel Rose

To focus so much on the Spitfire in talking about the Battle of Britain may seem rather unfair. Ranged against it was a fighter pretty much its equal, the Messerschmitt Bf 109. Furthermore, while the Spitfire gets so much credit for the British success, the Hawker Hurricane flying alongside it was, and remains, the great unsung hero of the Second World War. It lacked glamour, but more than delivered results – knocking out of the sky more German aircraft than the Spitfire (which it outnumbered by three to two) and anti-aircraft batteries put together. History, though, is rarely fair, and being glamorous, and on the winning side, has given the Spitfire an untouchable reputation, a reputation it actually began to acquire long before that summer of 1940. From the moment people first laid eyes on the Spitfire Mark I, they knew they were looking at a classic aircraft, with its sleek, modern lines, those innovative elliptical wings, that unmistakable coughing roar. People still recall the excitement of that first encounter, and it made every other propeller-driven plane seem like an also-ran.

If spectators could thrill to the look and the sound of the Spitfire, how much more of a charge it was to those who actually got in it and flew it. Bob Doe was trained as a bomber pilot, but he can still recall the first time he saw a Spitfire and how he was soon enthusiastically becoming a fighter pilot.

'We were sent to a squadron up in Beaconsfield in Yorkshire, which was a new squadron being formed, and it had Blenheims. Then eventually they took those away and sent them to Finland to help them fight the war and we were given Fairey Battles. And this was a time when they were being shot down in France like flies. And I was very worried. And then one

day a Spitfire landed on our airfield – we had a grass airfield then – and taxied over to our hangar. We walked over to this thing, we looked at it, we stroked it. Sat in it. I fell in love with it. We just had one Spitfire at first but then, a couple of days later, fifteen more turned up and we were a fighter squadron.'

Members of No 32 Squadron at Biggin Hill refuel a Hawker Hurricane while the pilot waits in the cockpit

For Doe, the Spitfire was so much more than just a machine.

'You're not flying an aeroplane, you've got wings on your back. You are just flying. It's a dream. It's the most wonderful sensation I have ever known. That is the Spitfire. It's the only airplane I know where you don't climb into it, you strap it on. It's a dream. The very early Spitfires were the best ones to fly ever because it was before we had armour plate put in them. I've actually brought one in to land at 65 miles an hour, which is almost an impossible task, unbelievable, but I've done it. If it started to stall, it just stalled flat, you opened the throttle and it pulls away. It's the most viceless aeroplane I have ever flown. I loved it.'

Geoff Wellum also has vivid memories of the first time he set eyes on a Spitfire.

'The first time I ever saw one was when I was training on Harvards. We had a maintenance unit and a Spitfire flew in for storage, I think. I saw it then, and I went and had a look at it, and was told by an ugly-looking man who was trying to guard it not to go too near it. Don't know what he thought I was going to do, or whether he thought it was going to bite me. I don't know. But that's the first time I saw one. The next time I saw one was when somebody said go and fly it. When I first saw it, I was struck by the line. Not a straight line anywhere. Beauty of line. It looked right. It looked like a fighter. It looked – it was – wonderful. It looked a beautiful, beautiful little aeroplane. Oh yeah, I wanted to fly one. I was jolly lucky to do so, too, actually. Of course it was the highest bit of technology, it was right on. We were lucky to get on to Spitfires. Out of the whole of the course at flying training school only two of us went straight to a Spitfire squadron, a fighter squadron. Many of the others went to Hurricane squadrons, but I went to a Spitfire. It was the latest and fastest thing, and a little bit daunting when somebody said there's one, you know, go and have a go at it, see how you get on.'

> '*We walked over to this thing, we looked at it, we stroked it. Sat in it. I fell in love with it.*'
>
> Bob Doe

The glamour of the Spitfire has intensified over the years, not diminished. Yet its success, and fame, rests on more than just the accident of sweet lines; it would prove itself one of the great campaigners of the Second World War, by lasting longer and undergoing more development than any other Allied fighter. Indeed, it would share one thing with its German adversary: both were in production all the way through the war, though by the end, later variant Spitfires had long left the Bf 109 behind.

For a plane that worried many as being too difficult to produce in volume, it would end its career having been built in greater numbers than any other: over twenty thousand in twenty-two different versions. Sold off by the RAF after the war, they worked their way through the world's smaller air forces, and so Spitfires would continue carrying out operational flying duties until the late 1950s. The Indian, Italian and Burmese air forces would all make use of the Spitfire, and many of the planes changed hands several times. The last Spitfires to be destroyed in combat would in fact be destroyed by other Spitfires as, during the first Arab–Israeli War, the Egyptian, Syrian and Israeli air forces were all making use of Spitfires. This wasn't simply for want of alternatives, but powerful testimony to just how superbly designed and conceived this aircraft was.

Even before the Second World War, the rate of fighter plane development was accelerating rapidly; when war broke out, that acceleration went into overdrive, and yet still the Spitfire kept up. As the new-version Mustangs, Tempests and Lightnings became familiar sights in the skies over Europe, they never succeeded in rendering the Spitfire obsolete, as happened to the Hurricane. Nothing short of the jet engine would do that, and it would sweep away all propeller-engine fighters, not just the Spitfire.

Of all warplanes, it's the Spitfire that's most likely to be the one we secretly yearn to be allowed to fly. Not just to experience the sensation of speed and living history, but because the Spitfire pilot represents the most potent question many of us ask ourselves: if we had been that age, in 1940, would we have risen to the challenge? And what a challenge! It's what those photographs of Battle of Britain pilots say to us; as though even then they knew theirs was some kind of ultimate experience, a benchmark that would challenge future generations.

In an age that has become jaded, even cynical, about historical myths, embarrassed by the distortions they require to work, uneasy about the sentimentalities they play to, the Spitfire legend has remained impressively resilient. There is still something special about the Spitfire, something that goes beyond how good it looked, or how iconic it became in the British imagination. The Spitfire deserves its status as one of the great artefacts of British history. Of course much of this is symbolic, but symbols are powerful, too, and the Spitfire is one of the most powerful. Above all, the Spitfire is symbolic of the arms race that preceded the war, the arguments about rearmament and appeasement that tore the 1930s down the middle: symbolic of the battle the British very nearly lost, the battle against time; symbolic of the technology that could live up to the rhetoric of opposing slavery and the great nightmare of being subjugated to Nazi rule, something that could be put where Churchill's mouth was.

After all, air warfare is peculiarly unforgiving for technology; the second-rate fighter will always lose to the first-rate one. The Battle of Britain deployed many planes besides Spitfires, Hurricanes and Messerschmitt 109s, and many of them simply didn't achieve the results. Both sides were forced to fly aircraft that were well behind the cutting edge, and the result was a massacre for their pilots. In some cases, as with the RAF's Fairey Battle plane, there had been the opportunity to foresee their short-comings and withdraw them from service. Built in large numbers from 1933, the Fairey Battle was never going to be the plane that would win a war; its main attribute appears to be that it was ready to roll off the production line at a time when politicians seemed keener to demonstrate the RAF's fighting strength in terms of numbers of planes available than in actual combat ability. By the outbreak of war, it was all too clearly obsolete, and was taken off the front line in June 1940 after crews flying Fairey Battles in France had been annihilated. No wonder pilots like Bob Doe had been so worried about their prospects when they saw how the Fairey Battle had performed in France.

> *'When I first saw it, I was struck by the line. Not a straight line anywhere. Beauty of line. It looked right. It looked like a fighter. It looked – it was – wonderful. It looked a beautiful, beautiful little aeroplane. Oh yeah, I wanted to fly one. I was jolly lucky to do so, too.'*
>
> Geoff Wellum

The Fairey Battle was not the only second-rate plane in the RAF's service, and several other inferior types of aircraft were still flying during the Battle of Britain. The Boulton Paul Defiant, for example, was intended to be used only for defensive patrols, but was forced into action in 1940. While it could be effective if flying in formation with other planes, on its

GERMAN & ITALIAN AIRCRAFT

HOW TO SPOT THEM

ONLY COMPLETE ILLUSTRATED RECORD

1/- NET

UNIQUE COLLECTION OF PHOTOGRAPHS, SILHOUETTES & ILLUSTRATIONS, WITH EXPLANATORY NOTES DEPICTING ALL TYPES OF GERMAN AND ITALIAN AIRCRAFT

This booklet was sold for a shilling as a guide to enemy aircraft for amateur observers

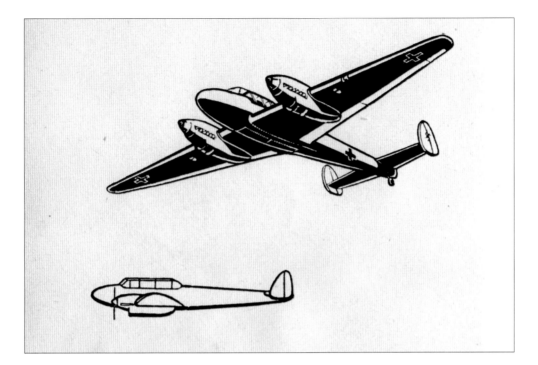

The Messerschmitt Me 110, as depicted in *German & Italian Aircraft: How to Spot Them*

own the Defiant was a poor match for the Messerschmitts and appalling casualties were inflicted on its pilots; and in an emergency a Defiant gunner had little chance of escaping from his turret. The Bristol Blenheim was a failure as a day fighter, easily destroyed by single-engined interceptors, and had to be relegated to night duties.

The Luftwaffe also had flying machines that were virtually guaranteed to produce fatalities. The Messerschmitt 110 soon proved to be no match for modern fighters, its speed, manoeuvrability and defensive armament being completely inadequate, and worse, its very presence in a combat zone was often a liability for the 109 fighters escorting them. For pilots like Gerald Stapleton, the 110 soon became a welcome sight: 'The Messerschmitt 110 was not a very successful aeroplane, it wasn't fast enough, any twin-engined aeroplane wouldn't stand a chance against a single-engined plane.'

George Unwin also saw the 110 as an easy target for Fighter Command. 'The 110s weren't as manoeuvrable as the 109s, they were bigger targets anyway. The 110 was easy.'

The Junkers 87, the so-called 'Stuka' dive-bomber, the plane so synonymous with the early Blitzkrieg successes, was also in fact easy prey for the Hurricanes and Spitfires it would face in the Battle of Britain. Once separated from its fighter escorts, the Stuka was helpless and, like the Fairey Battle before, it proved to be a death trap, proof that in the air second best was fatal.

> *'The Messerschmitt 110 was not a very successful aeroplane, it wasn't fast enough, any twin-engined aeroplane wouldn't stand a chance against a single-engined plane.'*
>
> Gerald Stapleton

The Junkers 87 or 'Stuka' dive-bomber that launched the Blitzkrieg attacks across continental Europe

Both were slow, and both placed excessive faith in the presence of a rear-facing gunner, and both paid the price. Like the Fairey Battle just weeks before, the Stuka would be pointedly withdrawn after suffering inordinate losses, and would be sent on only a few isolated raids during the Blitz.

The fact that the RAF did possess the Spitfire and the Hurricane, planes equal to those ranged against them, was absolutely crucial. Look what happened to Poland and to France, whose pilots were as brave as any but whose obsolescent planes were shot out of the sky. For both countries the price was total defeat. Fighter aircraft meet each other in combat much more directly than other weapons systems. In the eighteenth century, the Royal Navy could afford to have ships inferior to those sailed by the French and Spanish, because their officers were better. In the Battle of Britain, that was not an option. In a very real sense then, Reginald Mitchell and Sydney Camm, architects of the Spitfire and Hurricane respectively, deserve their places among the pantheon of those without whom Britain would have lost the war.

Above all, the Spitfire remains symbolic of a great national effort, spearheaded by a shockingly tiny cadre of pilots, but men on whom the eyes of the world were turned. Churchill, as always, got it just right: 'the Few'. Not since the legend of Horatio on his bridge has so much turned on the efforts of so small a number, even if, in typical manner, pilots would deprecate the sentiment. The war would never be like that again. Perhaps there is another reason it remains possible to think warmly about that period, nostalgically even. The Spitfire represents the impossible – the defiance of historical odds, winning not just one of the innumerable battles that have littered British history, but the one that, had it been lost, would have thrown our world into unimaginable darkness.

The potency of the Spitfire as an object of desire hinges on where it sits in the history of technology. It is perfectly pitched between rudimentary and space-age. It is a quantum leap more sophisticated than the canvas and wire of the First World War biplane that pre-dated it, but hasn't yet become the jet-fighter you guess would take a lifetime to master. So for those who don't have flying qualifications, it represents the peak of aerial fantasy. Here is a plane that only two generations ago represented the absolute apogee of aerial technology – and yet is capable of being flown with only hours of training. In the end, this was to prove utterly crucial. Many pilots were forced to master it in days – and had they not been able to, Britain could well have lost. But nine hours of training put you at the controls of a machine that could fly at over 350 mph, turn on a sixpence, climb in minutes to 25,000 feet, and deliver 3000 rounds of ammunition in 14 seconds of devastating fire.

What a contrast with twenty years earlier, when the technological restrictions of aeroplanes meant that their primary function of military flying in the First World War amounted to little more than observing the enemy, and doing what you could to prevent the enemy from observing you. It had been the information-gathering potential of aeroplanes that had first attracted the interest of the military. A war game played in September 1912 at army manoeuvres in East Anglia involving an airship and twenty-four aircraft, used air components to support soldiers with airborne officers able to spot groups of 'enemy' troops and guess their direction of movement. The success of the exercise was reflected in a memorandum issued by the Director of Military Operations which stated that 'There can no longer be any doubt as to the value of airships and aeroplanes in locating an enemy on land and obtaining information which could otherwise only be obtained by force… Though aircraft will probably have several uses in war, their primary duty is searching for information.'

> *'There can no longer be any doubt as to the value of airships and aeroplanes in locating an enemy on land and obtaining information which could otherwise only be obtained by force… Though aircraft will probably have several uses in war, their primary duty is searching for information.'*
>
> Director of Military Operations memorandum, 1912

During the war that followed soon afterwards, aircraft became faster, and more sturdy, and the weapons they carried more powerful, but the role of observing the enemy, and predicting its next move, was still the most useful one. This was beginning to change, though, and in May 1918 Hugh Trenchard, the Chief of the Air Staff who had played a crucial role in establishing the RAF, set up 'The Independent Force' within the RAF, created with the aim of the strategic bombing of Germany – the first time an air force section had been created anywhere in the world with the intention of conducting air war without reference or subordination to Army or Navy command. This, combined with the dogfights of the latter part of the war, meant that between January and November 1918 the RAF dropped 5500 tons of bombs and claimed 2953 enemy aircraft destroyed. The precedent of aerial warfare meaning bombing campaigns had been set; the consequences to be felt so fully two decades later.

The Great War did much to accelerate the early development of aeroplanes, and of flying for

Members of an early RAF
squadron, photographed
in 1919

military purposes. The Royal Flying Corps of 1914 with 62 aircraft had become the Royal Air Force of 1918, commanded by Hugh Trenchard, with over 22,000 aeroplanes and around 100 airships, organised by approximately 30,000 officers and flown by over 263,000 men in 188 front-line combat squadrons. In addition, there were 75 training squadrons, 401 aerodromes at home, 270 aerodromes overseas, and a fledgling Women's Royal Air Force (WRAF) service, established in 1918, which already had 25,000 members, all helping to make the RAF the largest air force in the world. The first proper fighter aircraft had been developed, planes such as the Bristol Scout, launched in 1915, with a top speed of 86.5 mph at 10,000 feet, a level that could be reached in 21 minutes; and the Sopwith Camel, which at the end of the war could reach 10,000 feet in just 10 minutes – and then fly at that altitude as fast as 112 mph.

The Great War also saw the first pilots beginning to attract a reputation that would endure, perhaps because their single-handed combat against the enemy conjured up old images of chivalry and honour, just when the war had become characterised by the bloody, muddy and seemingly endless horror of trench warfare. These pioneering pilots – and without precedents, textbooks or established tactics, they were the ultimate pioneers – were independent-minded and adventurous men who were able to make their own decisions. All very different qualities in fact from what made good infantry men. These first fighter pilots epitomised the new world of air warfare, even if their dogfights were considered to be of secondary importance to their observation work.

After the 1918 Armistice the RAF was reduced in size considerably, its 188 squadrons pared back to just 33. Public disgust with the war and the economic hardships faced by a country that had gone through four years of conflict dictated frugality in military expenditure. In any case, the Treaty of Versailles was designed to ensure that Germany could never pose such a threat again. So Trenchard set about shoring up the foundations of the Air Force, giving it a more permanent existence than had been possible during wartime, hence the training college at Cranwell for pilots, along with technical colleges at Halton, Cranwell and Flowerdown. He was encouraged by the man who held the post of Secretary of State for War and Air from 1919 to 1921, none other than Winston Churchill. Writing in the first issue of the Cranwell College magazine in September 1920, Churchill was quick to establish a sense of what the developing RAF was going to stand for:

> *Nothing that has ever happened in the world before has offered to man such an opportunity for individual personal prowess as the air fighting of the Great War. Fiction has never portrayed such extraordinary combats, such hairbreadth escapes, such an absolute superiority to risk, such dazzling personal triumphs… It is to rival, and no doubt to excel, these feats of your forerunners in the Service that you are now training yourselves and I, for one, look forward with confidence to the day when you who are now at the college will make the name of the Royal Air Force feared and respected throughout the world.*

Cranwell's rigorous training produced the first generation of professional RAF pilots, there for a long-term career. Churchill's enthusiasm for the new RAF was not enough, though, to sustain the growth of the Air Force during the 1920s. It was due only to Trenchard's dogged persistence that the RAF was able to grow, survive even. The man whose strategy during the war had been to make the Air Force indispensable, even if that meant agreeing to meet the Army's most unreasonable demands, saw his project through until his retirement in 1929. But there was no getting away from the fact that the post-war decade had not seen significant investment in the service. Annual expenditure estimates hovered between £18 million and £19 million, but did not increase from that. A government promise in 1923 to build a metropolitan air force of fifty-two squadrons for home defence produced, six years later, only twenty-five home-based regular squadrons in service, supplemented by eleven auxiliary and reserve units. Meeting the rest of the commitment didn't seem to be at the forefront of anybody's mind in Whitehall.

Nevertheless, the RAF was now able to draw on trained men, professional fighter pilots who would form the backbone of Fighter Command in 1940. Professional pilots would, however, need the best possible equipment. By the 1930s the development of aircraft was taking on a more militaristic agenda. The middle of the decade saw a revolution in the design of fighter aircraft. In fact by now the challenge was clear: modern air forces had reached the end of the road with the biplane, a much-loved, and familiar, model of aircraft. The future belonged to the low-winged, all-metal monoplane. The classic biplane had to be transformed.

First to go would be the open cockpit. Although it would cost the pilot a lot of his visibility, especially when misting up, it would allow the aircraft to fly much, much higher. It would also, of course, offer him a modicum of protection against enemy fire. Next to go would be the fixed undercarriage, replaced by a retractable one. Although requiring complicated hydraulics, the gains in cutting down drag would be immense. Next up – the materials used. The era of canvas and dope was surely over. The next generation of fighters would need to be built from metals like steel and aluminium, resilient enough to house the new engines and their unheard-of power. But the real jolt would be to lose that second wing. Not only did this drastically reduce the amount of lift available, but the single wings would have to house numerous machine guns *and* the undercarriage, while at the same time being strong enough to survive the power dives and steep turns the new air combat would demand. It's hard to appreciate today, but in the early stages of monoplane development there were many in the RAF who were utterly loath to lose what for them made the biplane the default word in fighter design.

The Air Ministry threw down the challenge, issuing a series of specifications in the early 1930s for new low-wing monoplanes that would incorporate all the features that would separate the new generation of fighters from the old. Two British companies, in the forefront of aircraft development at the time, were in a position to take up that challenge. Hawker was the first; its chief designer, Sydney Camm, would go on to develop the Hurricane. A small company in Southampton, Supermarine, also responded to the same tender, under the auspices of its chief designer Reginald Mitchell. Mitchell was a prodigy, appointed head of design at the age of only twenty-four; he had already made his name by designing the aircraft that had finally won the Schneider Trophy outright for Britain in 1931 – and this experience was crucial for the development of the Spitfire.

The Schneider Prize for seaplanes had been launched by Jacques Schneider, the French Under-Secretary for Air, in 1911, designed to encourage progress in civil aviation. It soon became a contest about speed, and in the 1920s did much to advance aircraft development as rival nations competed to win the prize. The rules stated that the trophy would be won outright by any nation winning the annual, and later biennial, contest three times in succession. The British Supermarine company first won victory in the 1922 race when their Sea Lion reached the speed of 145 mph. The Americans and the Italians won in subsequent years, but in 1927 Supermarine was firmly back in the contest, with Mitchell's latest aircraft, the S5, which took first and second place with a winning speed of 281 mph. By the time of the next contest, in 1929, the Supermarine S6 was ready, powered by a new engine from Rolls-Royce that was capable of producing an incredible 1900 horsepower.

Opposite: A Sopwith Camel in flight, one of the most successful aircraft of the First World War

The so-called 'R' engine helped the S6 reach a winning speed of 328 mph. By 1931, the British Government had withdrawn support from the competition, and it was only thanks to a generous gift of £100,000 from Lady Houston that Supermarine was able to enter once again.

Her support turned out to be enough to secure the Schneider Trophy for Britain for ever: the S6B was the only entry, and with an 'R' engine now boasting 2000 horsepower, was able to reach an astonishing 340 mph. Two weeks later, the S6B was breaking its own world speed record, with a recorded top speed of 407 mph. It is too easy for the contemporary mind to underestimate what an enormous achievement this represented. Less than 20 years previously, in 1913, Maurice Prevost had won the first Schneider Trophy in a Deperdussin at an average speed of just 46 mph.

In designing the new monoplane, armament was crucial, for what drove fighter development was an obsession with bombers. It was standard wisdom that the bomber would be the decisive weapon of aerial combat, and that the only requirement a fighter would have to meet would be its ability to counter the threat it posed. Fighter-to-fighter dogfighting, the style of combat that had dominated the experiences of the flying aces towards the end of the First World War, was not the principal aim; being able to decimate slow-flying, armoured bombers was. It was this that forced the Ministry and its suppliers to face up to the question of armament. It was clear that the one or two machine guns that had been standard during the First World War would be simply inadequate to the task of taking on multi-engined planes,

'By dint of much blotting paper, arithmetic and burning of midnight oil, I reached the answer of eight guns as being the number required to give a lethal dose in two seconds of fire.'

Ralph Sorley

especially those using metal in their construction. It was Squadron Leader Ralph Sorley, posted to the Operational Requirements Branch at the Air Ministry in 1933, who made the calculations that pointed to eight machine guns being the minimum necessary to deliver the killer blow. As a flier himself, he had correctly realised that no fighter could hope realistically to be able to keep a target in sight for longer than a couple of seconds, so the rate of fire would have to be intense and lethal.

In his account of the origins of Hurricane and Spitfire development penned in 1957, Sorley recorded his thinking:

'By dint of much blotting paper, arithmetic and burning of midnight oil, I reached the answer of eight guns as being the number required to give a lethal dose in two seconds of fire. I reckoned that the bomber's speed would probably be such as to allow the pursuing fighter only one chance of attack so it must be destroyed in that vital two-second burst.'

The most obvious implication of this would be a complete rethink of where to house the guns. Previously, they'd been placed in front of the cockpit, which conveniently kept them within reach of the pilot who was able to clear the frequent jams. With eight guns, this would now be impossible. It would also help if they could be kept clear of the propeller. It was technically feasible to fire through propellers (the Messerschmitt 109 would do so, with lethal results) but at a cost of firing rate. The answer then was obvious: it had to be in the wings. This of course demanded far greater reliability; if they jammed there was nothing the pilot would be able to do. It also required a new firing system, culminating in a trigger in the control

column. This meant pneumatic controls, not the traditional mechanical ones.

Peter Brothers flying a Hawker Hurricane, the plane that became the backbone of Fighter Command's war effort

However, all of Sorley's work on these problems would have remained theoretical had it not been for two other men: Hugh Dowding, appointed head of Fighter Command in 1936, and Max Aitken (Lord Beaverbrook), the Canadian newspaper magnate who would be made Minister of Aircraft Production in 1940. Both reached the same conclusion on their own: namely, that the future belonged to fighter monoplanes, and that it would be their job to ensure Britain had them. So when Sorley approached Dowding with his explanation of why eight guns were essential, he was rapidly sent off to visit both Hawker and Supermarine, and he readily persuaded them to abandon their first plan, using the fuselage as the gun-base. Instead, both companies agreed to try designs following his suggestion that this was a job for the wings.

The Hawker Hurricane was the first plane to be developed with all these innovations, while remaining rooted in conventional aircraft technology. Just one look at it makes its lineage clear: this is basically the Gloster Gladiator (the first fighter to be built with an enclosed cockpit, and with its debut in 1936, the last biplane introduced into RAF service) stripped of a wing, its cockpit replaced by the cucumber-frame canopy, and big, wide wheels that could be retracted after takeoff. The Hurricane embraces modernity, without abandoning tradition. Its frame was constructed from tubular steel and Duralumin, but wooden runners and fabric were also used. But look at the root of that wing – big, blunt and very thick. This gave the

Hurricane great virtues. Its pilots grew to love the stability those wings offered, its steadiness as a gun platform, the strength and volume to allow the machine guns to be placed close to one another. Peter Brothers was one of those appreciative pilots.

'At first, I was flying the Hurricane, which was a lovely aeroplane, rugged, wide, stable undercarriage, particularly comfortable for rough ground. And a very good solid gun platform, and it could take a lot of battle damage. Later, I was flying the Spitfire, which was a more delightful aeroplane to fly and control but had its disadvantages with a narrow undercarriage, which made it a little unstable on the ground, and it wasn't such a good gun platform.'

> *'At first, I was flying the Hurricane, which was a lovely aeroplane, rugged, wide, stable undercarriage, particularly comfortable for rough ground. And a very good solid gun platform, and it could take a lot of battle damage.'*
>
> Peter Brothers

Although Brothers agrees with most pilots that the Spitfire had better performance, he stresses that the Hurricane's gun platform was a considerable advantage.

'The Hurricane's nose curved down slightly, the result being that when you were taking a deflection shot, in other words, pointing well ahead of the target you were shooting at, with the Hurricane you could observe it the whole time. With the Spitfire you could lose your target on to the nose, so you couldn't see him. When you pressed the firing button, you hoped he was still there but, of course, you weren't sure that he was.'

To this day, Christopher Foxley-Norris also has the warmest memories of the Hurricane: 'It was a dear old thing. It had a sort of maternal feeling. You relied on it to get you home. More likely than not, a Hurricane could be counted on to get you home. I think you felt enormous confidence in a Hurricane.'

Foxley-Norris was a Hurricane pilot throughout the Battle of Britain with No 3 Squadron, later serving as an Air Chief Marshal. When he did have the opportunity to fly a Spitfire, it proved to be more of a challenge than he'd bargained for: 'I did fly a Spitfire once and I broke it. I made what they call a below average landing, and they had to put a new propeller on it. Disappointing, really.'

In fact, the Hawker Hurricane was nothing short of a major leap forward compared to the biplanes in service at the time, the first operational RAF aircraft capable of a top speed in excess of 300 mph. First flown on 6 November 1935 by its test pilot, P.W.S. 'George' Bullman, the first fleet of fighters were delivered to No 111 Squadron at Northolt in December 1937. In terms of numbers, the Hurricane would become the most important plane for the RAF in the Battle of Britain – a total of 1715 of them flying with Fighter Command, far more than all the other types of British fighter combined. Unlike the Spitfire, the Hurricane was a fully operational fighter in July 1940 – no wonder that it's estimated to have been responsible for four-fifths of the enemy aircraft destroyed between July and October 1940.

Tom Dalton-Morgan flew both Hurricanes and Spitfires during the Battle of Britain, and is also keen to recognise the important contribution made by the Hurricane.

'The Hurricane was a good aircraft to fight in. I soon learnt how to fight it – you know you can fly an aeroplane, but you've got to learn how to fight in it as well, and I found it a good fighter and it could carry a lot of punishment from enemy aircraft and still come back. I brought one home once with a chap who got on my tail. It looked like a colander, but they were able to repair it and I was soon back on the line in the squadron. I've fought in the Spitfire, too, and there's not much between them. I think the Hurricane could take more punishment, because it had an airframe underneath the skin. But there wasn't much in it. They were both good aircraft to fly for fighting. The Spitfire gets all the glory, it's still said in some places the Spitfire won the Battle of Britain. Well, that's quite untrue. Most of the squadrons in the Battle of Britain were Hurricanes.'

The advantage of Sydney Camm's great pragmatism – build on developing the achievement of the past – was to be crucial. It gave the RAF numbers, and it gave them reliability. In the end, these were the qualities that would prove just as crucial as the superiority of the Spitfire, if not more so. The Hurricane was built in numbers, which gave Fighter Command its backbone. The Hurricane was easier and quicker to build than the Spitfire would be, because the materials it used were familiar, the technology of their construction much less sophisticated. The Hurricane was also sturdier in the air. The stressed metal used by the Spitfire would only need a few bullet punctures to require a complete and time-

> 'The Hurricane was a good aircraft to fight in. I soon learnt how to fight it – you know you can fly an aeroplane, but you've got to learn how to fight in it as well, and I found it a good fighter.'
>
> Tom Dalton-Morgan

consuming overhaul; the fabric and wood of the Hurricane could be endlessly patched up. The Hurricane was easy to fly, especially for novices. Its wide outward-sloping undercarriage was a boon for the beginner having to negotiate bumpy grass runways, especially when landing. The Spitfire was far, far trickier on the ground, with its very much narrower wheelbase. Until a pilot got used to managing the powerful torque that would insist on pulling the plane off to the side, there was always the very real fear that the Spitfire could be tipped over. No wonder that by the end of the Battle of Britain it was the humble Hurricane that accounted for the lion's share of kills. Many of its pilots remained its most fervent fans, right to the end, adamantly refusing to relegate it to second best compared to the Spitfire.

However, while the Hurricane was undoubtedly robust and capable of sustaining considerable combat damage before being forced on to the scrapheap, it lacked manoeuvrability and finesse, and was undoubtedly inferior in terms of speed and climb compared to the Spitfire; most pilots would see a bigger difference between the Hurricane and the Spitfire than Tom Dalton-Morgan does. The Luftwaffe certainly saw the Hurricane as an inferior model, jokingly calling them 'tired old puffers'. The Hurricane would have only a year or so of unrivalled public adulation, before it was forced into the shadows by the arrival of the Spitfire.

It would fall to the Spitfire, built by Supermarine and benefiting from the technological breakthroughs the company had made in pursuit of the Schneider Trophy, to be the

encapsulation of Sorley's master vision. It's hard to take so mythologised a thing, and not assume it wasn't the product of mythological processes. Reginald Mitchell's early death at the age of forty-two, just in time to see his creation in the air, its lineage back to the glamorous world of seaplane racing, the overcoming of government indifference thanks to rich private individuals – all of this has become part of the Spitfire legend and, although none of it is completely untrue, this goes far from telling the whole story. In fact, much that characterises the long-haul process that led from drawing board to airfield took on the all-too familiar forms of endless government bureaucracy, and equally endless engineering and technical refinement.

The design of the plane was beset with many mundane problems. How to organise the cooling plant, deciding on the number of guns it could take, and furious debates about the size of the tail fin. So even in the 1930s, the production of a revolutionary new aircraft, at the absolute outer edge of technology, was a long, protracted and deeply complex mixture of science, intuition and government red tape. There were enough buccaneering spirits who played a role in the story of the Spitfire to keep the less attractive elements to a minimum, and indeed edged out of the legend altogether, but no matter how glorious the end-result, the Spitfire was the product of tried and tested methods.

But most importantly, it was a plane Britain nearly didn't have at all. Although it had its origins in a trophy-winning seaplane, the transformation of a prize-winning thoroughbred into a bread-and-butter front-line fighter was a bitterly political and economic one. Those who conceived the plane, and helped to pay for it, were working in the highly charged climate of 1930s politics; at a time when Britain was racked by economic hardship – and a yawning ideological divide between a minority convinced that war with Germany was inevitable, and those who would do anything to avoid a repetition of the Great War. They didn't know it, but they were locked in a battle against time, one Britain very, very nearly lost.

Reginald Mitchell began work on what was to become the Spitfire in 1934, a year after Camm started on the Hurricane. The story goes that a visit to Germany had alerted him to the growing threat that would be posed by German airpower. Whatever the genesis of his interest, it soon grew all-consuming. He had cut his design teeth on revolutionary monoplanes, those entrants in the Schneider Trophy, single-winged seaplanes that had only one purpose: to fly their pants off, in the process breaking all records for speed and astonishing the world. While the exact lineage between the Schneider Trophy seaplanes and the Spitfire may have become exaggerated in the growth of the legend, there is no doubt that they do share one very distinctive thing – their elegant outlines. Despite the immense amount of tinkering and trial and error that the Spitfire required in its development phase, what is particularly striking is just how early it appeared on the drawing board as looking like the virtually finished Spitfire we have all become so familiar with.

Mitchell's ambition wasn't evolution but revolution, a plane that in one leap would take the whole idea of the fighter forward, not by increments, but to a whole new level of sophistication. The break

Opposite: An early Mark I Spitfire, its distinctive elliptical wings in clear view

between monoplane and biplane would be absolute. The sheet of paper he started with was blank compared to Camm's. The journey from that sheet to operational flying was both longer, and more exacting – but the result: complete vindication.

Mitchell's first stabs at a fast monoplane interceptor ended in failure, though – a stubborn reminder that what they were attempting would require a great leap forward in both design and building know-how. The problem was the engine. He needed power and reliability, and the Rolls-Royce engine he was using, the Goshawk, gave him neither. What Mitchell needed, in fact, was the Merlin, Rolls-Royce's next great advance in engine technology; a V12 intended to produce 1000 horsepower, and, like the Schneider Trophy series of monoplanes, a private venture. Royce was dead before it was perfected, but it meant Mitchell had his missing piece, and now work could start in earnest in producing that revolutionary new aircraft, one that went well beyond government specifications.

The result would be the Supermarine Type 300 – or Spitfire, as it would very quickly come to be called. And that iconic name? Mitchell didn't approve of the original name, the 'Supermarine Shrew'. The chairman of Vickers, the company with a controlling interest in Supermarine, Sir Robert McLean, described his daughter as a little spitfire and so the new fighter was named after her. Mitchell was less than impressed, commenting 'just the sort of silly name they would give it'.

> *Spitfire (noun): a quick-tempered or volatile person.*
>
> The New Penguin English Dictionary

Taking the Spitfire from the drawing board to the production line was no mean feat in itself. It had proved to be almost unmakeable, suffering endless setbacks, and increasing scepticism in the Air Ministry, who were beginning to doubt the need for such a troublesome thoroughbred at such a vital moment in the numbers game. Even at full production, it was a plane that required the skill of true craftsmen to build, taking three times as many man-hours as the Messerschmitt 109. Was this a case of the best being the enemy of the good? There seemed no end of issues in need of being ironed out before the Spitfire could go fully operational. The question of engine cooling was resolved by the decision to replace water with glycol, which was much better at the job and required less heavy apparatus. The ailerons were covered with metal, not fabric, which gave them the strength required for steep dives.

Nowhere was the Spitfire more revolutionary than in its wings. Like Camm and his Hurricane, Mitchell faced an enormous, double challenge: to make the single wing do more work in lift and drag control than two could do, *and* make it strong enough to house four machine guns and an undercarriage. But Mitchell wasn't even content with that. His ambition was to produce a wing that owed nothing to the world of the earlier biplane, that made no compromises in performance whatsoever. Above all, it would be thin, where the Hurricane's was thick, and it would incorporate one of the hardest shapes to produce in bulk, the ellipsis, or oval.

He was drawn to the elliptical shape, not just because of its appearance but because of its aerodynamic advantages – though they were advantages that came at a price. He knew this

Spitfire MkI

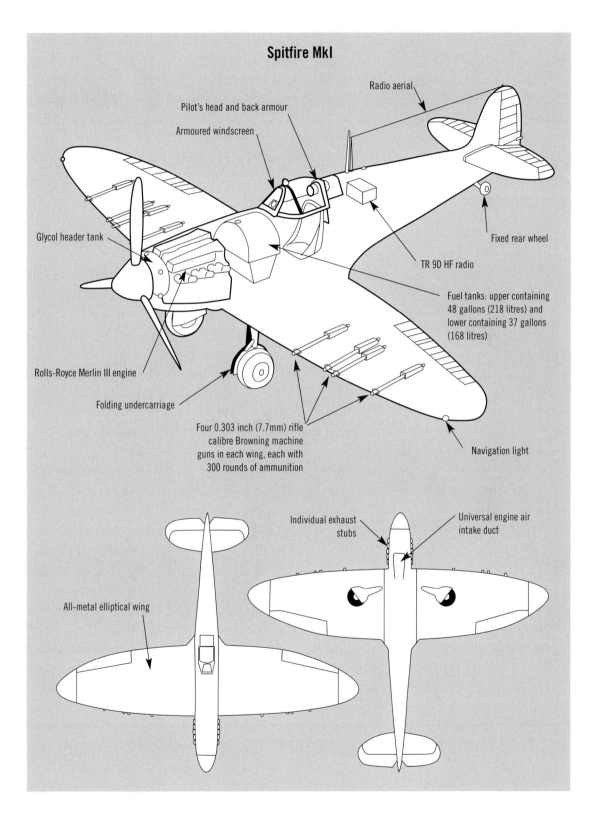

Radio aerial

Pilot's head and back armour

Armoured windscreen

Glycol header tank

Rolls-Royce Merlin III engine

Folding undercarriage

Four 0.303 inch (7.7mm) rifle calibre Browning machine guns in each wing, each with 300 rounds of ammunition

Fixed rear wheel

TR 9D HF radio

Fuel tanks: upper containing 48 gallons (218 litres) and lower containing 37 gallons (168 litres)

Navigation light

Individual exhaust stubs

Universal engine air intake duct

All-metal elliptical wing

would make life difficult for him. The geometry was highly complex, but nothing as compared to the business of building it, never mind mass-producing it. Beverley Shenstone, Mitchell's aerodynamicist, would later recall the development of the elliptical wing: 'The elliptical wing was decided upon quite early on. Aerodynamically it was the best for our purpose, because the induced drag, that causing lift, was lowest when this shape was used: the ellipse was an ideal shape, theoretically, a perfection.'

While the initiative and the impetus for the Spitfire belong to Mitchell and his single-minded concern that war with Germany was inevitable, the Spitfire was also the product of a powerful team of collegiate-minded men, all working to the same end. This was a period of endless refinement and scrutiny, decisions being made with one end in mind, namely, how to make this the world's finest fighter. It took two years simply for Supermarine to tool up for the new design. There were compromises. The cockpit was kept low, restricting the pilot's view, but reducing drag. There was little alternative to the need for a long nose to house the lean dimensions of the Merlin engine, which drastically interfered with forward vision. When you remember that the Spitfire is a tail dragger – stationary on the ground, its nose points steeply upwards – you appreciate what a challenge simply taking off becomes. No wonder the experienced Spitfire pilot learnt to weave left and right, giving him glimpses of what lay in front of him. But, as with everything, it remained simply something to grow accustomed to, a sacrifice well worth making given the performance advantages it produced. Cyril Bamberger, who flew with 610 and 41 Squadrons, can remember some of the operational issues the new Spitfire pilots faced.

> '*One probably disconcerting thing about it was that its nose was high up in front of you. You had very little visibility. So you had to swing the nose of the aircraft from side to side to see where you were going.*'
>
> Cyril Bamberger

'By the time I encountered my first Spitfire, I was lucky compared to some. I'd flown 280 hours on an assortment of aircraft. But all fixed wing, with no sophistication of any kind. But I had the hours, I had that experience. So when I climbed into a Spitfire for the first time, I wasn't in awe of flying, but the Spitfire had a retractable undercarriage. The ones we were flying at that point had a two-speed propeller control and the aircraft had flaps. But one probably disconcerting thing about it was that its nose was high up in front of you. You had very little visibility. So you had to swing the nose of the aircraft from side to side to see where you were going. Remember, we're in grass airfields again, where we're trying to stay on taxi tracks or runways. And so I'd studied the handbook well, and obviously been given some advice, and lined the aircraft up for takeoff.'

He remembers the experience of taking off in a Spitfire for the first time.

'When you open the throttle, it had not what I'd call a delicate undercarriage, but a fairly light undercarriage. The aircraft swung around a little bit to start with. So you opened the throttle to full throttle. You chose from fine pitch and you started bouncing, because you did in a Spitfire on grass. And it was rather good when you felt you were getting lift, when you could bring the tail up a little. And you were bouncing quite a lot and you were getting airborne, and you eased the control column back and you were in the air. And then a slight problem arose. Not really a problem, but it made you think. Because on the earlier Spitfires, the ones that I was doing my first solo on, you had to pump up the undercarriage. So you had your right hand on the control column and your left hand on the throttle. You'd make certain the throttle was tight open, you had a nut to tighten it up. Because then you had to transfer your left hand to the control column and your right hand to pump up the undercarriage. Now, the actions were opposite. You had to pump the undercarriage, which made your hand control of the column also move marginally backwards and forwards. So you went off in rather an undulating fashion. This is only in the earlier flights. Until you got used to this pumping the undercarriage up. And you were in the air. Beautiful.'

'It was totally different to any other aircraft you'd flown, the speed in particular, and the handling qualities. And it was a wonderful thrill.'

Cyril Bamberger

After takeoff, comes the landing.

'It was totally different to any other aircraft you'd flown, the speed in particular, and the handling qualities. And it was a wonderful thrill. You were airborne in a Spitfire. But of course you had then to come down. And you went to the circuit to land and you came in on a curved approach, not a straight approach, so you could see better where you were landing, but of course you had to remember to put your undercarriage down, and also landing flaps to slow yourself down. While you'd been flying around you've been in coarse pitch. These things may not seem a lot when you're dealing with modern aircraft, but they were things you'd never done before and you had to remember to do them. And you came in to land and once again you didn't have to aim for a three-point landing because you would land on your wheels. So if you're a little bit fast, it didn't really matter, as long as you didn't bounce. So you tried to get your speed correct for landing. And you touched down and kept the aircraft running straight. Obviously you'd cut all the power off by then. Got the aircraft running straight by use of your rudder. And you were down and, well, you'd done it once, you knew you could do it again.'

For pilots used to fixed undercarriages, it would be particularly important to remember to lower the undercarriage before landing; during the Battle of Britain, several Spitfires were damaged because pilots had forgotten to do so.

The Spitfire's test pilot, 'Mutt' Summers, was so impressed after his first flight, at Eastleigh Aerodrome on 5 March 1936, that he famously told the design team 'Don't touch anything.' Summers may actually have meant by this that he wanted to ensure that his measurements on the next flight were accurate but, even at this relatively early stage in the plane's development, the Spitfire was clearly a hit. The first operational Spitfire entered service with No 19 Squadron at Duxford in June 1938, a year after Mitchell's death from cancer. Others would continue to develop the fighter throughout the war, with twenty-two versions built by the end of production in February 1948, a total of 20,400 aircraft. Continual improvements were made: the propeller was upgraded, a bubble canopy added to improve visibility, and bullet-proof glass to the windscreen. It has been suggested that, had Mitchell lived, the evolution of the design would have been even more radical, the brilliance of Mitchell's mind rarely matched by his colleagues.

As Mitchell's vision was made actuality, pilots felt the excitement of seeing a Spitfire for the first time, and the sense of working with the very latest in aircraft design. Tom Neil still has vivid memories.

'When the Spitfires arrived at Church Fenton, I'd never been near a Spitfire in my life. And it was the early part of the war, and they came in all different stages of development. We didn't have constant speed propellers, for example, we had two-pitch propellers, that is fully fine or fully coarse. Some of us had undercarriages which came up by themselves, other ones you had to pump like mad. Every aircraft was virtually different. It was only a little later on that they became more or less standardised with the Spitfire, that they all had the same engine. They were very reliable, though, and they were delightful aeroplanes, they really were. And it didn't worry us a scrap except they were rather skittish on the ground, whereas a Hurricane wasn't quite so skittish. Flying a Spitfire was rather like being a kid and being asked to drive a Bugatti with somebody else paying for the fuel. It was a wonderful thing, and particularly, in those days, one could fly round the country virtually without restriction. So a lot of our training was low flying, and being in Yorkshire, we used to wander round the Yorkshire Dales at nought feet.'

> '*Flying a Spitfire was rather like being a kid and being asked to drive a Bugatti with somebody else paying for the fuel.*'
>
> Tom Neil

Neil remembers fondly the pre-war days of training, and getting used to the Spitfire, before the rigours of combat.

'I remember a wonderful occasion, where I was leading a formation of three, in Spitfires, and somewhere around Giggleswick, up in the Dales, and I came across a chap up a telephone pole who was mending the wire, or doing whatever it was, so, of course, we aimed ourselves at him, and he didn't know whether to jump or stay put. And I remember going round in a circle and coming at him a second time, and as he passed over the top, he decided to jump. All I remember was seeing him, spread-eagled arms, as he leapt from the top of the pole. He was obviously damaged but that didn't worry us a scrap. A nineteen-year-old pilot doesn't worry, of course. I also remember, after that, we went down and there was around Leeds a wood with a big lake in the middle. And in the middle of the lake in a sort of canoe affair, were a courting couple, doing what courting couples do in canoes. And I remember going down, leading my trio of aeroplanes and nearly knocking the chap out of the boat. And I remember looking back into the mirror that we had above our heads and seeing the boat was – well, not exactly upturned but not going the way it should have gone, with nobody in it. I thought, "My God, they've jumped overboard or done something like that," and I was dead keen to get away from this as quickly as I possibly could. And so I remember climbing up and taking my motley crew of three away and circling for half an hour until we begun to run out of fuel, before going

home. And then we exchanged glances on the ground and decided we wouldn't tell anybody what we'd just done. But those were the things that happened to one, when you're a nineteen-year-old Spitfire pilot with a lovely aeroplane.'

Nigel Rose and his first Spitfire, 'the most beautiful aircraft you'd ever seen'

Allan Wright first came into contact with fast, single-seater monoplanes when he joined his squadron.

'I remember that we were near London – Croydon. And I can remember this line-up of Spitfires and thinking, "My goodness, that's going to be something," because there's no dual. You sat in the cockpit a long time, with a chap over your shoulder showing you everything, and saying how they behaved, but you didn't know how it was going to behave until you actually flew it.'

Indeed, taking off in a Spitfire for the first time remains a memorable moment for Wright.

'Big gulp when you start off, because, of course, when you take off, you'd got to land, you know. It's a big moment in one's life, no question. The first flight went all right, though. It was a grass airfield, which is an advantage in a way, because you've got a wide area in which to land on, whereas when you're landing on a

> *'You've got fifteen hundred horsepower just six feet away from you, in the front there. And the exhaust pipes are only this long, and they're out here, and they're pointing straight at you.'*
>
> Allan Wright

runway, you've got to pick a circle, in such a way that you're going to be pointing in the right direction at the end of the runway, it might be a tight turn or it might be a wide turn. But with grass, you can afford to make mistakes and not worry too much, because you've got a wide area on which to land.'

Wright was also struck by the power of this new machine, and the contrast between the Spitfire and other planes he'd flown.

'The Spitfire was a very powerful aircraft, oh yes. I sat in one not long ago and started up the engine. I was amazed at the vibration, a terrific din. You've got fifteen hundred horsepower just six feet away from you, in the front there. And the exhaust pipes are only this long, and they're out here, and they're pointing straight at you. So, if it weren't for the cockpit being closed, it's almost unbearable. How the airmen coped with it, I don't know, because they're usually pretty close, or hanging over getting your straps on, when the thing is ticking over. We felt very privileged, actually, to begin to fly the Spitfire, in our case, rather than the Hurricane, because a Spitfire has obviously cleaner lines and will obviously go faster, and therefore it's going to be a better – so we thought, and probably rightly – fighter, than the biplane for fighting 109s, which were also not dissimilar from Spitfires. And I certainly wouldn't have liked to have had to cope with 109s flying a Hurricane.'

This love of Spitfires that is apparent time and time again in the veterans of Fighter Command is genuine, and not just driven by patriotism. Ludvik Martel, the Polish exile who flew with No 603 Squadron, was just as passionate about Spitfires as his British comrades.

'I felt extremely happy to fly Spitfires, because the Spitfire was an extremely pleasant aircraft to fly. There were practically no vices, providing you observe all the rules and regulations, which were published by the manufacturers. It was the fastest thing we'd ever flown. So that was quite nice, when you open up and then you reach practically a new level just touching 300 mph, and you realise that you are in something super. You could do exactly the same in a Spitfire as in the planes you had been trained in. The Spitfire was fully aerobatic. That was obvious, there's no fighter aircraft which is not fully aerobatic because all the dogfights are full of aerobatics. And then you feel so happy being able to fly. You flew like you were a part of that aircraft. I mean, whatever you do, the aircraft responds to your wishes.'

Martel is clear in his mind that the Spitfire was a big improvement on the Hurricane: 'Well, I always consider the Hurricane as an old lady. But the Spitfire is a lovely young girl, you know,

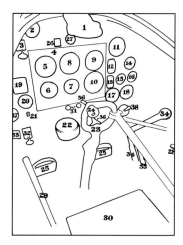

Inside a Spitfire cockpit (key to photo opposite) 1: platform for gunsight 2: flap position indicator 3: flap lever 4: instrument flying panel 5: airspeed indicator 6: altimeter 7: directional indicator 8: artificial horizon 9: rate of climb indicator 10: turning indicator 11: revolution counter 12/13: oil & fuel pressure gauges 14: engine boost gauge 15/16: oil & temperature gauges 17/18: fuel gauges19: chassis position indicator 20: flying position indicator 21: lights switch 22: compass 23: control column 24: gun button 25: foot stirrups on rudder bar 26: reflector sight light switch 27: dimming switch 28: key for downward recognition lamp 29: radiator flap control 30: seat31: floodlight switches 32: lever for landing light 33: throttle 35: undercarriage pump 35: undercarriage selector lever 36: pneumatic brake lever 37: air pressure control (for guns and brakes) 38: fuel cock

with the beautiful lines and everything and a wonderful performance which looks entirely different to the Hurricane.'

Tom Neil remembers the speed of the Spitfire, even if it wasn't quite as quick as expected.

'When the aircraft came out, in 1936, it was in the paper, this aeroplane will do 362 miles per hour. In fact, there were very few occasions when one flew 300. I always fondly thought that you flew around at 362 miles per hour, which was not the case. A Spitfire cruised at about 240, 250, and you weren't conscious of power, or at least I never was. And at altitude, I ought to explain that your speed is told to you by the airspeed indicator in the cockpit, which is only correct at nought feet. As you go up, and the pressure gets less, the airspeed indicator indicates a lesser figure than what you're actually flying. So, the true airspeed at twenty thousand feet, for example, is much more than is indicated on the ASI. So no, I was never conscious of the aeroplane gaining speed very quickly, and you could very quickly get up to 450 miles an hour on the airspeed indicator in a Spitfire, which, of course you couldn't do in a biplane or anything like that. But I was not conscious of any violent speed. You had to open fairly gingerly, otherwise the aircraft veered on takeoff.'

> 'A Spitfire hurtled into the wide blue yonder, dragging me along with it almost. I was hanging on to everything. The acceleration – that was a little bit awe-inspiring.'
>
> Geoff Wellum

Geoff Wellum recalls the most daunting part of flying a Spitfire:

'The takeoff was something like I'd never experienced before. And it soon became rapidly apparent that the aeroplane was flying me and not me it. A Spitfire hurtled into the wide blue yonder, dragging me along with it almost. I was hanging on to everything. The acceleration – that was a little bit awe-inspiring. But once you got it into the air, you obviously had a beautiful aeroplane. And you settled down in it very quickly. You got the wheels up and took it up a little bit and played around with it, and it did everything you wanted. You didn't subconsciously do something, you thought I would like to try a roll and the aeroplane did it. You know, what you thought transmitted itself to your hands, to your feet and to the aeroplane and it did it. That was the sort of thing I heard. Landing was a bit tricky, because you couldn't see out of it. It had a big nose in front of you. And if you were undershooting a bit and you wanted a little bit of throttle, the nose used to come up and it used to fly along in a tail-down attitude. And of course you had to get used to looking out at an angle. Once you mastered that you could three-point it on a threepenny bit. Absolutely docile. Nothing vicious about it. A beautiful aeroplane. I got to love the Spitfire.'

Iain Hutchinson, who'd been at the No 12 Service Flying Training School at Grantham, can remember the thrill when his squadron acquired Spitfires for the first time.

'At flying school, we were split up into single-engined pilots, designed to go to fighters, and multi-engined, and I was put in the multi-engined one, where we flew Ansons, and a more pedestrian aircraft you can't imagine than an Anson. So I did my advanced training squadron

A member of the ground crew re-arms one of No 19 Squadron's Spitfires at Duxford in September 1940

course there, and then I was posted to a Blenheim fighter squadron, No 236, at Martlesham Heath, which is, again, a twin-engined aircraft. And the third posting was to Duxford, No 222 Squadron, where they also had Fighter Blenheims. It wasn't until March 1940 that I came back from leave to find a whole squadron of Spitfires there and the Blenheims were no longer our steeds. It was Christmas, several times over. So, converted onto these, you were really on front-line aircraft of the first class, equal to anything the opposition might have. Our Squadron Commander took us up in a two-seat training aircraft, and he just took us around. We had to read the manual. He took us around and checked we were capable of flying it, sent us off solo, and after a couple of solo flights and that, we just went into a Spitfire and flew that. It was wonderful going on to the Spitfire. It was like a really powerful sports car.'

The Spitfire was a world away from the other planes Hutchinson had flown.

'The Spitfire differed from other aircraft in that it was highly manoeuvrable, it was nose heavy. It had a narrow track undercarriage, and it had two-pitch propellers, so that you had to be careful taxiing, you had to be careful taking off, because with the powerful engine it had, there's an enormous amount of torque – while the propeller was trying to turn round the aircraft, the aircraft was trying to turn round the propeller. That meant it put a lot of weight on one wheel and that wheel therefore tended to drag, therefore you had a tendency to swing to one side. So you had to counter that carefully. When you opened up the throttle you had to open it up gently. And you had to make sure that you were in fine pitch, because if you didn't, the airfield runway wasn't long enough to take off in. I remember once we were taking off in formation, I found I was falling further and further behind the squadron, and I couldn't understand it, because I had full throttle, until I realised that I was in coarse pitch, everybody else was in fine pitch. So it made a tremendous difference, really, on takeoff.

> '*With the powerful engine it had, there's an enormous amount of torque – while the propeller was trying to turn round the aircraft, the aircraft was trying to turn round the propeller.*'
>
> Iain Hutchinson

Once you were in the air and airborne and got up to speed, there was a plunger-like thing on the left-hand side of the aircraft, just partly behind you, and you put it into coarse pitch – I can't remember whether you pushed it in or pulled it out, at this stage. And then the aircraft went into coarse pitch and she was fine. And then, later on, when we went up to Kirton-in-Lindsey, and we converted to a constant speed propeller, it saved all that problem, and it looked after itself from then on in.'

Pilots flying the Spitfire for the first time largely had to work out these characteristics for themselves because, as George Unwin puts it, it was a case of stepping into the unknown.

'There were no pilot's notes in those days. There were no duals. All we were given was a quarto sheet of paper with the climbing speed, stalling speed, cruising speed and cruising revs, that was about it. And of course we had been flying Gauntlets, where nothing moved except the throttle, nothing. No hood, no undercarriage, no flaps, everything was static except the throttle. Here we get a thing where you've got a throttle, there was still only one throttle, there was no pitch in those days, so this dreadful two-bladed propeller – but you had things that went up and down and round about, an undercarriage that went up, flaps that came down and all this kind of thing, well, you're completely unused to them, and Duxford had only got about eight or nine hundred yards of runway. I'll never forget the takeoff. It was the most frightening thing in the world. Once you got it up it was fine, but it must have been a lovely aeroplane to fly because despite all that, the whole squadron went through without the slightest trouble. We used to fly an hour and a half trips, time after time. It was a lot of fun because they had a radio that worked. We'd never had one before, and you could go up to Newcastle or something in this thing and then say to the blokes on the ground, get me home, I'm lost, you know, and it worked. We'd never had this before.'

So although it was the Hurricane that bore the brunt of the combat in the Battle of Britain, it's Mitchell's Spitfire that gets the pilots' vote in terms of design and glamour. Even the Germans quickly latched on to the charisma of the Spitfire, and it was *'Achtung, Schpitfeuer!'* ('Look out, Spitfires!') that became the standard cry of Luftwaffe pilots, even when they saw Hurricanes approaching.

The RAF, however, needed fighters in numbers, not just world-beating prototypes. With time fast running out, as Britain's European allies fell to Nazi occupation, there still weren't enough Spitfires and Hurricanes being built, or even enough facilities to help build them. It was Lord Beaverbrook who would help to turn Dowding's plans and Mitchell's vision into front-line military reality. After being appointed by Churchill to run the newly formed Ministry of Aircraft Production in May 1940, he slashed his way through military red tape, forcing on Britain's aircraft factories the latest production methods. He brought in top business talent from the car industry, and helped spearhead popular campaigns to raise money for Spitfires, including the most famous, 'Buy a Spitfire', which produced a nationwide donation of pots and pans from which (ostensibly) to cull the aluminium.

> *'I'll never forget the takeoff. It was the most frightening thing in the world. Once you got it up it was fine.'*
>
> George Unwin

It's striking that the campaign was deliberately angled 'Buy a Spitfire', not 'Buy a Hurricane'. The campaign was an immediate success, with villages, towns and cities up and down the country collecting funds to purchase 'presentation Spitfires', an immediately recognisable way for individuals, communities or organisations to demonstrate their commitment to the war effort. Never mind, of course, that the true cost of a Spitfire was nearer £12,000 than the £5000 quoted by Beaverbrook's campaign, or that Beaverbrook knew from the outset that the pots and pans wouldn't be used for aircraft production. It was a propaganda triumph, which made the British public feel involved in the war, and it paid for nearly 1000 Spitfires to be built, representing around 11 per cent of the total production.

Both Beaverbrook and Dowding, in fact, brought a very un-British ruthlessness to the task in hand – very reminiscent of the way Dowding would run Fighter Command. They acted as scourges to everything that stood in their way: amateurishness, bureaucracy, patronage, complacency. It was Beaverbrook who gave the all-important second Spitfire factory at Castle Bromwich a complete overhaul immediately after his appointment to the Air Ministry, seeing the new Mark II roll off the production lines by the beginning of June. It was a similar story in other factories he took control over: production soared, efficiency peaked, and Britain got the air force it needed, by the skin of its teeth. Beaverbrook and Dowding formed a formidable and close-knit alliance, speaking daily throughout the course of the Battle of Britain. Interestingly, both had sons who were flying fighters, so the commitment to winning was deeply personal. And it was largely thanks to Beaverbrook that all these lessons remained in practice during the battle, ensuring both repairs and replacement aircraft kept ahead of the losses.

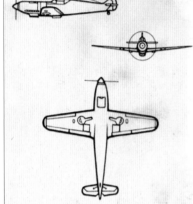

The Messerschmitt 109, built at Willy Messerschmitt's Bayerische Flugzeugwerke factory. From *German & Italian Aircraft: How to Spot Them*

What spurred on British endeavours was the news filtering out from Germany. In 1935 Hitler had revealed to the world what so many had suspected: Germany was now in possession of a military air force, his Luftwaffe, equipped with many hundreds of fighters and bombers. Everybody knew from then on that it would be a race against time. In fact, many of the figures were inflated by the Nazi propaganda machine, but this would backfire on the Luftwaffe: the RAF, hearing the size of the threat involved, were spurred on to equal the German air force.

The genuine growing strength of the Luftwaffe had only been too apparent during the Spanish Civil War, as Gerald Stapleton notes: 'The Germans were in Spain, and that's where they formed their tactics. And they were very much more experienced than we were, they'd been firing at enemy aircraft, and they were very, very good.'

Nigel Rose was equally aware: 'Certainly one knew that they'd had experience in Spain, which the RAF hadn't had. And that counted for quite a lot. I mean, the chaps who came over the Channel, a lot of them had had experience in Spain, and had built up their fighter squadrons accordingly, and bomber squadrons, too, of course.'

Since the Spanish Civil War, the Luftwaffe had continued to build up its fighting power and, in particular, it had developed the plane that would cause the greatest consternation during the Battle of Britain: its star fighter, the Messerschmitt Bf 109. Like Camm's Hurricane and Mitchell's Spitfire, this too was the product of the skill and obsession of one brilliant designer – Willy Messerschmitt. Conceived in the same year as the Hurricane, it had virtually the same performance attributes as the Spitfire, and there was little to choose between them. It was powered by an engine even more sophisticated than the Merlin, a Daimler-Benz with fuel injection. This gave it one distinct advantage over the Hurricane and the Spitfire. Because of their cruder gravity-operated carburettors, the British fighters couldn't fly upside-down, or dive by simply lowering the nose; both manoeuvres were negative gravity, which stopped the flow of fuel, cutting the engine. That gave escaping 109s a few invaluable seconds' start when diving to avoid attacks. The pursuing Hurricanes and Spitfires would have to peel off first, before diving, or dive by corkscrewing. Either way, the 109 maintained an important advantage.

The Bf 109, though, had its share of compromises – as did all these fighters pioneering the demands of speed, altitude, robustness and the single wing. If Mitchell had been driven by the quest for perfect aerodynamics, then Messerschmitt's obsession was with size. His plan was to keep the airframe as tight and lean as he could, the minimum necessary to house his powerful engine. Like Mitchell, he designed thin wings but, unlike the Spitfire's, his weren't able to operate safely at low speeds, requiring a whole series of slats and flaps, which in turn limited their capacity for housing guns. Shorter and stubbier than the RAF fighters, with far smaller wing areas, it was faster than the Hurricane by around 30 mph, and pretty much the same as the Spitfire, with a top speed of around 350 to 360 mph. It was better at higher altitudes, and could dive faster. But all Mitchell's work on the elliptical wing had paid off: the Spitfire could out-turn the 109, which was crucial. It even had a bonus, a slight twist that gave the pilot advance warning of a possible stall. With its massive wing area, so too could the Hurricane.

The 109's worst flaw was its spindly, narrow wheelbase, which made it even harder to land than the twitchy Spitfire. Hundreds of them were written off, all through the war, in this manner, and it accounted for the lives of many young pilots, losses the Luftwaffe could ill afford. In the plane's early days, pilots weren't even allowed near it until they had clocked up over 100 hours of flying experience, so fearful was its reputation on the ground in the hands of a novice. Its cockpit was also much less kind to pilots than

> *'The fighters on the two sides were more or less very similar. One was possibly slightly faster, another was possibly slightly better at manoeuvring.'*
>
> Hans-Ekkehard Bob

that of the Hurricane or Spitfire, being much more cramped, restricted to one-size-fits-all (the Spitfire pilot seat could be raised or lowered), and having a pivoting rather than sliding canopy cover that was easily damaged in combat, making parachute escapes especially hazardous. But once flying a Bf 109 was mastered, this aeroplane engendered the same levels of affection and loyalty among its Luftwaffe pilots as the Spitfire and Hurricane did with the men of Fighter Command.

Hans-Ekkehard Bob was one of the Luftwaffe pilots flying a Bf 109 in the summer of 1940.

'The fighters on the two sides were more or less very similar. One was possibly slightly faster, another was possibly slightly better at manoeuvring – the Spitfire was slightly more manoeuvrable – but as far as speed was concerned, they were all almost the same, the Bf

109 was probably slightly faster. The Hurricane was probably the least suitable for the conditions. I don't want to denigrate the Hurricane, it's a good plane, but in terms of speed it was slightly slower and in terms of manoeuvrability the Spitfire was better, and the 109 was probably the fastest of them all, but it was also the least manoeuvrable. I once compared the 109 to a diva. The 109 isn't just externally beautiful – even now the 109 is considered to be a very beautiful, handsome, racy machine. It has qualities, it handles very impressively when it's in the air. On the ground it's a bit stiff, the undercarriage is problematical because it's too narrow for the plane. So this is a bit of a problem when taking off or landing, but when the 109 is in the air, it's reliable. It has an engine, a twelve-cylinder Daimler-Benz engine, which runs like clockwork, and it's powerful and reliable and easy to control.'

Bob can clearly remember his first encounter with a Spitfire.

'The Spitfire had received advance publicity as being a superior plane and there was some apprehension about what this was going to be like, the 109 against the Spitfire. But for me personally, my feeling was that I was in control of my plane and the Spitfire won't be a problem for me. As it turned out, I was consistently successful in aerial battles, I shot down eight Spitfires as well as six Hurricanes. So for me there were no concerns that the Spitfire would be superior to us. It was obviously an entirely different matter for pilots who might not have been in control of the 109 to the same extent. The problem was simply that the Spitfire was extremely manoeuvrable, albeit the 109 being still a bit faster, but you really had to bring to bear all of your skill and all of your feeling in order to be able to cope with the opponent in situations like this. During all of these aerial battles I managed again and again to outwit the Spitfire and to score air victories.'

The 109 was an aircraft that gained the respect of RAF pilots, too, like Nigel Rose.

'Generally, the ones I fired at were 110s, the, twin-engined aircraft, which they abandoned after about October or November on our front, as they reckoned they were too vulnerable. But the 109 was as good as the Spitfire and getting better all the time – every time the Spitfire got a bit better, there was a pause and then the 109 got a bit better and so it was leapfrogged, really. The 109 was a very neat plane, not as well finished off as the Spitfire, I think, and not as pretty as the Spitfire, but it had this central cannon in the nose, which was a fine piece of armament, no doubt about it. The Spitfire later got two cannon and four machine guns but very few squadrons had it during the Battle of Britain. There was a Spitfire Mark II, but not a lot of them at this stage.'

Key to the 109's success was its engine, as Tom Neil explains.

'I was never conscious of this enormous engine that the Spitfire had in flight. In fact, it was quite a small engine, and when we began to run into the Messerschmitt 109s, we found that it was a smaller aircraft than a Spitfire, but had a much bigger engine than we had. The Daimler-Benz 600 series engine was thirty-nine litres, the Rolls-Royce Merlin was twenty-seven – our engine was only about two-thirds the size of theirs. Theirs was much heavier and theirs, of course, would produce the power at much lower revs and much less a boost than ours. We

had to flog our engines a bit in order to be competitive, so to speak. People tend to overlook the fact that the 109, being a smaller aircraft, had a much bigger engine than we did.'

Nigel Rose (second from left) and members of his squadron

Keeping the engines – and all the other parts – of fighting planes in good order was a considerable job in itself. The RAF was not just about flying men, it was also about the 'erks', the armourers and fitters whose round-the-clock job it was to keep the aircraft armed, fuelled and, as close as possible, in one piece. These men were often as enthralled by the Spitfire as the pilots. Fred Roberts remembers the novelty of it.

'I finished my armourer's course, at Manby in Lincolnshire, and was posted to No 19 Squadron. I didn't know what they had or anything. And there were two of us out of the sixty-odd armourers that finished the course. We were posted to No 19 Squadron on a Friday, and when we got there, we were surprised to find that we had Spitfires, not only that, we were thrilled. Spitfires were something new. On the second day, arriving at Duxford (No 19 were based at Duxford), that was the Saturday morning, the NCO in charge of the armoury told one of the older armourers, one of the chaps who'd been there some while, to take us out and show us around. And you'll never believe the feeling, to sit in a Spitfire for the first time. Not only be sitting in a cockpit of a Spitfire but to sit in the cockpit of any aircraft then.

I had flown at Manby but only in the back seat of a Wallace or a Fairey Gordon, one of the old biplanes. There was nothing like the Spitfire. In fact, I'd go as far as to say that my first love is Spitfires, even today, and I've got pictures of them, books on them.'

Roberts' enthusiasm for the Spitfire remains, even though he found the Hurricane was much easier to maintain from an armourer's point of view.

'On a Spitfire, to do the daily inspection and put the plane to sleep at night, you had to take eight panels off the top of the wings, eight panels from underneath the wings and when you rearmed it, you had an additional four flaps covering the underside of the ammunition tanks. Now, in the Hurricane, you only had five panels altogether, one each covering four guns and one covering the ammunition tanks. They were much, much easier to maintain, but the Hurricane couldn't be armed as quick as a Spitfire, because in the Hurricane you didn't take the ammunition tanks out and put a new full one in, you had to put the belt of ammunition in the tank whilst it was in the aeroplane. But from a point of view of maintenance, the Hurricane was a much, much easier plane. Another thing with the Hurricane, you could kneel on the top of the wing and do all the maintenance. On the Spitfire, you couldn't, you had to get on your knees on the wet grass and take all these panels off to do the maintenance. But, nevertheless, for all that, having worked on both Hurricanes and Spitfires, the Spitfire is my first love, no other plane like a Spitfire.'

Joe Roddis was also in awe of the Spitfire.

'It was out of this world, we just could not believe it and it was so beautiful. On the ground, standing still, it looked as if it were doing 400 miles an hour.'

Joe Roddis

'I went on to my flight mechanics' course, which was wonderful, and a pal of mine and I went for a walk across the airfield one day and standing in one corner of the airfield were four aeroplanes. We'd never seen the likes of this. Big head straight up on to the wing and looked in and there on the rudder bar it said, "Supermarine". We knew what they were. We'd heard such a lot of talk about them, especially after the Hurricane had been doing 300 miles an hour and that. Then the Spitfire came out, we thought oh my God, and that was the first Spitfire I ever saw, parked on St Athan Airfield, brand new, never been let off, you know, nothing on the clock. But I knew it was a Spitfire by Supermarine and I thought, my God if I only get on these. Because at St Athan, for training all you had was Hawker and Avro tutors, biplanes, but to get on a Spitfire was the ultimate. It was out of this world, we just could not believe it and it was so beautiful. On the ground, standing still, it looked as if it were doing 400 miles an hour, but I never actually saw one flying until I'd gone on to No 234 Squadron that I was with in the Battle of Britain. We didn't have them, we had biplanes and Blenheims and Fairey Battles to play with until we could get our Spitfires, but the squadron next door to us, in the next hangar, No 609, they had their Spitfires and they were the first I saw flying. I was open-mouthed. And the sound of that Merlin! Brilliant, brilliant.'

The job of the 'erks' was often dangerous, and Roddis was to find that accidents would happen in the best-regulated airfields.

Corporal FAJ Marriott (on the wing) and his fellow 'erks' pose with a Hurricane

'The pilots all used to say that it was the kindest aeroplane to them that they'd ever flown. Not that they'd flown many but it would never hurt you, never do you any harm, that their job was purely flying it. We sometimes got into situations where if you didn't watch what you were doing they could hurt you and they often did, at times, but that was purely through carelessness or familiarity breeding contempt. You did things that you knew you shouldn't do and you got hurt. We've had a bloke walk into an airscrew turning taking the starter plug out. We've had an aircraft tip up on its nose and the propeller flew off and cut a bloke in half. I've still got this funny mark on my chin, because I walked into a propeller tip when it was stopped. It was an excellent aeroplane and providing you treated it with the respect it deserved it wouldn't hurt you.'

He describes his duties as a flight mechanic with No 234 Squadron.

'My responsibility was to nursemaid the engine. When they landed after a flight I'd refuel it, put oil in it. Other people would do their job with regard to armament, oxygen, radio and all that, but my job was purely engine. If there was a snag and it was within my capability to fix it, I would, and then I'd have the great job of running the engine up to see that what I'd done had resolved the problem. Whenever it landed I would do what they called an after flight. That was to give the engine a real good going over. I mean you look at it and say, oh nowt's happened there but a bullet could have gone through the carline as bullets would go through the propeller and it was my job, because they were wooden ones in those days, covered with a rubberised fabric with copper wiring, to get a rat-tail file and smooth it out. It used to whistle like hell when they started up and I often wonder why

> 'The rigger had a lot to do, his responsibility was all the wheels and tyres and airframes and the hood, he had to polish the hood so much because if there was a speck on the hood it could be mistaken for a German aircraft.'
>
> Joe Roddis

it didn't cause some imbalance, but it didn't matter, Spits didn't last very long anyway them days. After flight, and then I'd refuel it, recoil it, check around as much as I could, resolve any problems that the pilot had reported and they'd bring us back on readiness when all the other trades had finished their job. That was after a flight. Before a flight I would do what they call a pre-flight exam on the engine. I'd check everything thoroughly, see as we'd missed nothing, the oil tank was full, there was eighty-five gallons of petrol in the petrol tank, everything was all right in the cockpit, that was it. We were ready then and when everybody was ready they'd bring the aircraft on to readiness.'

Each Spitfire had its own ground crew.

'It would take about half an hour after flight to have it ready, about the same pre-flight, providing there were no problems to be solved or any repairs to be done – some people's jobs took longer than others. I mean the armourers had a lot to do stuffing the wings full of ammunition. The instrument man had the same, he had to replace the oxygen bottles, the radio man had to check such a lot. The rigger had a lot to do, his responsibility was all the wheels and tyres and airframes and the hood, he had to polish the hood so much because if there was a speck on the hood it could be mistaken for a German aircraft, you know. They were very very keen on that, polishing that hood. Might sound daft but they attached a lot of importance to it. So the ringo was running round with his bit of cloth and metal polish. But anyway, between us we could have it ready in half an hour.'

Sometimes, though, preparing a Spitfire for its next mission wasn't so straightforward.

'When it came back we would know immediately whether it had been in action because if the red patches were blacked out on the gun ports, he'd fired. We knew we had something to deal with. A lot of the time they'd got away with it. There was no problem. It just needed an ordinary after flight refuel and that. Other times there was damage. I had very very little damage to the engine. It was mainly airframe, air screw, perhaps radio instruments, but the engine would take a hell of a battering before it would pack in, and as regards the fuel tank it had a great big armoured plate over the top of it so we knew we were all right there. If I'd no problems I'd go and help my rigger and if we'd both got no problems, we'd go and help the armourer. We were a team there to look after that Spitfire, to nursemaid that Spitfire – the Spitfire on the ground is a useless aircraft. Our aim was to get it back up there as quick as we could. Quick as the pilots wanted it. They always wanted it a lot quicker, obviously.'

Peter Brothers plays with his dog Merlin

Peter's wife, relaxing during a picnic in the summer of 1940

A crowd of airmen and ground crew survey a crashed Hurricane

Although members of the ground crew never left the ground, all too often they found themselves the targets of air attacks. They suffered terrible casualties first in France supporting the Hurricanes sent over by Churchill, and later in the British airfields that took the brunt of the German bombing. Their job was one of almost total hardship. Their accommodation rarely rose above the rudimentary, sometimes not even that – they would make do with tents, outhouses, anything with a roof. Their daily regime involved servicing the aircraft that were undamaged, before facing the Herculean task of repairing the many, many aircraft that limped home riddled by bullets and scarred by fire. Squadrons were flying four or five sorties a day, each time requiring the fitters to refuel, rearm, and cover the gun ports (to protect them from freezing) before moving onto a host of engine checks. Oil, coolant and oxygen supplies had to be replenished – and all of this in half an hour. Their work never ended. Much of it had to be done out in the open, exposed to all the weather could throw at them, and invariably way into the night. Sleep was something snatched in bursts, or discarded altogether.

During August and September, the ground crews were being bombed and strafed by the Luftwaffe that had made the airfields their principal target. What scant accommodation they had was as often as not among the first structures to be destroyed by bombs and machine gun fire. It would then be their job to emerge from the smoking ruins, and get the airfield working again as soon as possible, filling holes in the runway, before transferring to the satellite fields, which acted as substitutes for the planes still operating.

As a flight mechanic, Joe Roddis was right in the firing line when airfields were being bombed.

'Whilst the first stage of the Battle of Britain was on we were bombed out of existence at St Neville. All our accommodation was bombed, people were killed, a Dornier and two Junkers 88s really did the place over. But the worst bombing we took was at Middle Wallop. We left St Neville on the 11th of August just as the airfield bombing started, and we got overhead at Middle Wallop and the ground was erupting and there were German aeroplanes everywhere. The pilot knew there was a raid on and there's us in a Hadley Page Harrow sat in long lines down the side on funny seats, and of course the pilot went straight down to the deck and off we went, hedge-hopping to get out the way. And he flew around for about half an hour and then he got word that the raid was over and we went and landed where we could. So we thought right, that was a good opening.

'Now our Spitfires weren't there yet, they were at St Neville. Our job was to get to Middle Wallop, find out where our dispersal was, which incidentally was in the bomb dump with a tent and nothing else. We dug slit trenches but if they'd decided to bomb our dispersal we'd have gone up anyway because the bomb dump was behind us. But when we got out the Hadley Page Harrow and got our kit the first thing they said was right, go and get a meal then come straight back because the Spitfires could be coming. 609 Spitfire Squadron were there and they were the big aces, we were the newcomers and we took some stick from them in the dining room as we walked in – and when I say a meal, what we got was a great big white china mug full of hot sweet tea and as many slices of bread and butter and tins of plum jam, turnip jam as you wanted, and we loved it, we ate it.

> 'We sat there talking and the next thing they were dropping everywhere. Lumps of masonry were flying about, tables were erupting, we were right in the middle of it, so we shot outside as quick as we could, mug of tea in one hand, bread and jam in the other.'
>
> Joe Roddis

'Anyway, we sat down all talking away and we were taking some stick from 609 ground crew and the siren went and the place emptied like mad and we thought what have we got here? We never used to run when the siren went at St Neville. They'd all gone and disappeared and we sat there talking and the next thing they were dropping everywhere. Lumps of masonry were flying about, tables were erupting, we were right in the middle of it, so we shot outside as quick as we could, mug of tea in one hand, bread and jam in the other. We were only kids mind you, seventeen, eighteen. We didn't know where the shelters were, we didn't know where anything was but running round the cookhouse were all the heating pipes and steam pipes and the tops had been taken off, we dived down there with the cups of tea and bread and jam. But they knocked hell out the place. They flattened the hangars, a string of bombs came through the top of the hangar, hit the hangar door and lifted it and dropped it on a crowd of people running past, yes, we took a lot of bombing.

'And one day at dispersal the planes were away. What had happened was they'd sent over a real gaggle of 109s, dozens, high up. Now it took a Spitfire nearly twenty minutes to get to thirty thousand feet, so they knew they were safe, playing about and weaving about. But eventually our Spits started to get near to them, then they moved off to Southampton. When they had gone the Junkers 87s came in. Oh, knocking hell out the airfield. We were getting short of fuel and the Flight Sergeant, the bloke in charge of the ground, said we need some fuel, go and get some, to me. I'd have done anything to drive the tractor which was towing a fuel bowser so I jumped on and off, I went across the airfield, all hell going on. Didn't worry me, I never thought for one minute anything could kill me, you didn't think that way. I got to the petrol dump, positively empty, nobody about. Went into the office, found the key board, got a key, went out, got the hundred-octane tank going, filled mine up, came back out and I'm trundling across the airfield with this tractor and a full bowser behind me, there was no perimeter track or anything, you just kept close to the edge. I'm going along and I looked up and there's a Heinkel 111 and as I looked up I could see the bombs leave it and the tractor wasn't going fast enough for me, I got off it and ran, I ran and ran until I couldn't run another inch. I was totally out of breath, I dropped down on the thing and as I dropped I heard these bombs drop in the main camp. Then I had to catch the tractor up and drive it back to dispersal.'

> *'I never ever knew anybody to be frightened. Perhaps we were stupid, I don't know, we might have been. I would be frightened now, believe me.'*
>
> Joe Roddis

Roddis particularly remembers the sound of the Stukas.

'Sometimes you could see them drop two bombs chained together. You could see them leave, you know, as they pulled up, they'd let them go and they're chained together. Make hell of a row. Used to frighten the life out of you. I don't think they had anything like sirens but the speed that they got to in the dive and the airscrew, they really made a hell of a racket, frightened the life out of you.'

Another unfortunate incident that Roddis remembers occurred while the ground crew were attempting to close the hangar doors at Middle Wallop during a bombing raid when a Junkers 88 dropped a bomb through the top of the hangar roof.

'That was sheer bad luck that that little gaggle of people, WAAFs and airmen, happened to be running between two hangars. I mean I never ever saw another hangar door blown off like that. Collapse inwards as the walls went, yes, but not blown off like that. This hangar door flopped on to this crowd of airmen and WAAFs and we ran down to see if we could do anything but we couldn't. There was a WAAF's arm sticking out with a wrist watch on, still going. It was nasty, but as I say we were kids, we lapped it up, we couldn't get enough of it. I never ever knew anybody to be frightened. Perhaps we were stupid, I don't know, we might have been. I would be frightened now, believe me.'

Pilot Iain Hutchinson remembers his ground crew having to work while under fire.

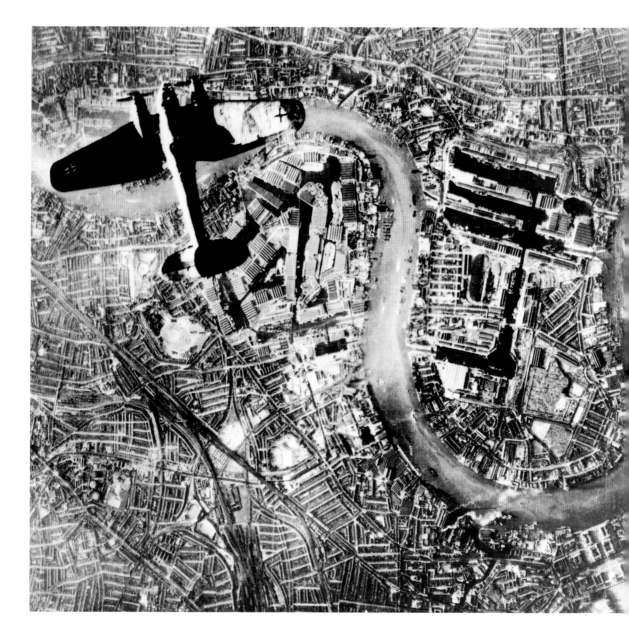

'I thought they were terrific. One of the times when I landed to rearm and refuel, the airfield was being attacked. I got out the cockpit and they got the machine gun rounds out. And I could hear this banging going on all over the place. I got under the wing, ostensibly to look and see if the guns had been reloaded, but basically I was trying to keep clear of any shrapnel that might come our way. Then I was very glad to get back into the aircraft and take off again, I may say. But they were out there in the middle of it, ignoring it all, and they were really fantastic. You could depend on them to the last man. And the great thing

A Heinkel 111 flies over Wapping and the Isle of Dogs during the Battle of Britain about it was that they were engineers of skill, they did an absolute precise job – there was no skimping any job, every job was done to perfection. They looked after their pilots better than anybody else could have done.'

Even without reckoning for repairs and damage, theirs was a full-time job. Just keeping the operational planes at readiness was time-consuming and arduous, warming the engine at regular intervals, checking the canopy was well lubricated, and the guns fully maintained. It would then be the fitter's job to help the pilot strap himself into the cockpit, and remove the chocks. No wonder many pilots had the most intense respect for their ground crews, striking up the closest of relationships. For their part, ground crews had to undergo the daily trial of seeing their charges take off, and, all too often, fail to return.

Geoff Wellum certainly appreciated his ground crew.

> *'The salt of the earth. Lovely, lovely people, great friends. You relied on them implicitly for your safety and they were wonderful young men, who had great affection for their pilot.'*
>
> Geoff Wellum

'The salt of the earth. Lovely, lovely people, great friends. You relied on them implicitly for your safety and they were wonderful young men, who had great affection for their pilot. Because as much as possible you used to fly their aeroplane, one pilot got used to the aeroplane. You had your own aeroplane. But it was their aeroplane, you see, and you were their pilot. And they were very proud of you, and I was very, very proud of them. Wonderful comradeship. Wonderful. Salt of the earth.'

The ground crew's imperative was to get the plane back in the air as soon as possible, even if there was a bombing raid on.

'Normally we didn't land when the thing was being bombed. I would never land it on an airfield when it was being bombed. But you'd land and you'd taxi in and they'd run out to meet you, and they'd grab each wing tip and guide you back into your dispersal pen. "How'd you get on, sir?" that sort of thing. "Oh, not much. Sprayed bullets all over Kent." "What, again, sir?" That sort of thing. The armourers would descend on their aeroplane and rearm you. You'd have about four or five people clambering over the aeroplane. They're wonderful people.'

Tom Dalton-Morgan also had a close relationship with his ground crew, acknowledging the need for a good team spirit.

'No 43 Squadron, right from its formation in the First World War, as I understand it from several of the pilots from that era who were in No 43, always had a good spirit in the squadron between pilots and ground crew. Now I regarded it as the first priority job to maintain that squadron spirit and indeed the squadron became well known for it. I had an extremely good relationship with my crew. I encouraged the view that we were a team of three. Tommy Poole, my rigger, and Bill Littlemore, my fitter, and me, the pilot. I said we're a team of three and I encouraged that through my flight sergeants in the flights to have that, the other pilots and ground crew to have the same sort of camaraderie. And this squadron was known for this close camaraderie. I lost trace of Tommy Poole, my rigger, after the war. Bill Littlemore and I were friends until he died, and he was a darn good fitter but he was a very nice chap. And that spirit, I think I could say, was reflected through the squadron. Not only on the flight line where there was a pilot and two, but back in the hangar where they'd take an aircraft in and they'd work on it all night to get it serviceable for the next morning. So we did have the right sort of spirit.'

For Fred Roberts, it was during the Battle of Britain that ground crew first worked with individual pilots.

'We had our own planes. Up until Dunkirk, that wasn't so. Prior to Dunkirk, there was never any action taking place, and we'd be in the armoury of a morning, the NCO in charge of the Army would say, "They want so-and-so", or "They want JNM and N ready for flying", and we would just go out and carry out the morning inspection, the daily inspection then, sign for it, and that was it, any available armourer would go out. We didn't have assistants before the war, you see. And any available armourer would go out and do the necessary. But when we moved to Hornchurch to cover Dunkirk, I fell in with George Unwin and from then until the time I left the squadron, in October 1940, I was his armourer.'

George Unwin and Fred Roberts built up a particularly strong relationship based on total mutual respect for the job the other was doing. Unwin is the first to admit, however, that the ground crew were often at the receiving end of a pilot's frustrations.

'One day the Germans had altered their tactics, they were now bombing fighter aerodromes instead of bombing the cities, and being methodical Germans, they attacked the most southern one first and gradually worked their way up so we knew perfectly well when it was our turn. And sure enough, the squadron was whistled over, and I go to get to my aircraft and it's not there. And it's in a blister hangar, a canvas hangar, having a minor inspection. Well, it's nothing, it's just routine. Doesn't mean to say there's anything wrong with it. And I could see the armourers underneath working on the guns and so, according to old Freddie Roberts, he said I arrived cursing and swearing, saying where the bloody hell's my airplane?'

This outburst, though, was a rare event in a working relationship that both Unwin and Roberts remember as being 'very good indeed'. Roberts also remembers that the ground crew 'never liked to see them go, we used to think to ourselves, "Is he coming back?"'

The Spitfire's teeth, like the Hurricane's were its guns, initially eight .303 Colt machine guns built under licence from America. The British version (of which over two thousand a week were being produced) had to be slightly adapted to take British ammunition – but, once done, it proved itself a reliable weapon. It was a good job: each of the eight guns carried three hundred rounds, delivered by belt, and stored in drums. The two-second burst so favoured by Sorley delivered three hundred and twenty rounds from his array of

'The Germans had altered their tactics, they were now bombing fighter aerodromes instead of bombing the cities, and being methodical Germans, they attacked the most southern one first and gradually worked their way up so we knew perfectly well when it was our turn.'

George Unwin

A damaged Hawker Hurricane is transported away from its crash site

barrels. The recoil was so intense that it took between 25 and 40 mph off the airspeed, and made the nose dip dramatically down. There were problems with icing at high altitude, but these were remedied by first covering the gun ports with canvas, and later by redirecting radiator heat into the gun ducts. The ammunition would comprise a mixture of three different types of round: armour-piercing, incendiary and tracer. Later, thanks to a contract with the Belgian De Wilde company, ammunition was standardised to a combined round, both incendiary and armour-piercing.

As an armourer, Fred Roberts was one of those responsible for loading up the guns.

'There were 300 rounds in each gun at a time, that's 2400 rounds for a full rearm on a Spitfire. In the later cannon Spitfire the magazine fed the Spitfires, and they had sixty rounds in each drum but, of course, they hardly ever fired sixty rounds, as they jammed. But later on, the cannons were set in the proper position and, they had belt-feed mechanism and a tank with the ammunition in, and they carried 120 rounds. The Hurricane had 300 rounds a gun.'

Roberts remembers that harmonising the guns was another part of the job.

'We used to take the Spitfire down to the firing range at Duxford, put it up on trestles, level it fore and aft, and laterally, and then sight the guns. We had a target in front of the firing range, and we sighted the guns on the target and the gun sight was harmonised with the guns, and then we got the pilot along. And he went along all the guns and we had a little microscope that we put on the breech of the guns to sight them, and he went along, on the wing, to be certain that the guns were sighted on the target and to his satisfaction, and the same with the gun sight. And then we locked all the guns, wired them up, blocked them up and that was it. But they did change that after Dunkirk, yes, it was after Dunkirk, a lot of the pilots disagreed with this method of sighting, and they had their guns harmonised on a dartboard kind of target then, about three hundred yards in front of the Spitfire, and all eight guns were harmonised on this one central point.'

Roberts never fired the guns himself, though: 'That was a pilot's job. When they wanted to fire the guns, we went along there, three or four of us hung on to the tail of the plane – it was up on trestles, of course – and a couple more on each wing, to keep it steady on the trestles, while he fired the eight guns. The noise was terrific, frightening.'

The patches put over the wings, where the guns were placed, were an important part of the plane.

'We put patches over the wings to stop the guns freezing up in high altitudes, because that was possible. And without the patches there, it did slow the plane down perhaps two or three miles an hour. Of course, pre-war, they didn't have patches, not the Spitfires, because the Spitfire guns, the two outboard guns on each Spitfire, had flash eliminators, which stuck out two or three inches forward of the gun ports, so you couldn't put patches over them. But on the outbreak of war, we changed the guns to a new mark of Browning gun, and they didn't have flash eliminators, they had what were called "muzzle chalks", which increased the rate of fire and also enabled patches to be put over the leading edge of the wings.'

It comes as no surprise to find that ground crew men, like Fred Roberts, felt as much a sense of achievement as the pilots when an enemy aircraft was shot down.

'I was part of it, proud of it, they were my guns, they weren't his guns, they were my guns, he only fired them for me. Yes, I think George [Unwin] got about fourteen altogether. People say to me, did you shoot any Germans down? I said, "No, but my guns shot fourteen down, but it was George that shot them down for me." We got very attached to our planes. Out of five planes, five Spitfires I had, in 1940, five that George had, and the first one was the best of the lot, best set of guns I had were in an old Mark I, which was replaced. George was taxiing on the aerodrome and one of the pilot officers taxied into the back of George and tore the tail off his Spitfire. That was the best set of guns I had all through the war, those eight, they were lovely guns. They were pre-war, made by BSA, in Birmingham.'

> *'I was part of it, proud of it, they were my guns, they weren't his guns, they were my guns, he only fired them for me. Yes, I think George [Unwin] got about fourteen altogether. People say to me, did you shoot any Germans down? I said, "No, but my guns shot fourteen down, but it was George that shot them down for me."'*
>
> Fred Roberts

Peter Brothers remembers that the firing power of the Spitfire and the Hurricane was very similar.

'The armament was the same on both aircraft, eight machine guns, a .303 machine gun. The rate of fire was about twelve hundred shots a minute, and you had a duration of fire something like thirty seconds at the most, then you were out of ammunition. The Hurricane's guns were in two clusters of four, on each wing, the Spitfire's guns were spread out over the wings, some towards the wing tips. And I did wonder at times whether wing flexing, when you were pulling a lot of G, whether in fact, of course, with the wing twisting a bit, the gun was quite pointing the way you really wanted it.'

> '*The German planes had small cannons, 3-centimetre cannons which used special ammunition, and we only needed to score a few hits to bring an English plane down. In other words, with just a brief burst of fire, in just a fraction of a second I was able to shoot down an enemy aircraft. If I could hit a Spitfire twice, I could destroy it.*'
>
> Hans-Ekkehard Bob

This difference in the gun layout came from the different wings of the two planes. The Hurricane's thicker wing allowed the machine guns to be grouped tightly together, as close to the propeller arc as possible. This was not achievable on the Spitfire, where the guns were spread out much more widely – making their fire harder to concentrate on a single target. This worked on the fairly basic principle of having enough mass and velocity to penetrate an enemy plane and wreck its vital systems, though they weren't in themselves explosive. The 109, however, was considered capable of delivering a heavier kick than either the Hurricane or the Spitfire, having cannon as well as two machine guns firing through the propeller, each with a thousand rounds. These had the virtue of far greater penetrative power – in fact a direct hit from just a couple of these exploding shells could destroy a plane on their own, as Luftwaffe pilot Hans-Ekkehard Bob points out.

'The English plane manufacturers opted for as many as eight machine guns, but of quite low calibre, whereas the German manufacturers opted for fewer weapons, but they were of high calibre. This meant that when an English plane shot at a German plane, it did not need to be able to aim as accurately because with eight machine guns, even if some of the shots misfired, you would still score a great many hits, which would enable you to shoot down the German plane. Whereas the German planes had small cannons, 3-centimetre cannons which used special ammunition, and we only needed to score a few hits to bring an English plane down. In other words, with just a brief burst of fire, in just a fraction of a second I was able to shoot down an enemy aircraft. If I could hit a Spitfire twice, I could destroy it. So the English had to score a great many hits with their machine guns, whereas with our heavy armament we only had to score a few. The English didn't need to shoot as accurately, whereas we did have to shoot as ccurately as possible.'

The RAF tried to upgrade their Spitfire, but without much success. Although they were trying to install a version of the same cannon used on the 109, loading and firing problems proved virtually insurmountable. Their resolution would have to wait until after the Battle of Britain.

However impressive the firing power of the planes was, the pilots still had to utilise considerable skills to be able to maximise their plane's fighting potential. Being a good pilot was not enough; the 'Few' would need to be first-class fighters as well. As Allan Wright recalls, shooting the guns effectively was not something many of the fighter pilots felt sufficiently skilled in doing.

'We'd only fired on ground targets before the Battle of Britain, and then the only other thing you could do was to fire at a drogue. You'd have an aircraft which would fly in a straight line and have a piece of rope behind it, about two hundred yards long, and a drogue on the end of that. A drogue is a piece of canvas, and he'd have a line, he'd go along it, and when he got to the end of his line, he turned round and came back. And when you'd go up to practise, you would put yourself the opposite end of the line that he was starting. And then, as he came towards you, you'd be out to the side and above, and then judge your position – and this is the difficult part – so when you turned in to come in after him, you wouldn't come on to him and be too close, or too far away, it's just how to come in right so that you'd get there, fifty yards behind. And then you'd use your camera gun, you see. The camera gun was a camera fitted into the wing, as close to the fuselage as possible. And you'd fill a whole reel with your firing and then come back, and they'd put it on the screen, where the reflector sight would be, and then discuss with your mentor or others whether you would have shot it down or not.'

The camera gun was an important instrument for pilots, as Nigel Rose explains. 'It was to give confirmation of your firing. I mean, either to show that you had disposed of an enemy or by how much you'd missed him, because you could see, as you do in one of my pictures, that there were times when you didn't allow enough deflection and were too much out of range.'

> *'The English didn't need to shoot as accurately, whereas we did have to shoot as ccurately as possible.'*
>
> Hans-Ekkehard Bob

Getting the right deflection angles would prove to be a decisive skill in the summer of 1940. The training that pilots like Allan Wright had received proved to be inadequate in preparing them for real combat situations.

'You didn't have a target which would nicely go up and down a tow line during the real battle. So, obviously, it was very different. And you could smell the cordite, and hear the guns. It's quite a surprise. It makes a terrific noise and the aircraft actually, as you're firing, pulls back a bit. In other words, the reaction of every gun firing out, an equal and opposite force is pushing it back, so you've got eight guns, all this ammunition going out, so the aeroplane is pushed back slightly. You soon forget about it, of course, but the first few times you do it, it's quite a surprise.'

Just as developing the Spitfire and Hurricane and maximising their firing power had engaged the very latest technology, it was clear that flying them would also require more from pilots than had ever previously been achieved. What exactly were the flying challenges posed by these new planes? For that matter, were human beings capable of what was about to be asked of them as pilots? Many thought not, believing that at these speeds the brain would simply black out. Even when it was proved that pilots could sustain this level of pressure, it was obvious flying had entered a new era.

Many of the pilots did experience blacking out during the Battle of Britain, including Nigel Rose.

'It was a thing that frequently happened to anybody who was flying. Naturally, with a fighter, any aircraft, if you pull in too tight a turn, the G forces mount up very rapidly and in a Spitfire you could get to 400, approaching 500 miles an hour in a steep dive, and if you were pulling out of that, you could feel the blood draining out of your brain and you got very fuzzy and eventually went unconscious. You could time this, curiously, as you tended to feel the pressure coming on, and you could almost feel it going off when you wanted it to go off, you know. It's the blood draining from the brain. But, you see, now, in modern aircraft, they wear these special G suits and they can stop the blood draining, when they get into a steep turn without loss of consciousness. In a Spitfire, you could get a pretty heavy G coming out at, say, 450 miles an hour, in a very steep dive, and you're pulling out, or if you were in a sharp turn in a dogfight, you could black yourself out as easy as anything. Or if you were doing a loop or something like that, I mean, it's very easy to black out. But you learned to control this, to some extent. I mean, you would fail before the aircraft did, usually, so I think a few people overdid it and got in such a dive that they couldn't pull out in time, if they were too low, I think.'

> 'In a Spitfire, you could get a pretty heavy G coming out at, say, 450 miles an hour, in a very steep dive, and you're pulling out, or if you were in a sharp turn in a dogfight, you could black yourself out as easy as anything.'
>
> Nigel Rose

All in all, the Spitfire and Hurricane pilots of 1940 were learning on the job. They'd trained on what once were front-line fighters, just to find that those planes were obsolete, so they had to start again, learning the new rigours imposed by the Hurricane and the Spitfire. Twenty years previously, pilots in their Tiger Moths would have found the journey on to operational aircraft a small and easy step. Not now. You had mastered the Tiger Moth – the rolls, loops, the discipline of safe combat flying – but now the real training would begin. But this was training without the safety net of instructors who'd been there, done that before. The pilots of 1940 were guinea-pigs, strapping themselves into the future, not taking part in some retro-thrill ride. They were literally in the vanguard, at the very limits of performance aircraft.

It was the combat that really would count, though, that would make the difference between whether the Battle of Britain would be won or lost. What pilots flying Spitfires now in air shows, or for television programmes, and their trainers, never have to face are the rigours of combat. No matter how superbly the Spitfire was designed, no matter how brilliantly it flew, the gulf that separated civilian from military flying is utterly unbridgeable. The gradations of skill that separate the inexperienced novice from the competent 'bread and butter' pilot from the squadron ace were many, and they were large.

Nigel Rose describes the particular demands of combat.

'When flying a Spitfire into combat, you had a number of things you must do. You might put these old aircraft into fine pitch, because you get a better response that way. But the propeller is fine pitch, you know, it would turn faster with the engine. Or, rather, you must switch on your gun sight which, in those days, was a reflector sight, it was a piece of glass on a slant with a red circle and a little cross in the middle of it. And the red circle, when you were flying with deflection, aiming in front of your target, would give you an idea of how much you should allow in the way of deflection. Then, of course, you had to turn on the gun button, which was a little knoll ring on the top of the control column. And you pressed the centre dot when you set the centre of the knob of the gun button when you wanted to fire your guns. Hopefully, all eight guns would fire together…'

For pilots like Rose, it was a case of making up their own rules as they went along.

'On the squadron, one didn't have the gunnery we used to put the pupils through on the operational training unit. So if you went straight to a squadron, you had to really make up your own lessons, or the Squadron Commander used to make up his own lessons, in a sense. One of them was ranging, which was deciding what an enemy aircraft looked like at various ranges, like three hundred yards, two-fifty, two hundred, one-fifty, hundred, right down until you were getting quite close. I found one tends to forget that little bit when you were in action, when you tended to open fire a good deal – in my case, I'm afraid – out of range. But the aces went in very close. If you're going to shoot down an enemy aircraft, the golden rule was to get in close, especially if it was a stern attack. And if it was a beam attack, to allow sufficient deflection, which is much harder, of course. But, at the same time the golden rule we were taught was, never lean on the button for more than three seconds at a time because there's somebody possibly on your tail or coming down at you. So if you were doing a close attack, you had to watch it.'

> 'If you're going to shoot down an enemy aircraft, the golden rule was to get in close, especially if it was a stern attack. And if it was a beam attack, to allow sufficient deflection, which is much harder.'
>
> Nigel Rose

And if you were shot at?

'Your first instinct was to turn as steeply as you could. And depending on what happened then, you'd either dive out of it or perhaps get into a turning duel with the enemy aircraft. The 110s, which were the aircraft I was mostly concerned with, had a habit of going into a circle when they were attacked. And it was a sort of protective circle, which was really fairly cunning of them. But, of course, in doing so, they left the bombers who they were escorting, perhaps to their fate. But they could preserve themselves and one of them certainly got me that way, by getting into this circular movement.'

The tail of a Hurricane after a dogfight over the Channel; the pilot landed safely

For Rose, the first he'd know of a coming attack would be when he looked in his mirror and saw something behind him, and tracer coming past.

'It made you feel very uncomfortable. And, of course, if you did see them, it was getting pretty late – it was better to have spotted them by having fired at the enemy than perhaps turning to see what there was about. But you have to realise there were aircraft flashing around, I mean, the Germans used to send over perhaps gaggles of a hundred, a hundred and fifty aircraft, of which, you know, perhaps forty or fifty were bombers and others were in two or three formations of fighters. And there was an awful sort of mingle of aircraft at times. If we were vectored on to a big raid coming into Portsmouth, Isle of Wight, Bristol, Southampton, that area, you saw these serried ranks of aircraft, especially if there was cloud below to show them up. And if you got into a scrap, it was incredible the amount of aircraft that were flashing around, some of whom you realised didn't see them any quicker than you saw them, and they used to flash past. There were some collisions, of course, of various magnitude. But at times it really was a bit of a free-for-all. And certainly a lot of haphazard flying, I think, that went on, a lot of lead flying around that never hit anything. And you were so obsessed with looking after yourself in your plane that there wasn't an awful lot of time to feel chronically frightened. I think you were scared but you tried to do what you were meant to be there to do, I think that was really it.'

Rose knows what he thinks made the difference between the very good and the not so good fighter pilots: 'I think I would say that it was the chaps with the guts and the killer instinct who got in there and did the business. Yes, it was determination to get their man and to get in close and get him.'

What was crucial for pilots like Gerald Stapleton was being both a good pilot and a good fighter.

'Can I use the expression "split arse pilot"? Because if you did a perfect turn, anybody firing at you would take the dot on his reflector sight, ahead of you, and his bullets and you would meet. If you did a split arse turn, you'd skid in it, that's where his bullets would be and that's where you'd be. Things like that, you picked up, and didn't tell anybody, because the Air Ministry was years behind, they didn't know what a combat pilot had to do to avoid getting shot down, and to run away when you're being shot at, not to follow the aircraft you were shooting at.'

Stapleton identifies a number of key factors that would lead to a pilot getting killed.

'Number one, never fly with a cold or a stiff neck. Number two, never follow the aircraft you're shooting at, because somebody will be shooting at you. Number three, check your oxygen, because we had reports of pilots just going in to the ground for no reason at all. Number four, the automatic flying of your aeroplane, you didn't have to think about. And the speed with which you reacted to any situation where you felt that you were in danger, if you could see an aircraft coming at you, and knowing the right action to take, to turn into him. And I'll give an example of that. I was following thirty 109s who were flying back to France, and I was trying to pretend to be one of them. To identify a fighter on edge is very difficult. But when you saw the Spitfire's elliptical wings, you could identify it straight away. And these chaps came down – four of them came down from the top of this echelon, and they were echeloned into the sun, it was in the evening, echelon to the west. And I saw them come down. And this chap started shooting at me when I was at right angles to him and he was pointing straight at me. And I'd turned into him, and I said to him, or to myself, "You damned fool, you can't hit me, you're pointing straight at me." So you do it automatically, that's the point I'm trying to make, you don't have to think. And the fourth one, who came down with the four of them who came down, I got onto his tail, but I was in such a steep turn I couldn't see him, because the nose was in the way, so I had to push the nose forward. And as he came into my vision, I went slap behind him like that and I was firing at him. I saw a bit come off him but I didn't see what happened to him, because by that time the other bloke had got into me and I went down in a spiral, down to the ground.

'I was very fortunate because I had to go through a cloud, I didn't know where I was. And I flew north, automatically, because I thought I might have been over the south coast

> *'Number one, never fly with a cold or a stiff neck. Number two, never follow the aircraft you're shooting at, because somebody will be shooting at you. Number three, check your oxygen...'*
>
> Gerald Stapleton

by then, and flew over a railway line which had Torbay Express on it. Now, I went to school down there, and I was on that train quite often, and I knew it went to Paddington, so I flew over there, then over Oxford Street, Regent Street, then down to Northumberland Avenue and to Whitehall, along the Thames, flying along the north shore, because the Thames had barges with balloons on it. And I got to the creek where it was the bad weather sign for Hornchurch Aerodrome. I turned left, flew for one minute, turned left again and there was the aerodrome.'

Being a successful fighter pilot wasn't even solely a question of experience, though clearly being an outright beginner couldn't help. Combat flying could not be further removed from even the most skilful and demanding aviation practised in peacetime. Firstly, it was a test of nothing more than eyesight. To the pilot who could see further, and first, lay the greater chance of survival. It was brutally simple. There was no such thing as a short-sighted fighter pilot. Even though the Battle of Britain pilot would be directed to roughly the right area and altitude by his controller, there would come a point when eyesight would have to take over. And then would come the nervous scouring of the skies around him – ahead to the horizon, up behind, below, anything that might betray the arrival of either fast-moving fighters or, best of all, a formation of lumbering bombers. Experience would help, of course, arming the successful pilot with a kind of sixth sense that could instantly spot that menacing dot, and spring into action. It would be the poor novice who would be wildly peering all around him but seeing nothing. Even more important was to have trigger-sensitive peripheral vision; nobody could search every bit of the sky, though it was important that you trained yourself to do it as systematically as possible. Weather and altitude made this even harder. The higher you flew, the more having to breathe in bottled oxygen played with your brain; your cockpit canopy was also prey to ice and misting.

Eating away at you would be the realisation that any attacking plane would be doing its utmost to conceal its presence; that would mean using cloud as cover, or worse, attacking out of the sun, which would render him almost totally invisible. The sun was a fighter's obsession, his greatest natural ally. Unlike Icarus, you simply couldn't fly too close to it. But with luck, the first visual establishment of enemy aircraft would happen at a distance of between one and five miles. Depending on the type of aircraft, and its course (and whether it was oblivious to you or not), that would mean you were only seconds away from combat – assuming, naturally, you had positively identified the intruder as hostile or friendly. From a distance it wasn't always easy to tell; RAF two-engined bombers, like the Blenheim, were easily confused with Bf 110s or Dorniers.

Luckily, the Spitfire's very distinctive wing shape helped to identify it, but so-called friendly fire, particularly in the earliest days, took its toll. Avoiding it relied on the razor sharp instinct of a pilot offered little more than the most fleeting of glimpses – a tail fin, a flash of wing, a glimpse of insignia. Worst offenders were the anti-aircraft batteries, on land but especially on ships, who could be relied upon to open up at anything that flew in range.

Then came decisiveness: it was a truism of the Battle of Britain that acting instantly and with resolution, even if tactically questionable, was better than hesitation. Again, and again, Battle of Britain diaries and accounts are full of tales of instant reflex actions. Dithering got you killed. The best situation of all, of course, was to avoid being noticed at all. Fighter pilots on all sides had no compunction whatsoever – indeed they actively sought it – in attacking planes that were oblivious to their presence. It's probably fair to assume that the vast majority of casualties had no idea of the plane that had shot them down. It's remarkable how many reminiscences there are of pilots realising they had been spotted only when their planes were rocked by enemy fire.

Only now would the pilot have to call on the rarest skill of all, the one that really set the aces apart from the rest – their aggression and their shooting ability. It's another commonplace of Battle of Britain literature that the opportunity to fire was fleeting and imprecise. Wheeling, ducking and diving, fighters made hugely difficult targets. Not only did they require lightning reflexes, but instant geometrical calculations in the head. This was the art of the 'deflection' shot – the calculation of the angle at which to shoot when not directly in front of, or behind, the plane you were attacking.

Famously, the Battle of Britain began with the conventional wisdom, endorsed by Dowding, that the point of convergence should be set four hundred yards in front of the Spitfire. This made sense; this was the place calculated to be the best compromise between attacking power and keeping the pilot as far out of harm's way as possible. It proved hopeless in practice. At four hundred yards, the bullets would be so dispersed, and their velocity so diminished, that a ferocious cone of fire would have been dissipated into a harmless spray. This was particularly true of the Spitfire, with its far less stable wing configuration than the Hurricane. The Spitfire's guns, more spread out than the Hurricane's, and its much more flexible wing, put even more pressure on the pilot's marksmanship; the Hurricane was always regarded as the much more effective 'gun platform'. But pilots of both planes quickly concluded that Dowding's four hundred yards had to be quietly dispensed with; two hundred and fifty – or even two hundred – yards, was much more effective, and pretty soon it was universally adopted as the conventional point at which to 'harmonise' the guns.

> 'Deflection shooting means you've got to aim your guns ahead of the enemy aircraft in order to shoot it down. It's like following a pheasant, as I had done, bringing your guns through the pheasant.'
>
> Archie Winskill

They were proved right, although it did require even more from the pilot to be able to get that close. Not all pilots had the icy nerve to be able to resist depressing the trigger too early, wasting ammunition and betraying their own location. But for those who did, results could be dramatic, though it should be remembered that even at this range a fighter plane, skidding violently in all directions, makes a negligible target. And remember, too, that at that range, even the rear and side gunner on the bombers could hit you back. The only consoling fact was that beyond three hudred yards or so, you were pretty safe. In all, pilots needed utter precision – the ability to position the plane ahead of the target, pointing into open sky, and the mental agility to have worked out that was where the flow of bullets and plane would meet. Not surprisingly, the great majority of planes shot down were victims of attack from more or less directly in line, or at most a few degrees off, from in front, or more usually from behind.

Little wonder that many Battle of Britain aces, on both sides, had spent their childhoods shooting and hunting. Archie Winskill, who flew Spitfires with several squadrons during the Battle of Britain, was typical of many in calling on his experience of game hunting for the fighter pilot's shooting skills. He found himself flying a very modern fighter aircraft in a combat situation with no combat shooting experience.

'Because the initial of my surname is "W", I was rather late in being called forward for this bombing and gunnery school. Although they'd plenty of pilots, the losses were high. There wasn't the time for training, so you really were learning to shoot on the job. I think what was missing, of course, was deflection shooting. Deflection shooting means you've got to aim your guns ahead of the enemy aircraft in order to shoot it down. It's like following a pheasant, as I had done, bringing your guns through the pheasant.'

> *'The pre-war pilots were well trained in shooting – but the sort of training that there wasn't time for with the many reserves of pilots who were brought in to cope with the losses.'*
>
> Archie Winskill

So Winskill finished up relying for his survival during the Battle of Britain on his pheasant-shooting skills – which admittedly were pretty poor.

'I'd done rough shooting, pheasant shooting, but I wouldn't call that shooting experience. I really only learned to shoot properly in a Spitfire when I went on a course right in the middle of the war, when one learned the finesse of deflection shooting. In a Spitfire, you have a ring sight which is a hundred miles an hour across, that is, crossing speed, and if, for example you're following a 109 down, at three hundred miles an hour, and the angle between your flight and his flight, say, is about thirty degrees, which is a fairly good average, the amount of deflection you must lay off is the sine of the angle of thirty degrees. The enemy's going at three hundred miles an hour, the sine of the thirty degrees is a half, so you halve his speed, which is three hundred, to a hundred and fifty, your graticule, your ring sight, is at a hundred miles an hour, so a ring and a half is the amount of deflection you must lay off in order to shoot him down. Now, that takes a lot of training. Of course, the pre-war pilots were well trained in shooting – but the sort of training that there wasn't time for with the many reserves of pilots who were brought in to cope with the losses. Later on, of course, when we got more experienced and built up a gunnery school, things were different.'

All of this accounts for why the 'bounce' would remain both side's favoured tactic. This involved diving, preferably out of the sun, fast and close to the target, squeezing off short decisive bursts of fire, rarely lasting more than three or four seconds, and quickly evading, either

in a power dive or climb, before wheeling round and having another go. The first the defending pilot would know would be the deafening, sickening explosions racking his plane, the smoke and flames, and the controls either going limp in his hands or dying completely. If he was lucky, damage was minimal and peripheral, and he could nurse his plane back to safety. If not, then he had no choice but to bale out or crash-land – assuming he wasn't too wounded to be able to do either. Many, of course, were killed instantly. Later in the war, this kind of hit and run would become the speciality of the Japanese Navy pilots.

Peter Brothers (fourth from left) and some of his squadron at readiness, making the most of the summer weather

Of course, in a sky full of planes this kind of ambush became much harder to execute – if only because no single plane would be doing anything as stupid as flying straight and level. In these circumstances, with the large formations of planes quickly splintering off into a myriad different encounters, the pilot's job was to avoid colliding, and present as small and mobile a target as possible, while trying to single out vulnerable targets of his own. Not surprisingly, most dogfights are recollected now only as bewildering blurs. Few had the luxury to 'pick' individual targets and clinically finish them off; this was much more a case of flying almost blind, lashing out at any plane that fortuitously crossed your sights, and guarding your

An RAF poster warning pilots to be vigilant against surprise attacks by the enemy coming out of the sun

tail as ferociously as you could. This was when the real crux of combat flying would come to the fore. Evasion. Now you really needed to fly by instinct. All that work that had gone into producing the ultimate elliptical wing now faced its sternest test. Could it produce a turn tight enough to save you from being slaughtered from behind? Would the wings, and the propeller, survive pulling out of a ten thousand-foot power dive? Would it stall? And could it take being hit without disintegrating? Now you would find out.

Needless to say, none of this was any use unless you flew the plane to the very limits of its technological – and your human – limits. Both the Spitfire and the Hurricane passed this test with flying colours; both served their pilots well. Anything less would have been fatal. But most of all, it bred a new type of flying. Those pilots who could translate their aerobatic skills into a kind of deliberately erratic style were most likely to survive. Those who had no aerobatic skills – who just did not know what flying to the limit meant – were not likely to make it. Those who had aerobatic skills, but were unable to adapt them to combat, did little better. The whole point about aerobatics is consistency and predictability – which made the perfect loop suicidal. But you did need to know just how tight that circle could go, how steep the dive, how violent the roll. Some pilots deliberately mis-set their rudder trims, with the effect of making their planes skid left and right. No points for elegance, but vital in the battle to make yourself as elusive a target as possible. Hence why, again and again, Battle of Britain pilots talked about making the plane part of themselves, of flying as some kind of direct extension of their own nervous systems.

None of this would have made any difference, of course, without courage and morale. Finally, the successful pilot is not one who simply survives, who flies only out of fear. At some point aggression has to kick in. And it is here that the fighter pilot, as a breed, comes into his own. It's about shooting down planes, and doing that required something altogether more remarkable than competence in the air. Even when you are defending your own country, you do so by attack. But pilots also knew only too well their own value; planes could be replaced, they could not. So it had to be controlled, calculated attack. Just diving in, or chasing lone enemy planes way out over the Channel, could be disastrous. Though that didn't stop maverick heroics quickly attaining the status of legend.

They were all brave, of course. You might argue nobody more so than those doomed novices who arrived at their squadrons with barely hours of training, only to be given the worst planes (why waste the good ones?) in fairly full knowledge that few expected them to make it to their second mission. But there were those pilots who took the art of aerial killing to new and clinical heights, the men who developed the tactic of the head-on attack. Or those who simply didn't let a small thing like the fact their plane was on fire stop them firing their own guns.

An elite of the most efficient killers, on both sides, started to emerge, their names destined to achieve star status in this, the most reported and eagerly described of wars. Daily reports, people watching from vantage points, the shrill crescendo of the propaganda war on both sides, made the skies over Britain, especially south-east England, a particularly intense colosseum.

Spitfire School *Roar of the Merlin*

We're actually going to be able to put these chaps through, as close as possible, the upper airwork training. The sort of flying that they're doing is designed to follow a pattern that was very similar to the sort of pattern that they followed in the war.'

Battle of Britain veteran Geoff Wellum has his own advice for young pilots flying Spitfires today.

'Go ahead and enjoy it. You have to go through so many things these days, as far as I can see, you have to be checked out on this, checked out on that, and that's good in a way, but there's nothing daunting about a Spitfire, except its value. I mean, you know, there aren't many of them. It's a very docile, straightforward aeroplane. You've got to get it right, mind you. Landing, like everything else, I suppose, you've got to get it right. There again, don't abuse it. If you do, nine times out of ten it'll help you out. But that's a Spitfire. Don't be daunted by it. Just go and enjoy it, and concentrate on what you're doing.'

It's the experiences of veterans like Wellum that continue to inspire young men like John Sweet to fly Spitfires today. 'I think any pilot who flies today would really give their eye-teeth to fly a Spitfire. It's such a classic aircraft, and so many people created such a lot of history in them.' So, having completed the Tiger Moth training, John and Dave now have three hours of hands-on flying on the dual-seater Spitfire that Carolyn Grace's late husband,

One week after undergoing training on a Tiger Moth, Dave Mallon, a private pilot, and John Sweet, a trainee RAF officer, arrive at Duxford Aerodrome, near Cambridge, for their first day flying a Spitfire. Duxford was one of the RAF's first airbases, established during the First World War. It was to Duxford that Supermarine test pilot Jeffrey Quill flew the very first operational Spitfire in the summer of 1938. The aerodrome was then home to a number of squadrons during the Second World War, and it was at Duxford that Douglas Bader pioneered his 'Big Wing' strategy. Today, Duxford is home to a large part of the Imperial War Museum's aircraft collection. Spitfire owner Carolyn Grace explains what Dave and John will be doing over the next few days.

'The young men who are going to fly in the Spitfire eventually will get something very representative of the sort of training that they would have done. They're coming from a Tiger Moth, they've got a relatively small amount of hours, and they will be coming on the Spitfire.

Nick, painstakingly restored in the 1980s. As the only operational dual-seater Spitfire in Britain, it's a unique aircraft. After their basic Spitfire training, Carolyn will be selecting one of the pilots for a full Spitfire operational training course. At the initial briefing, Carolyn prepares them for the week ahead.

'This week, you're going to learn to fly Spitfires. By Wednesday we will have assessed both of your abilities as fighter pilots, and we will then choose one of you who will go on to fly a full nine hours in the Spitfire of combat training. And at the end of that, you will have about the same amount of hours as a number of the Battle of Britain pilots had when they went to combat.'

Outside the briefing room, John and Dave get their first sight of the Spitfire. Encouraged by Carolyn, they eagerly go up and take a close look at this most ladylike of aircraft, inspecting the array of controls in the cockpit. John is surprised by the starkness of the interior of the plane. 'It's very businesslike on the inside. Not many frills around, not many cushions on the seat either.'

For his part, Dave can't conceal his enthusiasm for the plane, and his impatience to actually fly it. 'The plane as a whole is awe-inspiring. When you look inside the cockpit, it makes you feel nervous, if anything. The reality that I'm going to be flying this thing in a short while is strange. It should be fun. I'm very excited.'

After taking them on a guided tour of the Spitfire's controls, Carolyn straps Dave into his parachute. He'll be the first of the two pilots to go up in the Spitfire, but is worried that the parachute is too tight. Carolyn reassures him that's how it's supposed to be: 'It is tight. By the very nature of the parachute, you can't fall out of it!'

A few minutes later, Dave is finally sitting in the cockpit of the Spitfire. He straps himself in and takes a close look at the assortment of levers, dials and switches in front of him. Then he puts on his helmet and goggles. Dave Mallon is yet to leave the ground, but he looks every inch the Spitfire pilot, ready to fly for Britain. As he prepares for the takeoff, he feels confident.

'I'm a lot more relaxed now. After you've walked around the aircraft, you get to know it, but I'm sure it's going to be different when the big Merlin engine swings into action, all the noise. But I'm very excited now. I just want to get airborne and see how it feels.'

Then, the moment Dave has been waiting for. The propeller on this Mark IX Spitfire turns, and the noise of the Merlin engine reverberates around Duxford. It's the noise of legend – 1500 horsepower has been unleashed. Dave closes the hood of the cockpit, and Carolyn takes off.

As Dave and Carolyn fly over the Cambridgeshire countryside, Carolyn talks him through the controls, and how to handle the plane. Dave is flying in a Spitfire, fulfilling the dreams of millions of young boys, and he couldn't be happier: 'It's so much more relaxed than I though it would be.'

The flight lasts an all-too-short thirty minutes. It's been an exhilarating experience, prompting Dave to ask with a big grin on his face, 'Why can't all aircraft be Spitfires?' He notes, though, that it's been a world away from flying in the Tiger Moth the previous week at Headcorn. 'Stepping from a Tiger Moth into a Spitfire is a huge, huge

Main picture: Dave Mallon flying a Supermarine Spitfire for the first time

Left: Dave Mallon (left) and John Sweet waiting at Duxford to fly the Spitfire

Above: Carolyn Grace and Dave Mallon prepare for takeoff

John Sweet flies high above
the Cambridgeshire
countryside in ML407

step. These people who had to do it in 1940 were pretty special.'

An hour later, and John has also had his first Spitfire flight. He too is captivated by the experience. 'That was fantastic. I was a little bit twitchy to start with, but once I'd got the hang of it, it was an absolutely fantastic aircraft to fly. Very responsive to everything you do.'

Carolyn is delighted with the progress that both pilots have made, even on their first flight.

'They're both competent, surprisingly so. John has the advantage of being advanced with the variable pitch of the palate, so that was not something he had to take on board. But then you have to bear in mind that Dave had to take that on board, and did, and so I was pleased with that. John picked up the trimming quicker than Dave did, but there again, Dave took it on board, and by the end of the sortie they were both at the same level. They're neck and neck, there's nothing much to choose between them.'

Over the next three days, Dave and John spend several hours in the Spitfire, honing their flying skills in this remarkable machine. They soon share with the veterans of 1940 that enthusiasm for flying the Spitfires that is

rarely felt for other planes, as Dave explains. 'After fifteen minutes of flying the Spitfire, it's incredible how at ease I felt with it. It's an aircraft that immediately gave me a lot of trust in it. Its behaviour is impeccable, absolutely superb.'

For John, though, it is clear that there's a long way to go before they can really perfect flying the Spitfire. 'I think certainly the basics are coming along with the Spitfire. I think, like the Tiger Moth, it's quite an easy aircraft to fly to a fairly mediocre standard, to get you from A to B, but to truly get the hang of it would take quite a long time.'

It's a lesson that was learnt in 1940, sadly to the cost of many of the more inexperienced pilots. And, as Dave observes, flying the Spitfire was only part of the challenge during the Battle of Britain. 'You try and imagine what it would have been like for the pilots at the time. The most notable difference is the huge increase in the pilot's workload. You're not only trying to fly the aircraft, but also intercept bombers and fighters coming in, so you're constantly on the look-out for these aircraft, to make sure they don't intercept you first.'

Having mastered some of the basic flying techniques, Carolyn also introduces the boys to aerobatics, an essential skill for combat flying. It's a compelling lesson in the sort of physical strain that pilots were put under. The huge gravitational pull of one manoeuvre causes John to black out momentarily – another experience that was common in 1940. It is only for a few seconds, but nevertheless takes him by surprise. When he lands after the flight, John admits that he would be far from ready to engage with the enemy should this have been 1940.

'I don't think I'd like to go into battle just yet. I'd want a few more hours before I try doing that.'

The basic Spitfire training complete, Carolyn has to choose between the two pilots, to take one on to the advanced training stage. She takes some time to reach a verdict: 'It's a very difficult decision. There's nothing much to choose between them, they are both outstanding individuals.'

In the end, Carolyn resorts to a points system, taking into account all the skills that the two pilots have been working on during the previous three days. While John has the edge when it comes to physical flying, Carolyn cites Dave's obedient streak and analytical skills as being important too. Out of a total 200 possible points, Dave finishes up ahead, by just six points. Explaining her decision, Carolyn describes Dave as having the ideal team player characteristics that were essential for Fighter Command: 'I think that Dave will be the one that will always bring the aeroplane back, and just come back, land, and go into the squadron bar, and say, "Well done, chaps." He's very much a squadron pilot.'

For John, it's disappointing not to be going any further, but it's been an unforgettable three days, the chance of a lifetime. 'I've had three hours on the Spitfire now and it was fantastic fun. I'll probably never experience anything like it again.'

Reflecting on his time at Duxford, John is aware of what similar training would have led to in 1940, and the daunting prospects facing the newly trained pilots that summer. 'I don't think going into combat is something you can prepare yourself for at all. You can't think about it too much in advance, it's something that's going to be totally different from any expectations you can have of it, and it's something that everyone deals with in their own way.'

Dave is only too aware as well of what was required of the Fighter Command pilots. 'As a training pilot, you can only begin to understand what they actually went through then. They could be sitting on the ground waiting for a call, to potentially go up and meet their death every day.'

Not only potentially meeting their deaths, but going out to shoot down the enemy, to kill other pilots.

'Killing is something, to be honest, I haven't really thought about. Maybe these fighter pilots didn't think about it at first. I'm not sure how I would have dealt with that, but I imagine the anger and the sheer determination to save Britain from invasion would have been enough. And it was also a situation of kill or be killed, and I don't want to be killed, and I'm sure the guys in 1940 wouldn't want to have been killed, so it's me or him.'

For his part, though, Dave is 'really chuffed' to have come top of the class in this twenty-first-century Spitfire school. He now goes on to nine hours of advanced flying.

CHAPTER THREE

PLOTTING THE PILOTS

*'The best defence of the country is the fear of the fighter.
If we are strong in fighters we should probably never be
attacked in force. If we are moderately strong we shall probably
be attacked and the attacks will gradually be brought to a
standstill… If we are weak in fighter strength, the attacks will
not be brought to a standstill and the productive capacity of the
country will be virtually destroyed.'*

Hugh Dowding

By the middle of August 1940, the Battle of Britain was raging. It had taken around eight weeks following the disastrous humiliation of Dunkirk for the battle to reach its most intense stages, following a period of inconclusive action, usually over the English Channel and involving the attack of convoys. Now, though, the conflict had lost its early provisional quality and was being fought out at full pelt, directly between the RAF and the Luftwaffe. Many of the key Fighter Command airfields in the south-east – Lympne, Hawkinge, Manston, Martlesham Heath, Croydon and Tangmere among them – were at the receiving end of almost daily batterings by waves of German bombers. Radar stations at Dover, Rye, Pevensey, Dunkirk and Ventnor had also come under sustained attack. On the five days starting from 12 August, 194 German aircraft and 85 British fighters had been destroyed.

Previous page: Air Chief
Marshal Sir Hugh Dowding,
Air-Officer Commanding,
Fighter Command

With the Battle of Britain properly under way, the RAF pilots would fly countless missions. While every sortie would demand a whole raft of quick-fire decisions, taken in the white heat of combat, the overall strategy that dictated numbers and positions and flight plans had to be controlled by a central command, and at the centre in the summer of 1940 was Hugh Dowding, who oversaw the Battle of Britain with a small group of people based in Bentley Priory, near Stanmore in Middlesex.

Dowding is not one of the widely celebrated figures of British history; his name does not have the ring of familiarity that Nelson, Wellington or Walter Ralegh can claim. The same can be said for Keith Park, the New Zealander in charge of 11 Group and Dowding's right-hand man during the battle. In popular terms we still think of the Battle of Britain in relation to Churchill, the inspiring voice remembered across the country from those stirring radio broadcasts (even if what most of the country heard was often not Churchill at all, but the radio actor Norman Shelley who was hired to read out speeches Churchill had previously delivered to the House of Commons for broadcast). Yet it is Dowding and Park who were the driving forces behind Britain's success in the Battle of Britain, even if they virtually disappeared from view once it was over while the spotlight quickly turned to other people engaged in running the next stage of the war.

There is a memorial to Dowding, at the end of the Strand in London outside the church of St Clement Danes. The church was virtually destroyed on the night of 10 May 1941 when German bombers left just the steeple and walls extant. The incendiary bombs that burnt the rest of the church to a charred ruin were among the last to fall on London during the Blitz, and in the 1950s St Clements was restored, initially as a memorial to the fighter pilots who had defended the nation from the enemy raids of the Battle of Britain, and later extended as a memorial to all Allied airmen who had fought from the UK in both world wars. Outside this Central Church of the Royal Air Force are three statues. One is a large depiction of Gladstone; another is Arthur 'Bomber' Harris, head of RAF Bomber Command from 1942, who led the controversial area bombing strategy that destroyed large areas of German cities towards the end of the war. Next to them is a statue with the inscription 'To him the people of Britain and of the free world owe largely the way of life and the liberties they enjoy today.' This overwhelming sentiment goes not to Winston Churchill or Montgomery or one of the other better-known generals of the war. Instead it is a tribute to Air Chief Marshal Lord Dowding, Baron of Bentley Prior and Commander-in-Chief of the RAF's Fighter Command.

The British were fortunate that Dowding was still in place when the battle started. There had already been several attempts to retire him. He was a calm, even imperturbable, individual with a very clear view about the number of men and machines he needed for the job, and a very real sense of how important technology and communications would be if Britain was going to win.

It was Dowding, as George Unwin points out, who pressed hard for the developments in aircraft design that had taken place in the 1930s: 'The one thing that Dowding really needs credit for is insisting on the monoplane, namely the Hurricane and the Spitfire, because there was an awful bias against monoplanes. You know, they reckoned without a top wing bolted to a bottom wing, the wings would fall off. And he insisted on the monoplane and he does get full credit for that.'

Not only would the RAF be equipped, just in time, with the world's best plane, but for once the architect of its use was a man who had had the opportunity to prepare for its role. In fact, just the man for the job with, moreover, a genius for picking other individuals most suitable for the task in hand.

Dowding was not a man who attracted popularity easily. Indeed many recall him as a figure who put people's backs up during his time in command, and who attracted ridicule shortly afterwards, with his eager interest in spiritualism. He was in any case a distant figure for the pilots on the ground, like Allan Wright.

'I was absolutely concerned with getting as many aircraft down myself, I wasn't at all concerned about whether the leaders of Fighter Command or 11 Group were good or bad at their job. As long as they organised things, and then it's the controllers and the pilots who are doing the work. Perhaps I malign them on that, perhaps they were more important than I thought they were. They would visit squadrons, particularly Dowding. But I was too young and not in a position of power to understand what power meant. To me, they were just heads, I didn't feel that they had any influence on the actual fighting. I was probably wrong, but that's what I felt.'

Christopher Foxley-Norris, though, remembers Dowding more favourably: 'He was enormously fond of his pilots. He referred to them as his "chicks", and so forth, and he wept when they got killed. He was a grossly underrated man, and, unfortunately, underrated by people who saw fit to be his opponents.'

Nigel Rose is also more appreciative of the key role he played.

'Dowding was Commander-in-Chief Fighter Command, and very much, even in those days, a name to conjure with. He was known to all the squadron commanders and I suppose, through them, to us humble blokes on the squadron, and he used to go round the stations, too. But, of course, we didn't see him so very often, as perhaps the AOC of our particular group, who used to come round. I think Dowding did care about us, though. I mean, like Bomber Harris, I think, cared a great deal about his chaps. He was a remarkable person, because of course he was a carry-over from the First World War. And he was a very strong fighter for keeping the RAF up to strength, he did a tremendous amount with Trenchard to give the RAF some teeth at a time when the governments of the day were trying to really knock

> *'The one thing that Dowding really needs credit for is insisting on the monoplane, namely the Hurricane and the Spitfire, because there was an awful bias against monoplanes.'*
>
> George Unwin

the services down a great deal. And, of course, in the last two or three years before the war, then they were really on the ball, and production got started up, and the RAF grew stronger by the day, chiefly due to Trenchard and Dowding.'

Even Luftwaffe pilots like Ernie Wedding respect Dowding.

> *'I think Dowding did care about us, though. I mean, like Bomber Harris, I think, cared a great deal about his chaps. He was a remarkable person, because of course he was a carry-over from the First World War.'*
>
> Nigel Rose

'At the time I knew hardly anything about Dowding. I only knew that he was Commander-in-Chief of the RAF and that was it. Otherwise he wasn't discussed. Because we had enough of our own blokes to have discussed without going into the enemy camp. Later on I think Dowding was a very cool, calculated leader of the RAF. Even in France because they were screaming for Churchill to send fighters over to France, Dowding said no and rightly so. Because if he had sent fighters over there they would have been slaughtered the same as the fighters we had slaughtered which were already over there in France. The French Air Force was annihilated within three or four days, completely, but the British Air Force that was over there couldn't do much either because they didn't have the backing. The Army was retreating, so they had to move their airfields, and once you move backwards all the time then you're in trouble because you can't set up effective defence. And the other thing is, the morale goes when you retreat. See, attack and moving forward is a morale booster, but defend and move backwards, retreat, that destroys your morale. I'm not saying this because the RAF were defending Britain, no, the morale didn't suffer there, on the contrary, because of the successes that they had in shooting aircraft down, that boosted their morale. We are talking now more or less about ground troops when they have got to retreat.'

Whatever Dowding's personal reputation, and the sense in which he was famously immune to the 'romance' of the Battle of Britain, he was crucial to Britain's success in 1940. It was the fact he fought it so differently from the popular memory of it that is the key to his success, and the reason that Britain was able to win at all. He absolutely did not see it as a thin blue line of maverick heroes fighting against the odds, but a properly planned defensive strategy. He had the cool nerve to realise that the battle was in essence a systems campaign.

The thinking behind this modern war in the air had its roots in the previous global conflict. Of all the traumas suffered during the First World War, it was the experience of being bombed that was to prove one of the most deeply felt. In fact, the Zeppelin raids caused minimal damage and, in comparison to the carnage of the trenches, negligible casualties. But something in the national psyche was shaken to the core by the experience. Perhaps it was realising that the all but impregnable shield offered by the Channel was now obsolete, that Britain could be – and so would be – attacked by forces for whom the waves offered no obstacle. The newspaper baron Lord Northcliffe put it succinctly; Britain was 'no longer an island'. It was a deeply ominous concession to the modern age. And then there was the weapon itself, the

Nigel Rose in the cockpit of his Spitfire

bomber. Barely a generation old, and already the stuff of nightmare. It was, famously, Prime Minister Stanley Baldwin who summed it up with fearsome understatement: 'I think it well… for the man in the street to realise that there is no power on earth that can protect him from bombing, whatever people may tell him. The bomber will always get through.'

To make it worse, this time it would be 'the man in the street' who would be the front-line victim of this new escalation in the destructive power of warfare. There were those, Winston Churchill among them, who argued the other case, that civilian morale would be roused and quickened by the outrage of being bombed, rather than shattered and beaten. But at this point there was no way of knowing which way a large urban population would go. The widely held view was pessimistic on this score, apocalyptic even. Large-scale bombing would be like the end of the world.

The conclusions were two-fold. First, Britain must ensure that it could call on this fearful new weapon. It must have bombers. But there were those who also understood that now, more than ever, Britain had to start thinking long and hard about the challenges of defence. In 1934, badgered and hectored by Churchill, for whom the rise in German air power had become an obsessive mantra, the government agreed to start expanding the RAF. In 1936, only months after the official inauguration of the

> *'I think it well… for the man in the street to realise that there is no power on earth that can protect him from bombing, whatever people may tell him. The bomber will always get through.'*
>
> Stanley Baldwin

RAF recruits drilling at an Initial Training Wing

Luftwaffe, the RAF responded by reorganising itself. Crucially, it was decided to split the roles of bombers, air/sea reconnaissance and fighter defence, into Bomber Command under Air Marshal Sir John Steel based at Uxbridge, Coastal Command under Air Marshal Sir Arthur Longmore at Lee-on-Solent and Fighter Command under Air Marshal Sir Hugh Dowding based at Stanmore. A fourth section, Training Command, was set up at Ternhill under Air Marshal Sir Charles Burnett.

It was to be a momentous, and auspicious, decision, at one stroke highlighting and isolating the challenges that would later take the form of the Battle of Britain, freeing up each command from being fatally bound up with other aviation priorities. Hugh Dowding was given what would turn out to be the most significant of the jobs, the new head of Fighter Command, a job, incredibly, not even considered the best on offer.

At the time nobody had any idea just how perfectly adapted to the job he was. His background included service in the First World War, initially in the artillery but then in the fledgling Royal Flying Corps as a fighter pilot. He was the ultimate safe pair of hands for a job considered one step back from the real priorities facing Britain. As a classic backroom boy, there was nothing of the obvious dash and flair of the pilots whose fates he controlled. Even his name is apt; there was always something rather uncharismatic, even dowdy, about him. He was nicknamed 'Stuffy', not altogether affectionately, and in many of his photographs he looks more like an archetypal 1940s bank manager prepared for a stint in Dad's Army than the military mastermind he was. He spent many years involved in such issues as training, and supply and research – the less glamorous aspects of military flying but of course, in the end, utterly crucial. He was modest, slightly puritanical, non-smoking, teetotal, abhorring display and pomp. No wonder he was regarded as rather remote, aloof even, by his pilots, few of whom shared any of these attributes. He was eccentric, too, to the point of oddness, while his spiritualism would really spook the happily down-to-earth optimists of his squadrons who had no appetite at all for his line in talking to the dead.

In the end, though, the Battle of Britain would hinge on how well Dowding had done his job, not on how unlike a fighter pilot he was in temperament. What really counted was that one man now surveyed all of Britain's defence needs – a job whose brief was the perfect size: wide enough to call on his undoubted organisational and strategic prowess, with resources available, but focused enough not to bleed over into irrelevancies and distractions.

It may have been the Cassandra-like rumblings of Churchill that had led to Dowding's appointment, but ironically it was his alliance with Neville Chamberlain that was to prove decisive. Together, and in conjunction with his Minister for Co-ordination of Defence, Sir Thomas Inskip, they would oversee a shift of resources into building up fighter numbers, avoiding the temptation to put all their resources into bombers alone. Dowding was adamant: deterrence was the key to defence, and the key to deterrence was the fighter. 'The best defence of the country is the fear of the fighter,' he argued. 'If we are strong in fighters we should probably never be attacked in force. If we are moderately strong we shall probably be attacked and the attacks will gradually be brought to a standstill… If we are weak in fighter strength, the attacks will not be brought to a standstill and the productive capacity of the country will be virtually destroyed.' Not everyone agreed.

Dowding's first task was to calculate the size of force Fighter Command would require to provide Britain with its defensive shield. Initially he assumed this would be in the region of forty-five squadrons. He knew only too well that on its own this was meaningless. First, the fighters themselves had to be up to the job. Second, there needed to be enough of them. Third, their pilots had to be good enough – and so on. Dowding's genius was, to use modern parlance, his joined-up thinking, his understanding of the corollaries that linked one defence priority with another.

> *'Keith Park was right out of the top drawer as a leader, an example. He knew what he was doing. He stuck to his guns. He was the best CO of 11 Group ever.'*
>
> Geoff Wellum

He took pains to organise Fighter Command as logically as possible. It had been his idea to split his forces into 'groups'. Each of the four groups – 10, 11, 12 and 13 – covered a different area of the country and its coastline. Each group was then broken down into sectors, tied to key airfields and their operations rooms. In each sector would be a group of squadrons, usually two or three, but sometimes as many as six.

This complex organisation pointed up the vital fact that one man could hardly run Fighter Command on his own. Indeed, Dowding's most important decision was to realise that no matter how good his grasp of detail, the job of actually translating strategy into everyday operations had to be left to his group commanders. Dowding was widely credited with picking the right men for the right jobs, and that reputation is certainly justified in one particular case.

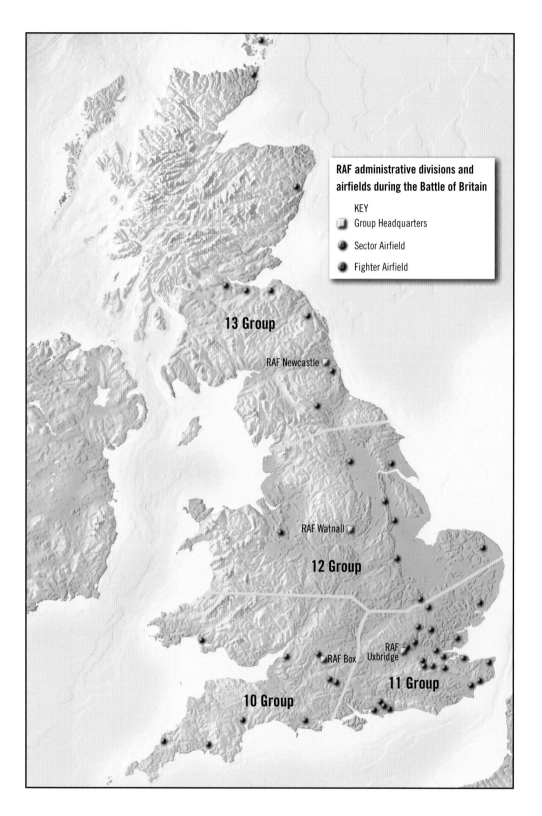

RAF administrative divisions and airfields during the Battle of Britain

KEY

Group Headquarters

Sector Airfield

Fighter Airfield

13 Group

RAF Newcastle

RAF Watnall

12 Group

RAF Box

RAF Uxbridge

11 Group

10 Group

For if ever the right man was in the right job at the right time, it was Keith Park, the New Zealander in charge of the critical 11 Group that covered the south-east of England. Park was one of the very greatest wartime officers to do this job, taking the brunt of the German attack in 1940, at the hot end of the assault.

Park was well liked by his men. Billy Drake calls himself 'very fortunate' to have served under him, while Bob Doe, whose 10 Group squadron was on loan to 11 Group for the defence of London, says, 'He was wonderful. He ensured that the pilots had all the latest information, what was happening.'

Geoff Wellum agrees with these sentiments.

'Keith Park was right out of the top drawer as a leader, an example. He knew what he was doing. He stuck to his guns. He was the best CO of 11 Group ever. He and Dowding were complementary. Dowding was very quiet, his nickname was Stuffy. Keith Park would turn up in his Hurricane at dispersal. He led from the front, did Keith Park. And he was a very fine air officer commanding.'

Gerald Stapleton enlarges on this, explaining that while Dowding was respected for refusing to allow Churchill to send more Spitfires to France, it was Park who they looked to for leadership.

'Park was very much closer to us. He used to visit us, quite often, and chat, no rank, he didn't want saluting or anything like that. He came in very informally in his Hurricane and found out how we were getting on. Dowding and Park were the architects of how the Battle of Britain was carried out and fought. And they deserve as much praise as anybody else who had anything to do with the Battle of Britain.'

> 'Park was very much closer to us. He used to visit us, quite often, and chat, no rank, he didn't want saluting or anything like that. He came in very informally in his Hurricane and found out how we were getting on.'
>
> Gerald Stapleton

Park was a remarkable commander with a very clear view of the battlefields, who displayed a notable flexibility throughout the battle in response to what the Germans were doing. This sound judgement was the benefit of all the time he had spent working with Dowding in the 1930s on problems of fighter defence and fighter tactics, allowing him to fully understand the capabilities of the systems available and exactly how they worked – or didn't. Radar, for example, was still far from perfect. Park fully understood that: he appreciated the quality of the data that radar would provide, and how much reliance could be placed on the information coming from the Observer Corps. He had a good sense of the capability of the pilots, he understood the unique principles of air warfare – and he was unafraid of lateral thinking.

To a military mind, the idea that you would do better by deploying fewer forces over a longer period of time is quite an alien concept. A traditional military approach is about concentration of force: to get a decisive impact, it's essential to employ all of your available forces at one point in time. The validity of Park's strategy, counter-intuitive as it appears, was demonstrated time and time again in 1940. The events would be typical in this respect on 15 September – the so-called 'Battle of Britain Day', one of the decisive days of the summer. In the morning, the RAF outnumbered the Luftwaffe by about three to two, but managed only relatively modest successes. In the afternoon the ratio was reversed, and the RAF did considerably better, inflicting much heavier losses. More German bombers meant more targets for Park's men; fewer Spitfires and Hurricanes meant that the Fighter Command pilots were able to get themselves in more favourable positions more easily to face the large unwieldy Luftwaffe formations. The lesson on this day, like many others, was clear: the more bombers Field Marshal Albert Kesselring sent over the English Channel, the more he lost. This may not be the expectation from conventional military thinking, but war in the air was proving to have its own rules.

> *'Not only were the tactics antiquated, but the formations we flew in were antiquated. We used to fly in threes.'*
>
> Tom Neil

Park's strategic foresight was vital, and was in stark contrast to the tactics that the RAF had been teaching its young pilots in the 1930s, as Cyril Bamberger recalls.

'Both squadrons I flew with during the Battle of Britain, No 610 Squadron and No 41 Squadron, flew in formations of three aircraft. There were four threes in a squadron. To my knowledge it goes back to pre-war training. That's how squadrons flew. It was very much the way we took off from the airfield and virtually, you could almost say, joined in combat. Now, the problem was that if you were flying in formation and trying to keep formation, you couldn't keep a good look-out. That meant there was only the leader and the leaders of the sections of three who could really look around, and the section of three couldn't look around too much if they're trying to keep in reasonable formation on the leader. But when it came to you being attacked, there was only one way you could really go, which is away from your leading aircraft. And so if, say, you were flying on the starboard side and the attack came from the starboard side, the only way you could turn was into that attack. Not being at all wise about using good tactics, but if you'd flown the other way you'd knock your leader out of the sky. With hindsight, of my later war experiences, it's the most stupid formation you could go into combat in. But I mean, that's being wise after the event.'

Tom Neil also recalls his training as being distinctly out of date.

'Not only were the tactics antiquated, but the formations we flew in were antiquated. We used to fly in threes. And then the Germans, who'd been in the Spanish Civil War of course, were pretty clued up as far as tactics were concerned and they taught us it's far better to fly in twos, and we gradually developed that. And all the standard Fighter Command attacks were just thrown out of the window as soon as we got down south, and it was a much more realistic business.'

These tactics also won the approval of Tom Dalton-Morgan.

'I am sure both Dowding and Park were right not to get us wasting time circling round and getting into formation. That takes time. There was a place for that in the later operations,

Peter Brothers (front centre) and his squadron in their 'Mae West' lifejackets at readiness

but it wasn't here. The time here was to get six in the lead and there were probably so few of us that they didn't really see us. The Luftwaffe would see a larger mass of aircraft coming towards them but not the little six that there were of us to start with.'

Dowding and Park's tactical skills are all the more remarkable when you consider that an air battle on the scale they were faced with was unprecedented. Today we're familiar with the concepts of air combat, but Fighter Command was deploying a system that had never been used before. The historical precedents, whether the dogfights of the First World War, or the bombing raids of the Spanish Civil War, would in reality be of very little use in 1940. Air fighting in the Battle of Britain was based on the ambush – a column of bombers coming in facing small numbers of fighters, often unseen, making their attack, inflicting a couple of casualties and getting away so quickly that it was impossible for the victims to even react. For this 'bounce' manoeuvre to work depended not so much on the number of aircraft available, but, as we have seen, on more subtle factors, such as height and being sun-up. Getting the right position trumped numerical superiority every time. So it was for pilots such as Allan Wright that there was no doubting the superiority of the 'bounce' manoeuvre over the traditional dogfight.

'If you could get in a position without being seen, obviously you could get closer, he'd be flying straight and level and you'd have a simple target. Whereas to shoot down an evading target is very difficult. Although you've got eight guns there, you're at least two to three hundred yards away – can't be closer because you just can't keep your sight on.'

Reacting quickly was also crucial. Park knew that when he saw on the radar reports a raid building up over the Pas de Calais and heading out over Cap Gris Nez, he had about twenty minutes to get his defence lined up. The time for decisions to be made in the control room was as short as it was for the pilots in the air. Sitting in a fighter, it would take around twenty or thirty seconds for a speck first spotted in the distance to transform into an enemy fighter.

In a war without precedent, it is perhaps no surprise that there would be bitter arguments about tactics. For while Park's innovative approach is celebrated in retrospect, its benefits were not universally acknowledged at the time. Heading up 12 Group in northern England was a vastly different man to Park, one who in his own way also played a crucial role in helping the RAF to punch above its weight: Trafford Leigh-Mallory. It is no secret that Park did not see eye to eye with him. Park was convinced that the German bombers should be intercepted ahead of their objectives, so forcing them to use more of their fighters, while Leigh-Mallory maintained this would leave RAF fighters overstretched and vulnerable, likely to be caught on the ground when refuelling. In the old debate on whether to fight in huge, massed strength, or with speed and flexibility, even at the cost of numbers, Leigh-Mallory was among those who came down on the side of massed strength – what could be called the traditional military approach to warfare. He advocated the 'Big Wing' approach: intercepting the Germans with a massive concentration of many fighters. His star pilot, the flying ace Douglas Bader (who famously lost his legs in an accident and continued flying with tin ones), agreed with him, which made this theory prominent, while Park and 11 Group continued to argue for the more flexible policy of taking advantage of radar and positioning fighters accordingly.

> '*You're right in the middle of a ding-dong battle with aircraft everywhere turning in all directions. You engage someone, you slip away to starboard, and then you turn round to port and everybody's gone.*'
>
> Iain Hutchinson

You can see the rationale of each approach. With Leigh-Mallory's growing confidence that maybe the RAF was just holding its own, and therefore should think about ways of maximising its power in the air, the answer, for him, was to take Dowding's confidence in coordination a step further. Keith Park stood firm. He continued to have no time for the Big Wing tactic, arguing it wasted time and effort. While these tactical arguments raged, many of the pilots who would translate decisions into action were not aware of the controversy, and for many of them, like Iain Hutchinson, big strategic debates were largely irrelevant when the practicalities of fighting air battles were considered.

'If I'd known about it, I wouldn't have agreed with it, for two reasons. The first reason was you had to stop the enemy, you had to attack them, even if you were outnumbered, and I think we were outnumbered most times, but you had to go in there and do your worst, or your best, whatever way you looked at it. It didn't matter whether you went in a squadron – in fact, I took off by myself, once, when I came down to land and rearm and fuel, and off up again into the battle. So the fact whether you went singly or a group of three or a squadron, didn't matter, you had to hack down the enemy. Now, the other point that's not in this theory was that rendezvousing at twenty-five thousand feet with anyone was extremely difficult. You've no idea how big the sky is. A common experience of a fighter was, you're right in the middle of a ding-dong battle with aircraft everywhere turning in all directions. You engage someone, you slip away to starboard, and then you turn round to port and everybody's gone, the sky is suddenly clear, everybody has beetled off. Things just change so quickly. So, getting up there, waiting until you got up, in a big unit, forming up into a big unit would have been extremely difficult, keeping that unit together to go into battle. It was bad enough with a squadron keeping it together. You could only keep it together for the first engagement, then you were broken up, because you attacked, you defended yourself, you attacked, and it was a fluid battle. So, squadron by squadron was quite good enough.'

Geoff Wellum, however, was aware of the argument, but agrees that the reality of fighting situations was very different to the theoretical approaches behind the Big Wing controversy.

'We just did what we were told, really. We went off in squadrons, we didn't think about this Big Wing thing. Thinking about it afterwards, if you're going to form up a wing, you can't just do it like that. It takes time. And time's not on your side. You've got to stop them getting to the target, not hit them after they've got to the target and gone back. No, we thought we were doing the right thing. The trouble was that we were never scrambled in time to get up to their height. So what we tried to do initially was instead of going straight up into them, turn 180 degrees to them, clamber for height and then try and get them before they got to the target, when you were nearer their altitude. But you were normally a little bit short of height and the 109s had the jump on you. I was aware in my own mind that there was some nastiness going on. I was quite convinced, all nineteen years old of me, that we were right, and that Park was right. And that by going in, in small batches and hitting them, going back, going away if you got away with it, and then going back and doing it again, I'm convinced that was the right way to do it – under those circumstances. You didn't have time for a favoured tactic. You had to assess a situation, because they were normally escorted by 109s that were going to have a go at you anyway, so you just took the line of least resistance and sorted out the best way of attack. Head-on was useful. But the only trouble was it was a bit quick, because your closing speed was, say, 600 miles an hour.'

So while 11 Group stuck by their guns, Leigh-Mallory's 12 Group began to experiment

> *'The big trouble with the "Big Wing" is getting sixty aeroplanes going in the same direction together. Both Park and Leigh-Mallory were wrong.'*
>
> George Unwin

with the Big Wing. It wasn't altogether successful, though, and Fighter Command became dangerously divided at a critical moment – as Joe Roddis recalls.

'We'd heard from pilots that Bader was involved in something at Tangmere called the "Big Wing" and a lot of the pilots were against it. Having had no experience in it I don't see why they could be. They must have had their reasons but the first time Bader got permission to use the Big Wing it was a total disaster, because the weather was against them. They never got to where they were supposed to be, half of them got lost and it was an expensive exercise. But I think he carried on doing it somehow, I don't know why but as far as we were concerned it was in another world, it was Tangmere, it was somewhere else.'

For George Unwin, it's the geographical and strategic differences between 11 and 12 Groups that made the Big Wing a credible option for Leigh-Mallory's boys but inappropriate for Park's squadrons based in the south-east.

'When Churchill said, "Where are your reserves?" and he [Park] said, "There aren't any", absolute nonsense. He had sixty of us waiting – waiting ten minutes' flying away and an awful lot of lives could have been saved, I think, and a lot more damage done.'

George Unwin

'It was the most ridiculous argument ever. They were both quite wrong and they were both quite right. Now, the big trouble with the "Big Wing" is getting sixty aeroplanes going in the same direction together. Both Park and Leigh-Mallory were wrong. You see, I had personal experience of this before the war, the final display at Hendon. The final display at Hendon was a flypast of two hundred and fifty aircraft to try and frighten Hitler. The most ridiculous thing. I was at that flypast. It was lead by Avro Ansons, at 120 miles an hour, in vics [V-formations] of five, and the last 70 aircraft were fighters and they were all Gauntlets or Gladiators at 120 miles an hour in vics of five. Now the last squadron of that lot were 19 Squadron and the last man on the left was me, at the end of two hundred and fifty aircraft, and we practised for weeks and weeks and weeks. They came from three different places and the trouble was getting going together – it was nearly impossible, we did it eventually.

'Now this was only sixty but you've got to be there in a hurry and it wasn't possible except at Duxford. Now you've got to realise the geographical situation. Here was me in Duxford. Due west, three miles west and slightly north is Fowlmere, which was our satellite which was where we were. Duxford had three Hurricane squadrons, Fowlmere had the two Spitfire squadrons. We were ten minutes from London, ten minutes to get in position. The Hurricanes were to line up and as they lined up for takeoff all three squadrons together, because you could do it in a grass aerodrome, and as they started to move we'd already been told they'd taxied out and we taxied out, we were in position at Fowlmere and as they went past us, we could see them – we took off. And we all got airborne and we all turned through 90 degrees on our way to London and we were all in position. Now you couldn't do that with Kenley, Biggin Hill. They're right – the enemy is on your doorstep, he's there before

you can do that, see. They couldn't do it, we could. But the net result proved itself that it was a great thing to do from Duxford because the casualties of the Hurricanes, three Hurricane squadrons went down to about four per cent and the casualties of the bombers and things went up enormously.'

A policeman takes down the details of a German airman, holding his parachute, after baling out during the Battle of Britain

Unwin believes that the bitter divide that developed over the 'Big Wing' between 11 and 12 Groups had a negative effect on Fighter Command's operations.

'Oh, the arguments that went on afterwards … Quite honestly, I emphasise my opinion is that Park was at fault in many ways. I'm sure it was just personal pride. We had sixty aircraft at Duxford, at Fowlmere, and we were never called out to help 11 Group on time. We were always called out too late and there's no excuse for it, except that he thought they could cope. And when he had that famous interview with Churchill, when Churchill said, "Where are your reserves?" and he said, "There aren't any", absolute nonsense. He had sixty of us waiting – waiting ten minutes' flying away and an awful lot of lives could have been saved, I think, and a lot more damage done.'

Reichsmarschall Hermann Goering talking to Luftwaffe pilots in January 1941

This dispute between Park and Leigh-Mallory, his two most able lieutenants, reveals a fundamental fault in Dowding: he didn't arbitrate decisively enough. He paid the price for this, and was quickly retired from duty on 25 November 1940, the Battle of Britain barely over. He had originally expected to retire in 1942, when he reached the age of sixty, which was the usual practice. However, in 1938 he'd been told that he would retire in the summer of 1939 instead, being seen by his superiors as obstinate and uncooperative, and unsuited to the most senior RAF posts. As the crisis in Europe intensified and the war progressed, though, Dowding's retirement date was continually extended, partly because no one knew Britain's air defences better than him, and partly because he had the support of both Churchill and Lord Beaverbrook. But once the direct threat to Britain had been broken, it was clear that the focus of the RAF's activities would shift to Bomber Command, and Dowding was released from duties. His dispute with Leigh-Mallory and his high-profile star pilot had done nothing to help Dowding find friends in the high echelons of the RAF. It seems an unceremonious way of dealing with a man who had achieved so much.

As policy and tactics were being debated and honed in Fighter Command, Dowding's opposite number, Hermann Goering, was contemplating victory. A military triumph for the Luftwaffe that would lift him to the level of the Roman Caesars he so worshipped. Apart from being a fighter pilot in the First World War, Goering had nothing in common with the diffident, conscientious Dowding. Flamboyant, high-living, self-important, to this day the porcine Nazi, at his peak second in power only to Hitler himself, remains instantly recognisable, with his field marshal's baton and bloated white uniforms, groaning under the weight of self-pinned medals.

Although Goering did have military experience, he was a politician first and foremost, a party boss before he was a fighter pilot. He'd been pushed into senior military office because of his Air Force background. His motivation in the Battle of Britain was more political than military, too. The victory in France had really been the Army's victory; now it was the turn of the Air Force. The English Channel would have to be crossed either by air or by sea, and the Royal Navy was still too powerful to make crossing by sea a realistic option; in any case the German Navy was relatively weak. The Luftwaffe was the force for the job. It had to be. So Goering promised Hitler that he would bomb Britain into submission.

Of course, it would turn out to be a promise that Goering couldn't meet, and from that point on his star went into decline in the Nazi firmament. He had been Hitler's deputy, but, with the debacle of Dunkirk followed swiftly by the failure to deliver the goods at the Battle of Britain, Goering would soon lose his favoured status. Any chance of a rehabilitation was firmly knocked back a year later with Stalingrad. He had promised to supply the encircled troops of the 6th Army until they could get out. This was followed by increasing pressure on German air defences by Allied attacks, during day and night, and Goering's credibility went into everlasting freefall, his Luftwaffe's star falling with the leader. Goering's reputation was no stronger among the German people than with the Nazi hierarchy; another pledge had seen to that. Goering had promised the German people early on in the war that no British bombs would ever fall on Berlin. Confident of his claims, he went so far as to tell the population that they could call him 'Meyer', and that he would eat a broomstick should he, as unlikely as it was, be proved wrong. When, as early as the autumn of 1940, a few British bombs were dropped on railway stations in the centre of Berlin, Goering inevitably left himself open to ridicule, and was quickly labelled the 'Meyer der Besen', or 'Meyer the Broom'. This was only the beginning, of course, of a British bombing campaign that would far eclipse the weight of the raids the Germans launched on London and British cities. Goering's status meanwhile would never recover.

However, decisive failure was still in the future. Now, for the Luftwaffe, just as for the RAF, the Battle of Britain represented something thrilling. Even though the Germans had the experiences of the Spanish Civil War behind them, it was for them as well a new kind of war, and it was one that Germany had been preparing for since 1935. The Luftwaffe had always 'belonged' to the new German Third Reich more than any other branch of the armed services, not only because of the continued novelty of air warfare, but also because quite simply Hitler had invented the Luftwaffe, and made it the international benchmark of his military ambitions. Germany hadn't been allowed an air force before 1933, and it was one of Hitler's first acts to authorise Goering to start the secret rearmament in the air. And it was Nazi Party members, and Nazi Party enthusiasts, who Goering would appoint throughout the 1930s to staff the Air Force and the Air Ministry. So it wasn't just an empty boast that the Air Force was more Nazi than the rest of the armed forces, and that its outlook was more sympathetic to the needs and aspirations of the regime. It was also largely in terms of air power that the growing rearmament of Germany was measured by the more sceptical international political and military bodies monitoring Hitler's movements during the 1930s. For Hitler, it was nothing less than a fetish of air power. Ever since 1935 the Nazi military elite, anxious to reverse the setbacks encoded in the Versailles treaty, had been itching to try out this new weapon; German greatness was going to be restored through conquest from the sky.

> 'For us, Goering did not come into the equation, we were not flying for him. We were flying for Germany. Even Hitler didn't come into the equation.'
>
> Ernie Wedding

Hermann Goering, more than anyone else, couldn't wait to deliver up this great victory to his Führer. It would be a personal victory for him, as much as for Germany; despite Hitler's undoubted enthusiasm for the skies, the Luftwaffe had very much become his concern – at least in Goering's eyes – and the pilots were flying for Goering's personal glory. This was an ethos that spread through the entire Air Force; aces itching to add to their already swelling totals gained in their heroic exploits in Spain, Poland and France. The Battle of Britain would, in the eyes of many Luftwaffe pilots, be the ultimate challenge. The Luftwaffe conducted the war of the future for Germany. It was a counterweight to the well-established Prussian homage to the Army and its traditions which had been the backbone of the military world of a previous generation. For Hitler, the Luftwaffe was not only more sympathetic to the regime than the rest of the armed forces, it was also representative of modernity, embracing as it did the most up-to-date technology.

Luftwaffe pilot Ernie Wedding puts some distance between himself and Goering – and indeed his ultimate leader.

'For us, Goering did not come into the equation, we were not flying for him. We were flying for Germany. Even Hitler didn't come into the equation. Yes, he was the leader and the big war lord, but we were flying for Germany and we were flying for the Air Force. Hitler was the leader of Germany, yes, but he wasn't Germany. Germany was bigger than he was. Later on, as the war progressed, and we thought more about it, then it was only Germany, not him at all.'

Later in the war, Wedding had the opportunity to meet Goering for himself.

'This was in Russia in 1943. I was coming back from a mission. I landed in a place called Stalino, which was a hundred miles west of Stalingrad, and we had to refuel because I wouldn't have got back to my station without refuelling and at the same time we wanted something to eat. Now we were on our way when we smell the cook house and who comes along with his entourage but the fat one himself, Hermann Goering, and we were walking in one direction and he was walking in the opposite and we did a sloppy salute and he could see on our faces that we were not too happy and he called us over. He said, "What's the matter with you?" "Well, sir, we haven't had anything to eat since this morning's breakfast. It's now two o'clock in the afternoon, we're hungry." And he got one of the officers from his entourage and he told them, "Take them into the officers' casino to be fed."'

Despite this gesture, Wedding remains unimpressed with the one-time Reichsmarschall.

'I think Hermann Goering himself played too much politics instead of looking after the Air Force. There was a man, Erhard Milch, Colonel General. He was actually the chairman of Lufthansa and he was top notch at organising, anything from a pin to aircrafts, and Goering didn't like it. And so the two of them clashed and he tried to put Ernst Udet into his place, but Udet committed suicide because he was not up to the job. And Milch got the job back again. But Goering was a politician. He was more interested in politics than he was interested in the Air Force. And he had quite a few clashes with outstanding pilots of the Air Force, and one of them was Adolf Galland. See, Galland was inspector of the fighter arm and after he clashed with Goering, he was told you're going now to a fighter squadron, a leader fighter squadron. You won't be inspector of the fighter any more.'

> 'He built for us pilots the most wonderful air bases with all mod cons and facilities, officers' flats. As a young second lieutenant, I had a two-room flat with a bathroom! Then the airbases themselves were beautifully fitted out, with wonderful casinos and swimming pools.'
>
> Hans-Ekkehard Bob

Another Luftwaffe pilot, Hans-Ekkehard Bob, recalls that Goering was highly regarded by his pilots before the war.

'Opinions about Hermann Goering do tend to vary somewhat, particularly depending on whether you're considering the time before the war, during the war or after the war. Before the war, in peacetime, Goering was of course someone who was highly thought of by the Luftwaffe. He built for us pilots the most wonderful air bases with all mod cons and facilities, officers' flats. As a young second lieutenant, I had a two-room flat with a bathroom! Then the airbases themselves were beautifully fitted out, with wonderful casinos and swimming pools. Goering also built the best planes, that's indisputable, if you think that the Bf 109 created world flight records even when it was at its developmental stage, back in 1935 or 1936, and it was the fastest plane in existence. Or the Bf 108, which was its forerunner, a sort of prototype. As a passenger aircraft, the Bf 108 was a four-seater passenger plane, one that is still considered to be elegant even today. If you're considering that period, then Goering was a highly respected man, very well thought of, someone who had also been awarded a top decoration as a result of his successes as a fighter pilot during the First World War, and at that stage the world envied

A Dornier 17 brought down by anti-aircraft guns.

From *The War Weekly*, 13 September 1940

us because of our Luftwaffe. Then came the missions in Poland, which were all quite bearable and easy to handle, and then France.'

However, his reputation changed dramatically during the Battle of Britain.

'When it was time for England, some doubts surfaced because Goering was not capable of forming any impression of the overall position there with regard to aerial warfare. He issued orders which were completely incomprehensible – we were expected to match our speed to that of the bombers, which rendered us completely helpless – or because we weren't scoring the same successes as before, he called the German fighter pilots cowards. At that point, Galland, the most highly decorated fighter pilot, stopped wearing his medals as a protest, because Goering, being totally ignorant of the reality of the situation, had branded us cowards. Situations of this kind certainly neither helped matters nor contributed to our continuing to have any respect for him.'

Bob also cites a number of strategic errors made by Goering.

'Aircraft development in Germany was assessed totally incorrectly. We didn't have any four-engined strategic bombers, that was something else he neglected. Another plane was developed as an alternative to the Messerschmitt, which was the Heinkel 112, which was in some ways similar to the Spitfire in its form, with those elliptical wings. This wasn't a bad development, but then they chose the Messerschmitt in preference to it. In other words, there were a number of situations where Goering, as commander-in-chief, thought things through completely wrongly, and the ensuing image that he acquired was damaging to him of course, and then it all just deteriorated from there. All in all I would take the view that Goering failed.'

For now, though, Goering was seeing the Battle of Britain as the pinnacle of a challenge that he had been gearing up to for over half a decade. In the ecstasy that swept over Germany following their wave of great victories, everything seemed to vindicate Hitler's 'big risk'. The amazingly rapid successes of Blitzkrieg had justified all that rearmament. All the propaganda about Germany standing on the threshold of an age of greatness was being borne out by events. The great Nazi dream was all coming true.

In 1940, thanks to Blitzkrieg, Hitler might have thought that he could afford to take pride in his victories. Western Europe had now been brought under control, apart from Britain, and surely it was safe to assume that the British would either fall quickly, or that, isolated without any allies left standing on mainland Europe, it would come readily to the negotiating table eager to make peace rather than risk being overrun. So what next for the great Blitzkrieg war? They were not going to stop now. No matter that nobody, not even Hitler, had any very clear idea of where this was leading. There was one thing that everyone could agree on: this was Germany's moment, this was Fascism's moment, a chance to sweep away the rubble of democracy and Anglo-French domination of Europe.

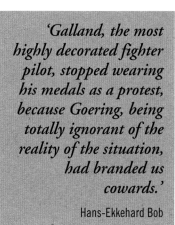

'Galland, the most highly decorated fighter pilot, stopped wearing his medals as a protest, because Goering, being totally ignorant of the reality of the situation, had branded us cowards.'

Hans-Ekkehard Bob

Certainly, this was not the moment to stop. But what next? The fall of Europe had been breathtaking, the whole thing had happened so quickly, that Hitler needed to catch up on where his ambitions now lay.

The stage was almost cleared, unbelievably, for the war Hitler had most wanted from the outset: the chance to take on the Soviet Union. Not long to wait now, the goalposts were in sight. Once the Western Front had been secured, Hitler would be able to turn his attention fully to the East. So the final stage was here, surely not one that would need to take up too much time or resources: Britain. Hitler may have had hesitations about fighting the British, he may have seen them as fellow Aryans – a kind of warped sense of racial solidarity clouding his thinking – and it may not have been an ambition to absorb Britain in the Nazi empire, but Britain would have to be neutralised before the next stage of the war could commence.

The problem was that, by June 1940, diplomacy wasn't working. Apparently Britain wasn't going to come to the negotiating table straight away, as might have been expected. Churchill, far from giving in, was making his sentiments quite clear in his public speeches. Hitler, though, on 19 July, had held out the olive branch of peace. In his 'last appeal to reason' speech on German radio, he said he saw no point in continuing the war, and offered to avoid dealing a final blow to the British government. Hitler's audience were no doubt convinced that the offer would be accepted. The offer was rejected in a BBC broadcast just an hour later. So much for Hitler's attempt to separate the interests of the British people from those of Churchill's government. Churchill himself stated that he had no intention of making a reply to Hitler himself as he wasn't on speaking terms with him.

So the British would have to be made to surrender. The battle for Britain was going to be a new chapter in Blitzkrieg war, but the elements would remain the same. The lightning strike, liquidating key centres of opposition and neutralising the enemy's ability (and will) to fight, would again be the key elements to bringing about victory. At this point the war was yet to become the total war of complete annihilation that it would after 1941. Amazing as it may sound, the Luftwaffe were actually forbidden to bomb London or civilian areas. It was only on 30 August that Hitler would lift the ban on the Luftwaffe bombing London after a number of bombs had fallen on the capital accidentally, and the RAF had retaliated by bombing German cities. This, combined with the growing realisation that the Luftwaffe was failing to break Britain, led to the first sustained bombing offensive over civilian areas in early September.

Thus for Goering, the pieces were in place, the strategy practised, even if the Channel made things different this time. Everything was ready to offer Hermann Goering his perfect opportunity to mastermind, oversee and take the credit for the great expansion of German power.

So the next stage of this Continental war focused on the work of two individuals in an unusually intense way. On the one hand there was Dowding with his meticulously planned strategies, as yet untested, including the radar system. On the other was Goering, whose Luftwaffe had more operational experience but who was personally most concerned with his own political advancement – or rather at this stage in holding on to the political power and influence he had, but with only a precarious grip. With the Navy and Army for the time being relegated to the sidelines, the skies over southern England for a few months *were* the Second World War as fighter pilots played out Dowding and Goering's battle plans.

In the ensuing battle, one vital piece of technology would make all the difference to Britain's chances, and it was a crucial omission from German forecasts: radar, or RDF (Radio Direction Finding) as it was called at first. The irony is that it was Germany who had helped pioneer it, but had then seen it as having a naval rather than air force use. During the 1930s, though, Hugh Dowding had been considering the last great challenge facing anyone charged with defending these islands: finding the enemy. War in the air made this, the oldest of all military problems, particularly urgent. Land armies, even naval vessels, have mass and move at slow speed. Detecting them, though not always easy, was not impossible. Spotting incoming airborne forces, laden with bombs, at speeds of over 200 mph, at altitude, hidden by cloud, was in a different league altogether – and the price for failure would be total. Dowding would create a system that would draw on every resource available to him at the time to counter this and, in so doing, create a blueprint for every command and control system that would come later. This, on top of his earlier contributions to the development of the specifications that resulted in the Hurricane and the Spitfire, would be enough to ensure his place as perhaps the key RAF figure in the Battle of Britain.

In this, Dowding revealed another vital strength, his ability to marry the very latest in technology with utterly pragmatic, low-tech backup. In addition to RDF, his other vital piece of kit was the so-called 'Mark I eyeball' – sixty thousand of which probed the coastal skies as

part of the Observer Corps, belonging to thirty thousand usually retired service men, armed with binoculars, charts and altitude calculators. One without the other would have been only partially useful; used together, radio detection waves and men in tin helmets

Nigel Rose, who served with No 602 Squadron, after the Battle of Britain

staring into the sky helped make Britain impregnable. It may not have been on the scale or grandeur of France's Maginot Line, lacking the big sweeping statement of defensive intent, but this was precision planning, isolating the key defensive problem, recognising the areas of greatest vulnerability, and finding solutions to them.

RDF had its origins in work done in the early 1930s. While the Germans had only been interested in its naval applications as a way of locating ships, the British were quicker to realise its greatest use would be as a way of detecting incoming aircraft. The fear of enemy bombing being well recognised, in 1934 the Air Ministry had set up a committee for the scientific survey of air defence. Some time later came a lurid rumour – that the Germans were developing nothing less than a death ray.

Sir Edward Fennessy was closely involved in early radar development, and he recalls the response to this rumour.

'Wimperis, Director of Scientific Research at the Air Ministry, decided to circulate all the research establishments, saying, is this possible? And among the research establishments was the radio research board at Slough, which was run by Robert Watson-Watt. He got his assistant, Arnold Wilkins, to do some calculations and it was clearly quite impossible to generate enough radio energy even to boil an egg, let alone boil a human being. Watson-Watt, who was a great opportunist, wrote a paper saying this is out of the question, but I believe I can offer a method of detecting aeroplanes. Now, he said that, or he wrote that, because he was doing ionospheric research, sending radio signals up into the stratosphere and getting reflections back. And they

> *"The third best gives you what you want today, the second best comes too late, the very best never comes." So he [Watson-Watt] started out with what he called the third best, and it did the job.'*
>
> Sir Edward Fennessy

had noticed that occasionally they got a blip, not from hundreds of thousands of feet up, but from ten thousand feet up, and they'd say casually, oh that must be an aeroplane.'

Watson-Watt was asked by Henry Tizard at the Air Ministry to demonstrate this concept.

'So in February 1935, he and Wilkins brought a van up from Slough, which was the radio research board, to a field near Daventry at Weadon. And on board they had an oscilloscope and they planned to use the radio energy from the BBC's Daventry Empire transmitter, which was a very high-powered transmitter, as the transmitter for their system, and a Hayford bomber was flown over Weadon and they watched for it on their oscilloscope and they detected it at about eight miles, which considering the lash-up they were using was quite remarkable. Roe from the Air Ministry was present at this demonstration. He hurried back and there's a meeting, I think, next day, when Watson-Watt was invited to submit his proposals for a radar system. He did that, and within a matter of a few weeks £10,000 had been granted by the Treasury, a remarkable sum of money for those days, to set up a research team at Orford Ness, which had been an RAF bombing range on the east coast. So Watson-Watt and about five of his radio research board team moved up there and started the development of radar. By the beginning of 1936 they could detect aeroplanes at forty miles – by July at seventy miles.'

He describes Watson-Watt's original concept as 'a relatively low frequency system in the metric band, broadcasting on a wide front, its energy not concentrated in a beam, and this was the quickest way of providing Fighter Command with a method of detecting aircraft. More sophisticated systems came later, using higher and higher frequencies, until we moved into the centimetric band with very narrow beams.'

'The quickest way' was a key requirement here, and Fennessy highlights the principle upon which Watson-Watt based his work – a principle that was to prove absolutely crucial in giving Britain a head start: '"The third best gives you what you want today, the second best comes too late, the very best never comes." So he started out with what he called the third best, and it did the job.'

It certainly did. The Germans, by contrast, aspired to use sophisticated techniques from the outset.

'They were trying to be perfectionist, and they had quite rightly, in some respects, gone for the use of higher frequencies, because that gives you a better radar system. But a better radar system too late is no use to you at all. What we got with Watson-Watt's concept was a radar system there for the battle we had to fight. The Germans were reaching out a little too far. Later in the war they had very good radar systems, but at a critical point they didn't.'

Fennessy also identifies another element of the German system which, he thinks, affected their efficiency. In the British radar research base, initially at Bawdsey Manor on the Suffolk coast, there were fortnightly meetings dubbed 'Sunday Soviets', a kind of free-ranging discussion group between civilian researchers and military personnel.

'The most junior person present had the full right to tell the most senior person present that he didn't know what he was talking about, and the most senior person had to accept that. It was all part of the "Sunday Soviet" procedure. There was a full-ranging discussion, usually leading to a conclusion. And when the morning's debate was over, you retired to the mess and had a drink.'

He cites one telling example:

'We were having very great difficulty in bombing Germany, navigation over a blacked-out country was proving impossible for Bomber Command. You couldn't get your bomber force within ten to twenty miles of the target area. You certainly couldn't find a specific target. And it got to a point where they were even debating disbanding Bomber Command and allocating the aircraft to Coastal Command and elsewhere. This was the subject of a "Sunday Soviet". A representative from the Air Ministry, Air Marshal Sir Philip Joubert, was there, and he outlined the problem. He said, "What can we do? Is there no radar method of solving this problem?" There happened to be at the meeting an old friend of mine called Robert Dippy, a research member of the team. Dippy said, "Well, in 1937 at Bawdsey I made a proposal for a blind landing system, which could have been converted into a navigational system. But because the priority was on the defensive radar, it was put in the ice box. And that's where it still is." So they said, well, get it out of the ice box fast and tell us more about it.

> *'Navigation over a blacked-out country was proving impossible for Bomber Command. You couldn't get your bomber force within ten to twenty miles of the target area. You certainly couldn't find a specific target. And it got to a point where they were even debating disbanding Bomber Command.'*
>
> Sir Edward Fennessy

Off Selsey Bill at 18,000 ft. 109s passed over but did not attack. Saw 110s circling below and turned to attack. Went for one chap and got white smoke from both his engines. Just missed hitting another head on. Followed another which was entering protective circle. B. fool! Cannon shell hit tail plane, and cannon and m/g bullets entered fuselage and stbd wing. Airbottle, wheeled and cockpit instruments shot up. A/p bullet thro' armour plating by left elbow, resulting in slight wound. Flew home feeling rather heroic,   !

Fired at 110

An entry from Nigel Rose's logbook, documenting when he was wounded

'So at a later meeting, he brought out the concept of what was to become G System. G was a method of equipping bombers with a radar receiver that received signals from three ground-based stations, which enabled the navigator to plot his position anywhere out to about three hundred miles from the English coast, deep into Germany. It had an accuracy of the order of two and a half miles, which was quite adequate for target finding. What it enabled Bomber Command to do was to get their entire bomber force to the target area accurately in space and accurately in time, because time is vital to get a concentrated attack. So the G system became the standard way of navigating bombers, not only over Germany but over many other areas, too. It all came out of a simple question at a "Sunday Soviet".'

The willingness of Air Ministry officials to listen to scientists may seem unsurprising, but Fennessy has discovered that the Germans had no such forum.

'I've spoken to German scientists after the war. They said as civilians they never actively participated in major discussions. What would happen if there was a major problem involving their particular field of science, which was radar, is that they would be summoned to the ministry, they would be kept in an outer office until the question was ready to be put, they'd be marched in, they would give the Hitler salute, the question would be addressed to them, they'd give the answer, they'd give another Hitler salute and they'd retire. There was no intermingling in the way of a "Sunday Soviet"-type discussion ever in Germany. And this led to a considerable failure in effective German development of their own defence system.'

The much more flexible and visionary Dowding seized on early experimental results as absolutely vital to the development of Britain's defences against aerial attack, 'a discovery of the highest importance', he declared. Fennessy, who had himself joined Watson-Watt's research team in 1938, pays tribute to Dowding's role.

'Dowding happened to have been the Air Member for supply and research at the Air Ministry at the time that the original Watson-Watt proposal was put in. So he was well aware of what was in the wind. Some time after that he moved to take command at Fighter Command, and he recognised that here was the weapon with which he could defeat the Luftwaffe. He had allocated some of his staff to work with Bawdsey, so that we were not just developing a scientific toy, we were developing a weapon of war, which met the operational requirements of Fighter Command. That close working liaison between the research team and RAF Fighter Command was a dominant factor in the rapid development of an effective weapon. Because what radar had to do was to bring the fighter force, at the right time at the right place and in the right strength, to attack the formation that was coming in. You therefore had to know where the formation is, what its speed is, what its composition is, how many aircraft, so that you know what defensive force you send off to attack them. That was all done and had been demonstrated by 1937–38 as an RAF weapon. By the outbreak of war, the liaison had become extremely tight and continued so throughout the war. And throughout the war Dowding's liaison was the closest.

'I remember personally being at a meeting at Fighter Command when we were dealing with a particularly complex problem and he said, "Look, I've got to fight a war, I want a better radar system than I've got, why can't I have it?" And the senior scientist there said, "Well, Commander-in-Chief, the scientists say it can't be done." Dowding – "Stuffy", as he was known – said, 'If the scientists say it can't be done, get me some other scientists." Well, we did it.'

> '*You ... had to know where the formation is, what its speed is, what its composition is, how many aircraft, so that you know what defensive force you send off to attack them.*'
>
> Sir Edward Fennessy

Radar not only gave Fighter Command an accurate indication of where an attack would strike, but also saved the RAF from having to organise standing patrols as they had done in France. This meant that the available aircraft could be sent directly to where they would be of most use. Fennessy is in no doubt about the significance of radar: 'Without radar he would have been so outnumbered that he would have had no chance whatsoever of winning the Battle of Britain. It was radar that gave him the means that his brave fighter crews could operate effectively and efficiently and destroy the German Luftwaffe.'

Furthermore, Dowding was just the man for the job.

'There couldn't have been a better Commander-in- Chief to fight the Battle of Britain, in my opinion, than Dowding. He understood the role of radar. There might have been another Commander-in-Chief who might have been dismissive of it. Dowding was a hundred per cent for it. He saw his staff recognised its value to Fighter Command and they cooperated to the maximum extent. He was the best man in the right place at the right time. And he was tough. You didn't argue with him.'

Within the space of just two or three years, the south coast was home to a chain of these RDF facilities (called 'chain homes'), built in great secrecy. Despite being rudimentary in their abilities, they were at least established and up and running in time to be useful – another illustration of Watson-Watt's pragmatic dictum. Of course, these early RDF facilities offered nothing like the resolution and certainty of later radar; for one thing the signals required detailed deciphering by very skilled operators, as well as an element of educated guesswork,

> 'Without radar he would have been so outnumbered that he would have had no chance whatsoever of winning the Battle of Britain.'
>
> Sir Edward Fennessy

but crucially the result of those interpretations was range of target, its direction or bearing, (more tentatively) the number of targets, and (most tentatively of all) their height. Just as fighters are useless without good pilots, so RDF was useless without good operators, only too aware of the price to be paid by making any mistakes, and under the added pressure of knowing they were themselves prime targets for the dive-bombers streaming over the English Channel.

It was because RDF was at its weakest in supplying details about altitude, the most important information that intercepting forces need to know, that Dowding then came to rely on his second chain of intelligence, the Observer Corps. It was their job to confirm, consolidate, and refine information about incoming formations. They also answered another flaw in the RDF coverage – namely, that it faced out to sea; once past the coast, aircraft inland of them became undetectable by their radio waves. The Observer Corps had been formed during the First World War, but had grown hugely both in terms of size and importance in the period before the Battle of Britain. They were vital too in detecting the arrival of the many low-flying raids that aimed to cause surprise by coming in under the RDF. They were the outer fringes of a dense and coherent network of communications, each linked by phone to the Observer Corps Centre at Horsham, which in turn passed the vital information along to Fighter Command headquarters at Bentley Priory.

In the hands of one of these trained operators, RDF truly became the RAF's eyes and ears. At an altitude of around twenty thousand feet, pretty standard for bombers, RDF could pick up formations from around a hundred miles, which gave just enough time to manage some kind of response, though with very little margin for error. British planes had been fitted with a device called IFF (Identification Friend or Foe), which was supposed to help the operators spot that they were friend not foe by changing the radar signature of British fighters.

Of course, the information provided by radar and the Observer Corps was only of any use if it could be interpreted correctly, and quickly enough for Fighter Command to act upon. So Bentley Priory became the centre of operations, containing the 'filter room'. The job here was to make sense of the flood of incoming sightings and data, separating it from information about friendly flights, giving each raid its own number before being disseminated back down the line to the group controllers, and then the sector stations. It would even get passed back down the line to the Observer Corps stations, where much of it had originated. In the filter room a phalanx of controllers and their assistants, with specifically delineated tasks and responsibilities, would process information and act upon it. All the key personnel were now linked into this web – from controllers all the way to pilots. As a command and control system it had many strengths. It was simple, clear, logical and resilient. It provided clarity where before had been utter confusion and chaos. And it did all it could to prevent key people being left in the dark. The technology it relied upon – telephone lines, maps laid out on tables – may have been familiar, but the organisational blueprint that lay behind it was altogether new, and had taken Dowding fully three years to get to something even close to working.

The apparatus and the procedures of this extraordinary early warning system have become so familiar a part of our picture of the Battle of Britain that it's too easy to overlook not just the contribution they made, but also the rigour and the vision of the thinking that created them. Just as much as the great leap forward in aircraft technology, this was what most separated the experience of combat flying in the two world wars. Much had remained the same: the grass airfields (allowing planes to take off in whichever direction the wind was blowing), the tents, the rudimentary buildings. But in every other respect there was much that was very, very new, and very modern.

In fact, with Dowding and Park, fighter defence was in the hands of two men who were the exact opposite of the mythical RAF pilot. Forget the idea of buccaneering amateurs – neither of those men fits that stereotype. Despite the image that has endured in the decades since the Battle of Britain, both Dowding and Park put all their trust in virtues commonly supposed to characterise the German approach to war: efficiency, preparedness, planning; in the utterly unglamorous business of logistics, priorities and technology. Above all, they had between them two decades of experience, from which they were determined to draw exactly the right lessons. So seamlessly have their contributions to the image of the Battle of Britain been submerged, it's hard to realise just how radical and indispensable they were. In virtually every regard, they marked the difference between the fate of the RAF compared to that of the Polish and French air forces before them.

Essential to the experience of the Battle of Britain pilots, so very different from any that had gone before, was the feeling of being part of a larger armed force. Although the pilot's world rarely went further than the limits of his squadron, maybe ten or twelve planes, he knew only too well during 1940 that his squadron was just one piece of many being assembled and reassembled as fast as possible to counter the fluid, and ever-changing, threat from the across the Channel. It accounts for those archetypal Battle of Britain vignettes – the pilots in their 'Mae West' lifejackets (named after the well-endowed actress so many of the pilots admired), playing cards, reading the paper or just snoozing in deckchairs in the dispersal area, waiting for the phone to ring. That was what connected them to the battle at large, and its sound would remain a powerful psychological totem for all Battle of Britain pilots, the moment they would be catapulted from rest to full combat – often not before they had been sick first.

It was what accounted for the strange new language they all had to learn, the fact the RAF (in distinct contrast to the Luftwaffe) had put VHF radio in all its fighters. (The Luftwaffe was

Peter Brothers in flying helmet, covering headphones, and oxygen mask, containing a microphone

influenced strongly by veterans from the Spanish Civil War, who thought radios unnecessary when hand signals had been perfectly adequate not only in Spain, but also for that great hero of the First World War, Baron von Richthofen.) The controller's voice, calm, impersonal and direct, became the great guiding force in the conflict. All those altitude and direction details, the tags and the slang by which squadrons would be scrambled, and led as accurately as possible into harm's way, were all a product of this new machinery of command and control that Dowding did so much to pioneer. Not just jargon, but proof that this was a battle not only being fought by more sophisticated planes but a much more sophisticated front line.

As a pilot, Gerald Stapleton relied on the command and control system for directions.

'The command and control system with us stopped at our controller. And we realised that there was a higher echelon of command and Park was the 11 Group Commander, Dowding was Chief of Fighter Command, and that's all there was to it. We realised that there was Observer Corps and the radar, and all that information coming in to 11 Group and to the various control stations, because they had a system of telling the control stations, one person would speak and the information would go to both, on the telephone, that's why they had these two control stations monitoring the German formations. That was at Biggin Hill and at Hornchurch, in 11 Group. In the cockpit over the radio, we're getting the instructions, in the beginning we were given to fly in a certain direction, to a certain height, to intercept the German formations. Because we were always looking for height, later on, maybe a month after we went down there, we were told to fly at 15,000 feet over Maidstone, which would give us time to get the necessary height to get above the German formations. And it was mainly to give directions on the radio.'

Nigel Rose recalls the change to VHF from the old TR9 radios as 'very, very valuable to us', the communication highly efficient. He paints a picture of a lone airman in his cockpit, keeping in touch with all concerned.

'There was one famous occasion when we were on the same wavelengths as the Germans who were coming in towards us. But, apart from that there was as little chatter as possible. When we were airborne we wore headphones, of course, and had a microphone with the oxygen mask, and we had our flying helmets, which came right over your head with earphones in a padded swelling on the side of the helmet, you see. And then clipped to it, usually on one side, unless you buttoned it up on both sides, was a mouthpiece and oxygen attachment, the oxygen tube went down to a clip which you could turn on when you were up at fifteen thousand feet and rising. And the microphone, I think, you had switched on all the time, I'm not sure about this point, whether you did have the actual microphone, because it had a little switch on the front. But you had the control box for your radio and with that you could switch off or on to your own wavelength. And then, when you were airborne, within the squadron, you tried to keep silence as much as possible. This was the rule, so as not to interrupt anybody shouting that something had been seen. And quite often it was the same chap in our squadron, when I was flying, he had the most wonderful eyes. He was killed later on, unfortunately, during the Battle of Britain, but he had the most terrific eyesight and he would yell, "Bandits at three o'clock high" or something like that. Whereupon the squadron commander would make sure he could see them, too, and we'd fly as a squadron, flying altogether, in the right direction. He might then tell us to break up into sections or flights, according to what was needed.'

> '*There was one famous occasion when we were on the same wavelengths as the Germans who were coming in towards us.*'
>
> Nigel Rose

Rose recalls that sometimes the language could get rather strong.

'During the ensuing scrap you got snippets of "For God's sake" – there was some lurid language used, and I'm sure they were blushing – well, perhaps to start with – down in the control room, because they must have heard a lot of things they'd never heard before. But there was some fairly swift language, naturally, used: "Get the hell out of it!" Or "Watch out behind!" Or "Red two", or whatever it was, "there's something coming up behind you." And, of course, that was a good warning, if you were told in detail what was happening, you could turn immediately.'

Gerald Stapleton confesses to breaking radio silence on more than one occasion.

'On the radio we could hear each other talking, and I used to do some stupid things. I used to sing a song called "Night and Day" over the radio, and George Denholm, the Squadron Leader, used to say, "What the hell do you think you're doing? Blocking the radio up." I sang though because I was exhilarated. I was excited, very excited. And tingling with exhilaration. And sort of keeping an eye on everything when we went on to fours. You had time to look around and at one stage, when I was on my own, I got up to 34,000 feet, and I could see Paris, I could see Plymouth and I could see Hull, it was a perfect day, and you could only see it by the haze in the distance.'

Members of the WAAF at work in the Operations Room of 11 Group at Uxbridge

All the RAF pilots appreciated the benefits of the control system. Gerald Stapleton calls the controllers 'unsung heroes'.

'They used to have the map in front of them, with all the girls [WAAFs] placing the German formations where radar was telling them, and they juggled the squadrons. They would have a list of how many squadrons were at readiness at various aerodromes in 11 Group. And they would decide which squadrons were to take off first, which to keep in reserve, or to have any reserve, or to decide whether it was a German feint with fighters only, because the Germans would come out in what they called a "free hunt". While they were over France and over the Channel, out of reach of the Observer Corps, radar couldn't tell if they were bombers or fighters, they could only tell by the speed, if the fighters were going fast, and, of course, they weren't, because they'd be cruising, and they'd be going along at the bombers' speed. And the controllers had to decide not to take any notice of those aircraft if they were fighters only – what's the point? They can't do any damage to you.'

Nigel Rose is equally appreciative.

'Radar was very efficient, and the WAAFs were absolutely wonderful, doing the plotting and so on. So we were kept aware by the controller in our particular section. We switched on to our own wavelength, although we weren't actually talking, we could hear calls made to the Squadron Commander by the Sector Commander down somewhere in a padded cell with the WAAFs all around him and the map of the south coast. And so we knew to some extent, what he was doing and he would say, "Villa leader, there's fifty plus coming in over Selsey at Angels" or whatever, and they would probably say how far out at sea, and that would give him a chance to position himself, ready to receive these people coming in, you see. We needed those particulars, the size of the raid and the height and the speed, the rate at which he was coming in over the sea or the land or whatever.'

The mention of WAAFs – members of the Women's Auxiliary Air Force – brings in a significant fact. For the first time, women were now involved in something approximating the front line. In a move then considered risky, they became the plotters, taking their place in the heart of the operations rooms, often, as at Kenley, in unprotected buildings above ground. It was their job to translate the information coming from the filter room, on to the map tables in front of them, courtesy of a long wooden rake similar to those used on roulette tables. Many were in their early twenties, having passed a psychiatric evaluation before being allowed to take on these duties – no one was quite certain in those patriarchal days whether these young women would be able to endure the crushing stress of being bombed, virtually every day. The vast majority did. There was a key day

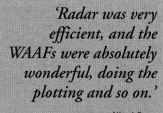

'Radar was very efficient, and the WAAFs were absolutely wonderful, doing the plotting and so on.'

Nigel Rose

early on, when for the first time, a 'hundred plus' symbol was used, to the incredulous scepticism of the group controller, who until that point hadn't seen formations larger than a dozen. Convinced it was an error, he bawled out the WAAF officer, only to find out it was true: the Germans were indeed coming in these previously unheard-of numbers.

Nobody, though, could be prepared for the hardest job of all – plotting the course of a major raid, which, it soon became clear, was heading straight for your airfield, and having to stay at the table until the very last moment.

It was on those Luftwaffe attackers that Dowding's command system had a devastating impact. Again and again, German pilots were struck not so much by the courage of the RAF, or the effectiveness of the Spitfires and Hurricanes ranged against them, but the plotting systems the British were employing. They had anticipated the courage and the planes – it was the RAF's ubiquity that unnerved them. Wherever they flew, from whatever base, at whatever time, it seemed they could rely on one thing: there would be RAF fighters scrambled to meet them, often with enough warning to have gained that all-important altitude. As the

Battle of Britain developed, and the Luftwaffe found itself attacking targets deeper and deeper into the mainland, this was compounded by the awareness that their position was being plotted and computed, all the way there, and all the way back. The RAF map of the skies was proving to be a terrifying reality for the incoming Luftwaffe planes.

Luftwaffe veteran Hans-Ekkehard Bob certainly believes that radar gave the RAF an important advantage.

'Once I experienced a Spitfire formation all of a sudden coming up from behind, having a clear line of fire, and we wondered how this was even possible. Having no visibility whatsoever, neither from above nor from below, how was it possible that an enemy formation was able to get into a firing position from behind? That was the first time we heard about radio direction-finding equipment, which was called radar later on. At the time we used the term radio direction-finding equipment, which was capable of exactly locating the position of the individual planes. The English were able to make the best use of this superior radar equipment, gaining an advantage, especially in bad weather conditions. So we very much had the disadvantage.'

Fellow Luftwaffe pilot Ernie Wedding also recognises the importance of radar.

> '*Once I experienced a Spitfire formation all of a sudden coming up from behind, having a clear line of fire, and we wondered how this was even possible.*'
>
> Hans-Ekkehard Bob

'I think it was fifty per cent of the victory of the battle. The radar was very important to the RAF because they didn't need to fly standard patrols. They could conserve fuel, aircraft time and flying time, because at any given time they knew exactly where the attacking forces were, which strength, which direction they were flying, so at the last moment they could send up the interceptors which were fresh and they had the shortest approach time necessary to get into a fighting position. And in my opinion that was half the battle to win the Battle of Britain. Without radar it would have been a different picture altogether.'

Sir Edward Fennessy had been convinced – erroneously – that the Germans knew all about Britain's development of radar.

'We were building the chain home system 1938–39. We built eighteen stations in readiness for the outbreak of war. They had 350-foot steel towers and 240-foot wooden towers. They were quite obvious. We said the Germans must have seen this. They were obviously flying reconnaissance, they must have seen it, they must realise what these stations are for, and therefore the likelihood is that they will attack when war comes. On the 8th of August 1939, the radar station just north of Southend saw a very large echo approaching from the east at sixty knots. It slowly came in at sixty knots, until about twenty or thirty miles off the coast, when it turned and flew northwards up the east coast, where it was successively plotted by each of the chain home stations all the way to Scotland. Before it got to Scotland, Fighter Command had come to the conclusion, quite rightly, that this was a Zeppelin. Nothing else could be flying at sixty knots. When it got to Scotland, RAF Dyce sent up a fighter, not to shoot it down, because we hadn't gone to war, but to have a good look at it, and it photographed it. It was the Graf

Zeppelin. It flew up, I think, as far as Shetland and it turned and flew back to its base in Germany. The conclusion at Bawdsey was that this was a reconnaissance, it would have detected and located all of our stations, it would have measured their frequency, their power, and therefore the likelihood was that they would be bombed at a very early stage of the war. Indeed, for that reason, we evacuated Bawdsey, which was one of the radar stations, as soon as war was declared.'

So Fennessy and his colleagues were surprised that radar stations weren't in the first line of attack.

'It wasn't until the 12th of August 1940 that this attack came. Five of the south coast radar stations, extending from the Thames estuary to Ventnor in the Isle of Wight, were attacked. Considerable damage was done at four of them, but we had all those back in operation by midnight. Ventnor was attacked by eighteen dive-bombers and very seriously damaged and was out of action for some weeks. Now, we said, they'll come back tomorrow and finish the job, and if they have to come back the day after that, they'll come back. Because if they can do to the other four stations what they've done to Ventnor, Fighter Command is blind for weeks on end and the Luftwaffe can pour through and wreak havoc with it. But they didn't come back. We never understood that.

'It happened that some time after the war I was at the Farnborough Air Show and Sir Robert Watson-Watt, as he was then, brought General Martini, who had been the chief signals officer at the Luftwaffe during the war, to the Farnborough Air Show, where I entertained him to lunch. After lunch we started talking about wartime things and I asked General Martini, "Why didn't you destroy the radar system at the outbreak of war?" He said, "You didn't have a radar system." I said, "How did we track the Graf Zeppelin from the Thames estuary to Scotland?" He said, "You tracked the Graf Zeppelin? Impossible." I said, "No, we tracked it." I then described in detail what it did. He turned to one of his colonels, he said, "How did this happen?"

'It was only afterwards, when we did some further research, that we discovered that what had gone wrong was that they had assumed that we were working on a much higher frequency, which the Germans were, and that they were not looking for us on the metric frequencies we were using. Secondly, all our stations were, for operational reasons, locked to the fifty-cycle grid. So this giant airship with thousands of rivets was being bombarded with heavy power radar, which was radiated all over the shop, completely confusing the receivers, but bearing the characteristic of a fifty-cycle power main, so they concluded that the noise they were hearing was not a radar station but was flashing over on the power system, and they dismissed any possibility of operational radar. It

> 'They could have destroyed the radar system … they could have destroyed Fighter Command. That decision of Goering not to continue attacking, cost him the Battle of Britain, in my opinion.'
>
> Sir Edward Fennessy

wasn't until the beginning of the Battle of Britain, when we started to shoot down the attacking forces with accuracy, that Martini, who was a very able man, realised we must have a radar system. And he tried to persuade Goering that their task, before they went on

A newspaper seller watching the ongoing battle overhead, the day's reported tally displayed on his blackboard

with the Battle of Britain, attacking airfields, was to destroy the radar system. Goering allowed him one day. That was the day of the 12th of August, when they half did the job. If Goering had allowed three days, they could have destroyed the radar system and it would have been out of action for weeks, if not months, and they could have destroyed Fighter Command. That decision of Goering not to continue attacking, cost him the Battle of Britain, in my opinion.'

So radar, and Germany's failure to recognise its significance, were key factors in Britain's survival. What a world away this was from the experience of the First World War. Aircraft had been used then as long-range scouting reconnaissance weapons; now they needed to be protected by them. Pilots during the Battle of Britain weren't being faced with a squadron of biplanes, the biggest air threat in the last world war. This time, the enemy came across as an armada of bombers. Positioning correctly was more essential than ever before: no matter how good the engine, or how adept the pilot was, the Spitfire was useless if he was 'blind', or if he was simply in the wrong place at the wrong time. Now, there were huge distances to be covered by patrols and also by navigation. This represented a very considerable challenge to aircraft equipped only with rudimentary compasses and the primitive radio beacons of the time.

It was therefore essential that navigation skills were gained by pilots at basic patrol level. The pilot needed to understand that the Spitfire had a limited range, and that fuel capacity meant that time in the air had to be tightly controlled. Running out of fuel was hardly going to be a welcome occurrence during combat. But the pilot also needed to understand that this was still time enough to get well and truly lost. The Luftwaffe pilots had even tougher restrictions, of course. They not only needed to be able to fly during combat time, but they needed to be able to navigate from their bases in France and fly over a country they didn't even know before they could begin to engage with the enemy.

Engaging with the enemy was of course what it was all about. The moment of combat was what everything else had been leading up to. The Battle of Britain would ultimately be about which side could shoot down more of the enemy's planes. After all, the RAF had been mauled over France, helping the British Expeditionary Force, and had been part of the humiliating evacuation from Dunkirk. The Luftwaffe had been triumphant, even though they had certainly had no easy ride of it, with even the French Air Force managing to inflict many losses. The truth about war in the air was that planes were always going to be shot down. It was going to be a numbers game – even though at the start there had been the confident boast that this would be Blitzkrieg all over again. Short and decisive, that was the ambition: to deal with Britain swiftly, just as Poland, Norway, Denmark, Holland, Belgium, Luxembourg and even France had been dealt with.

This time, however, the Luftwaffe faced a strong and resolute enemy air force that had all the possible back-up it could need from a highly organised command and control system. They faced the skill and daring and tenacity of the 'Brylcreem Boys' of Fighter Command, armed with their Spitfires and Hurricanes. This time, in the high summer of 1940, things were going to be different.

Spitfire School Formation Flyer

A few days after being selected as the pilot to go on a nine-hour advanced Spitfire training course, Dave Mallon arrives back in Duxford, and once again meets up with Carolyn Grace, owner of ML407, the only operational dual-seater Spitfire in Britain.

In the briefing room, Carolyn gives Dave a full rundown on what to expect from the course. As well as giving him advanced flying skills, Carolyn is also keen to give Dave a real sense of how his training relates to the experience of pilots in the summer of 1940.

'I thought it would be really significant now that you've got to this stage that we go down to the area where the battle was really at its peak. So we're going to take a flight down to the south coast.'

As they look at a map of southern England, Carolyn explains to Dave where the key areas were for the Battle of Britain, and how Dowding's operational groups worked.

'We're in 12 Group area here at Duxford. So we come down past Stansted, past Stapleford, and into the south via the Thames Estuary.'

For Dave, flying the Spitfire from Duxford all the way to the south coast is going to be a long flight, but it's his-

torically significant, covering many of the battlegrounds of the summer of 1940. Flying over Kent, Dave is in the heart of what was once the best defended airspace in the world, but also witness to some of the fiercest aerial combat ever seen. No wonder the pilots christened Kent 'hell's corner'. In 1940, this countryside was strewn with destroyed and damaged aircraft.

So, for Dave, it's both a demanding challenge as a pilot who still has just a few hours experience flying a Spitfire, and it's also an emotional journey. For Dave, the same age as many of the pilots in 1940, it's a unique experience too. What could be more resonant for a young pilot than flying over the White Cliffs of Dover in a Spitfire?

Although Carolyn is still flying in the front seat of the plane, Dave is now very much in control, flying over the most iconic piece of British landscape in the most iconic of aircraft. He's become much more assured of the controls, and confidently reads out the altitude and speed markings to Carolyn as they go. Not only can he now find his way around the cockpit dials quickly, but he can also immediately understand the significance of what they're saying. If ever a pilot looked at home in his plane, it is Dave Mallon.

The following day, Carolyn hands Dave over to Peter Kynsey, the instructor who taught her to fly the Spitfire originally. Peter was the British aerobatic champion for three years and represented the UK in the world and European aerobatic championships. After he stopped participating in aviation as a sport, Peter began training aerobatic pilots and has also for several years been an instructor for pilots undertaking display flying courses. One of the most experienced pilots of historic aircraft in the country, he's an examiner for the Civil Aviation Authority for display flying qualifications.

In the briefing room, Peter talks Dave through the next stage of his course.

'Today's exercise is that we're going to start off with formation flying, and talk about why we do formation flying and what the purpose of it is. Then we're going to

Opposite: Dave Mallon climbs into the
Spitfire, helped by Carolyn Grace
Above: Dave puts on his flying helmet
Right: Receiving a final briefing from
Peter Kynney
Main picture: In the air, shortly after
taking off

look at the responsibilities of the leader and the wingman – which will be you'

The pilots in 1940 not only had to look out for themselves, as part of a formation, they also had to look out for each other. This required a highly competent level of flying, and it was a real test of the pilots' skills when the formations, hard enough to hold together anyway, were intercepted by the enemy.

Peter teaches Dave how to fly in an Echelon formation, involving two Spitfires, with the wingman flying behind the leader at a 45 degree angle. Peter reinforces the importance of keeping the formation intact, pointing out that the 'wingman must maintain a very precise position'. If this had been 1940, Dave's ability to stay in line would be crucial.

Flying in a formation of two Spitfires with Peter is now giving Dave a real flavour of the training that a Spitfire pilot would have had in 1940. It's still, of course, a world away from combat flying, or the level of experience that was necessary to operate a 'Big Wing' formation successfully.

With basic formation flying under his belt, Dave has one final part of his course to complete: aerobatic training.

CHAPTER FOUR

BIG DAYS, BIG BATTLES

> *'It was the young fellas that came along that took the brunt of it and got most of the losses. I mean, a lot of the old people you talk to now were people who were in before the war …*
> *We had the experience.'*

George Unwin

From July to October 1940, the RAF and the Luftwaffe battled it out in the

skies over Britain. The young pilots on both sides, many of whom had taken up flying simply for the thrill of it, had found themselves on the front line. And before the fighting, the waiting. Waiting each day for the scramble call to come through, at readiness to go on another sortie. For Nigel Rose, the call to action is still fresh in the memory.

'We would be at readiness and suddenly the bells would ring, and somebody would shout, "Villa Squadron, Angels fifteen, take off immediately", or something like that, and so we would race out to our aircraft, climb aboard, get strapped in, and start the engines, which in those days involved a starter battery on wheels, which had to be unplugged by the chaps on the ground once she'd started. Of course, soon after that, we got automatic starting cartridges and you just pressed the button, but not during the Battle of Britain. Then you trundled out as fast as you could and got airborne, probably in sections, and formed up and went away

Previous page: Peter Brothers (centre) and fellow pilots discuss flight plans

Above: Peter Brothers (right) and colleague examine a navigation chart in the summer of 1940

behind the Squadron Commander, who was directing how and when to go. The controller would have told him – they were very good at this – what height to aim for and what direction to aim for, and how the enemy was approaching. They became very skilled at this. It was very much a team job, wonderful.'

The sound of the bell still resonates for Gerald Stapleton, too.

'When the bell goes, it's exhilarating, because you've got to hurtle off into your machine. "Uncle George", our commanding officer, who was thirty, used to get into his machine. The parachute was already there, so he'd jump into it, start up – the ground crew didn't always start your engines up if you'd got there first. He'd taxi out and say over the radio, "Come on, hurry up, you chaps." We always got in and put our parachute harnesses on first, and then taxi out, but he didn't. He didn't put any harness on, he'd just jump in and start taxiing out, and he'd always be out there first. As we were forming up, we'd get over the tannoy system, "603 Squadron, please get into the air as soon as possible." Uncle George would go, "Ah, 603 Squadron airborne." We'd all form up on him, and quite often, the chaps who were the last forming up were still taxiing, and you'd go round in a circle and everybody would catch each other up.'

For Stapleton, being airborne was an exhilarating experience.

'If you've got height, you can be in control, if you see any aircraft underneath you, you've got the advantage. And if you're going to be outnumbered or they outmanoeuvre you, you've got the speed to get away, so you're quite safe when you're up very, very high. And the Spitfire won't fly higher than thirty-four thousand feet, the air's too thin. It wallows about as if you're going to land. But it was exhilarating.'

Once airborne, the squadron would be ready for the sortie. These, though, were dangerous missions, the lives of each young man involved at huge risk. Gerald Stapleton remembers the experience of going on a mission.

'On one occasion I remember, we were vectored, or guided, on to fifty-plus bombers, with an escort. And we were climbing at the time – we were always at a disadvantage for height. Over Dover, when we got closer to them, we got to about twelve thousand feet, and they're at about fifteen thousand feet. You could see black dots in the sky, and you'd think, "Oh, Lord", because you could always see the anti-aircraft backdrops, so that doubled the number of aircraft that you could see, because you couldn't tell what they were, they were just black dots. As well as aeroplanes, there'd be anti-aircraft fire that would explode into black smoke. At that distance, you couldn't tell the difference between aeroplanes and the black smoke of the anti-aircraft fire. It was still exhilarating, though. You didn't have time to think, "What am I getting into?" You never thought that. You would be so down one line, of getting into a position which you could use to your advantage, even though you needed height. So you'd turn away and climb. The Messerschmitt 109s would stick with the bomber formation which was quite slow. You'd turn away to get more height, and if you had the chance, you could use the sun. Then the 109s would come for you, because they'd see you, and they had the height, always. But that manoeuvre of turning away to one side at a diagonal to the formation that you were going for would give you that little more height that you needed, because any aircraft diving down at you was far less manoeuvrable than you were, because he was going so fast. So therefore you had a chance. You could turn into them, and they would fly past you, they didn't have a chance to get really behind you.'

Once in position, the Spitfire pilot would have the opportunity to open fire on the enemy.

'To get a decent shot at any aircraft moving, you've got to shoot ahead of it. Now, if an aircraft is doing two hundred miles an hour, we had a hundred-mile-an-hour ring sight, a reflector sight, which had ninety degrees to you. If he was doing a hundred miles an hour, you'd put him on the edge of the ring and on the dot, but it was stupid to fire at anything at ninety degrees, because you wouldn't hit it – you'd have to fire so far ahead of him. So, the thing to do was to get behind him and get close, and that's the only way. Within ten degrees is the best way. We used to fire a two-second burst. We had thirty seconds of fire, just a brrrrr, brrrrr – it wouldn't be one continuous burst, it would just be, brrrr, brrrr, like that. To keep him in your sights, to have a chance of shooting him down, two seconds was too long, in

> *'If you've got height, you can be in control, if you see any aircraft underneath you, you've got the advantage.'*
>
> Gerald Stapleton

one long two-second burst, you couldn't hold it that long. Especially with a 109, if you could get underneath him and close and he didn't know you were there, then he'd had it. The rule is, get stuck in and get out, as quickly as you can.'

On one occasion, like so many of the RAF pilots in the Battle of Britain, Stapleton was himself shot down.

'We'd been in action, and over the radio George Denham said, "We'll re-form over Hornchurch at fifteen thousand feet." I think there were seven of us who went to fifteen thousand feet over Hornchurch, and we were flying south again. We weren't in a proper defensive formation, and over the Thames, we'd climbed from fifteen thousand to about twenty-two thousand feet, and that's when I got hit, because we were going straight. We thought we were out of range of the 109s but obviously we weren't. And the first thing that happened was that a cannon shell hit the starboard wing in between the two guns on the Spitfire wing, and flattened them, and the ammunition started to come out from its boxes, over the wing, with the pull of the lift, because an aircraft is dragged into the air, not pushed. There was more and more and more ammunition coming out of the wing. When that happens, one of the first things you do is to open the cockpit hood, if you've got to jump out. Then glycol came into the cockpit so then I knew that the radiator had been hit as well. I had no ailerons, so I couldn't turn. I saw a straw field, miles away, because I had my nose down, to gain speed, and that's what I aimed for. Anyway, I was going too fast when I hit this field – well, I didn't hit it, I overshot it, into a hop field. And those supports on those vines pulled up the aeroplane and it never touched the ground – it was sitting on all those vines, two feet from the ground.

> '*Suddenly hell fire broke all around me. I'd flown straight into the escort unwittingly and everything happened then. I came back with an aircraft full of bullets.*'
>
> George Unwin

'When I got out, with my parachute on, I had to be very, very careful that I didn't injure myself getting out of that aeroplane because of the very sharp supports of the hop vines. When I did get out of it, with the parachute over my shoulder, I heard some voices, and I went over to this little sunken lane where I saw a black baby Austin Seven, a man and his wife and two children. They offered me a cup of tea and I accepted it and said, "Thank you very much." Then we went up to the Red Lion in Sutton Valance – when I say "we", the sergeant pilot had dropped down in a parachute in the next field – we got together and up we went to the Red Lion.'

Despite setbacks like these, the RAF pilots were gradually winning the battle. The Luftwaffe needed not only to survive in the air, but to gain air supremacy. That meant not just destroying more RAF planes than they lost themselves, but achieving a high enough hit rate that they would greatly outnumber what was left of the RAF. Thanks to the skills of the Spitfire and Hurricane pilots, and the meticulous planning of Fighter Command, the Luftwaffe were far from their target. The German Fighter Commander Theo Osterkamp had calculated that the Luftwaffe would need to achieve a 'kill' ratio of 5:1 in order to gain supremacy with enough Luftwaffe air power left to launch an invasion. By 11 August, one month after the battle began, the Luftwaffe had destroyed 162 RAF aircraft, and damaged another 174. The cost, though, had been 301 losses of German aircraft and 196 damaged.

It was becoming clear that Dowding and Park's careful planning was paying dividends. However, not all of the RAF's successes were down to their tactical initiatives. George Unwin was one pilot who found himself taken by surprise on a sortie.

'We went over as usual and once you lose each other in clouds and then you look round and there isn't an aeroplane in the sky, marvellous, everything disappears. I was at about twenty thousand feet so I thought, well, I'll go looking for trouble, and I heard on the radio there was another raid coming in and so I started heading towards the coast and there I saw fifty or sixty bombers coming in. I was watching completely fascinated by the sight of them, because I could see Hurricanes going in and I was entirely on my own. And suddenly hell fire broke all around me. I'd flown straight into the escort unwittingly and everything happened then. I came back with an aircraft full of bullets. I went straight into a steep turn, with the stick back, and that's where the Spitfire had it on the Messerschmitt. You see, you get a stalling speed and the Spitfire, it was 74 miles an hour then she stalls, but you can get what they call a high-speed stall in a tight turn. Up goes the stalling speed and in the Messerschmitt once you got to that state it would viciously spin. But with the old lady Spitfire, when you got to that stage she'd shake herself, now watch it, you know, and you just ease the stick forward and you stop it. That's one of the things she had over the Messerschmitt.

'I just went into this and they sat there knowing they couldn't out-turn and shoot me. I actually got two of them by sheer fluke, shutting me eyes. It was sheer luck, I mean, they're all at ninety degrees deflection, I was just spraying them hoping for the best and trying to get out of the way of the things anyway. I saw one go

> *'I got two of them by sheer fluke, shutting me eyes. It was sheer luck, I mean, they're all at ninety degrees deflection, I was just spraying them hoping for the best and trying to get out of the way.'*
>
> George Unwin

straight under the cockpit. The other one went away with oil streaming and blue smoke and I claimed him as a possible, he was damaged but later on they confirmed that he had crashed, but anyway that was luck again, sheer luck. Eventually I broke away and went down and got home, but I was riddled with bullet holes all in the back, but that was sheer carelessness, I'd forgotten all about the escort. I'll never forget that one, that was the most dangerous time in my life.'

Claiming hits was not much of a science during the battle. It was all too easy for several pilots to report the same lost Messerschmitt, maybe because they'd fired at a plane already on its way down, or because they mistook a line of smoke and a plane diving away as a hit.

The fact that the RAF was flying over home territory gave them the edge over the enemy invader, as Gerald Stapleton points out.

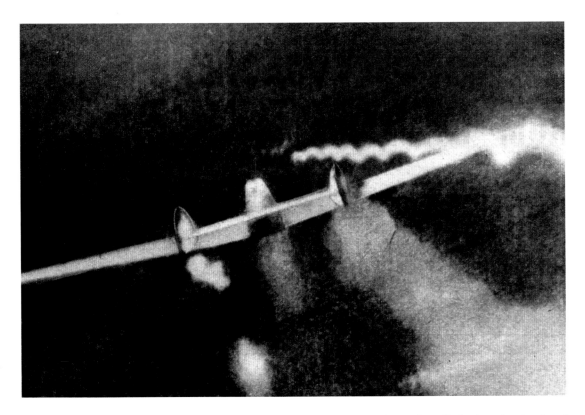

The first official photo published showing British successes in aerial combat, from *The War Weekly*, 14 June 1940

'The two disadvantages that the Luftwaffe had at the Battle of Britain was the Messerschmitt's short range and flying over enemy territory. We lost over five hundred pilots in the Battle of Britain, and we lost eight hundred aircraft, and the difference in those numbers were chaps who'd got out or crash-landed. So, if we'd been flying anywhere else – and this is where Dowding came in, not allowing any Spitfires to go over to France – we would've been at such a disadvantage. So that's the big advantage we had, we're flying over our own territory and fighting over our own territory.'

Flying over home territory allowed RAF pilots to fly two or three sorties on the same day. For Luftwaffe pilots, even if they had a successful mission, the time taken flying home made this far less likely, and even on the biggest days of the battle Ernie Wedding was able to go on only one sortie.

'I was stationed at Chartres. It is quite a long flying time to get there and back. It depended entirely how close you were to the target and how close you were to the coast. The further you were away, the less missions you flew because of the time. The closer you were to the Channel, the more missions you flew. The widest part of the Channel for our sector was about forty miles, and the narrowest was twenty-odd miles, at Dover. There were other units which came from Holland, and they had a long flying time.'

Getting home after a mission presented its own difficulties.

'The worst thing is actually, specially at night, when you're flying through an anti-aircraft barrage, after you've dropped your bomb load and you're heading for home. I would screw myself up as high as I could with the aircraft because the anti-aircraft predictors were aiming at the lowest-flying aircraft. With sufficient height, I could afford to put the nose down slightly and gain speed. In flying, speed is safety. Not just when you're flying in combat, but ordinary flying as well.'

His fellow pilot Hans-Ekkehard Bob sees another dimension to flying over enemy territory: 'The psychological situation was more favourable for the British. If you are fighting over your own country and you're shot down, you are still in your own country. We were above enemy territory, if we were shot down or experienced any other kind of difficulties, it meant capture or death.'

Death for vanquished German pilots didn't have to be in the flames of a burning fighter; another great fear for them was drowning, and 'Kanalkrankheit', or 'Channel sickness', reached epidemic proportions. An airman landing in the Channel had a virtual death sentence, with around four hours before hypothermia set in, and, although there were attempts at rescue with specially adapted sea rescue planes, the odds were not high. No wonder that many German pilots took pistols with them so that they could ensure a quick end if they landed in the so-called 'shit canal'. The problem was so significant that in early September the Luftwaffe authorities had to ban pilots from carrying pistols.

> 'If you are fighting over your own country and you're shot down, you are still in your own country. We were above enemy territory, if we were shot down or experienced any other kind of difficulties, it meant capture or death.'
>
> Hans-Ekkehard Bob

During those summer months, the mess became the centre of everyday life for RAF pilots. There wasn't much time off, and they could often be called to scramble at short notice, depending on what level of readiness they'd be assigned, as Nigel Rose explains.

'When the squadron was put on readiness, you could take off in a matter of seconds, well, hopefully, a matter of seconds, probably a minute or two. Or you might be at fifteen minutes available, or thirty minutes available. At thirty minutes, you could be up in the mess and still be brought to fifteen and then to readiness. But if you were released, then you could be off the camp. And, so if one was released, perhaps one did go off the camp and see friends or go to the flicks or do something else altogether. But if you were on thirty or fifteen, you hung around either down at flights to watch what was going on or perhaps at the mess, where they occupied your time.'

Unsurprisingly, the intense shared experience of being on the front line forged a great feeling of solidarity, and a great pride in the squadron you belonged to. Sixty years later, Rose still remembers the camaraderie of the squadron.

'Having arrived at the squadron, one realised after a little while that it was quite a privilege to join a sort of exclusive club. So one expected to be resented and talked down to a lot.

Not a bit of it, they were extremely friendly and welcoming altogether. And there were several of us posted from my flying training school to the squadron, raw, untrained in operational training units. They were very good indeed, all the chaps.'

Each squadron did become like an exclusive club, with intensive rivalry between the different squadrons – a rivalry that extended to ground crew too, as Joe Roddis recalls.

'Our pride was in being on a Spitfire squadron. Wherever we went invariably there were other Spitfire squadrons and there was a lot of competition. You always thought yours was the best outfit, and when we went to one place there was a squadron, an Australian squadron, No 452, and the CO was "Paddy" Finucane, a very well-known fighter ace. He appeared one day with his arm in plaster and all the girls were signing it, but what he didn't tell them was, he'd fallen off the wall at the pub and broken it. Of course we used to rib their blokes about this then, bloody CO that has to fall off a wall to get hurt, you know. But no, there was a lot of rivalry in as much that you all thought yours was the best. But they'd help you. If you needed help they'd help you. You were one big happy band, band of brothers if you like. But to be on a Spitfire squadron was the ultimate.'

The 'Brylcreem Boys' soon gained quite a reputation. Quite simply, they looked the part of heroes, dashing young men in sparkling uniforms, who dared to walk around with their top buttons undone with the casual touch of a cravat. Like all good legends, there's a certain amount of truth in this, but it's not quite as straightforward as the myth suggests. Keeping the top button undone could be a vital lifesaver for a pilot. The collar of the RAF's officer's regulation Van Heusen shirt would shrink on contact with sea water, which could be fatal for any pilot who found himself in the Channel. So instead pilots opted to wear silk scarves, which also helped to prevent chafing when they turned their heads to see behind them. So the look was not quite the affectation that many have since assumed.

Flying jackets have also become part of the mythical image of fighter pilots, but not for Nigel Rose.

'When you've turned on your oxygen, you could feel a sort of nice cool draught. And flying at 25,000 feet was perfectly normal, except that it was beginning to get pretty cold. And the trouble was that with these lovely ermine jackets which you were issued, these great furry things, you couldn't really move in a cockpit like the Spitfire one, because you had to keep your head turned all the time, and with this restriction, it was very, very difficult. These ermine jackets, great woolly fleece-lined leather jackets, are marvellous for watching rugby matches in cold weather, that sort of thing, but in a Spitfire it was too restricted, really, to wear it. So you couldn't really keep warm except by wearing a whole lot of jerseys, and I think most pilots wore a lot of jerseys. And as it got more into October, November, more and more jerseys, because up at twenty-five thousand feet, it began to get very cold, and at thirty thousand feet it was extremely cold.'

The memories of the veterans do concur more with the legends that have grown up around the Battle of Britain when it comes to the spirit of the times. Many a pilot has described the summer of 1940 as being all about 'beer, women and Spitfires'. In that order. Gerald Stapleton certainly remembers it as a summer of carefree days.

'The Battle of Britain didn't affect us. We weren't thinking about our wives and kids, we had no responsibility other than being in the Air Force. We didn't have any distractions at all, apart from the ones we made ourselves. It's a strange thing to look back on it and think, "Well, why didn't we grieve more for the chaps that were missing?" And you never knew whether they'd been killed or whether they'd jumped out or whether they crash-landed. And by the time the news came through that they had been killed, so much had happened in between that it had no effect on you whatsoever, none.'

While discipline was necessarily strictly enforced, there were certainly opportunities for distractions on the airfields. Joe Roddis remembers when one squadron celebrated shooting down their hundredth German plane.

'They were at Middle Wallop, that was the mob that were chiving us when we arrived, and I had particular interest in it because it was the West Riding of Yorkshire Squadron. It was a university squadron operating out of Yeadon at Leeds and as a result it was called the Leeds and Bradford Squadron, but it was made up of weekend flyers, university students and that. And they got their Spitfires before us at Leckinfield. When they got Spitfires we got short-nosed Blenheims, but fortunately for us, the Finns were fighting the Russians and the Air Minister gave all our Blenheims to the Finns, so we spent two nights painting out all the roundels and putting on the Finnish emblem. All our Blenheims went to Finland and three days later the Russians beat them, and as a result we got Spitfires, we were lucky. But No 609 Squadron was at Leckinfield with us and they went down to Hornchurch, they were really in the thick of it straight away, being in 11 Group. We went on 11 August, they went on the 14th I think, but there was more happening there and as a result they notched up a lot of kills.

> 'The Battle of Britain didn't affect us. We weren't thinking about our wives and kids, we had no responsibility other than being in the Air Force. We didn't have any distractions at all, apart from the ones we made ourselves.'
>
> Gerald Stapleton

'At Middle Wallop they were scrambled and as they came back there was a lot of shouting and cheering going on from their dispersal and they'd got their hundredth German plane. The crew of the plane they'd shot down baled out. And what's more they'd got the parachutes. They shot it down near the airfield. They'd got the Luftwaffe parachutes and all the pilots had cut these parachutes up and had silk scarves and they all dyed them different colours. That was their hundredth Jerry.'

George Unwin remembers another incident that shows how Fighter Command's control on the young men they'd recruited to fight the Germans wasn't always as rigorous as they might have imagined.

'Fredrick "Taffy" Higginson was a great pal of mine. He was a wonderful rugby player before he went to No 56 Squadron. He was a good pilot, Taffy, but he couldn't map read.

He couldn't find his way around at all. He was in No 66 Squadron later on and he kept getting lost, but all he did was find a railway line or a crossroads and he'd land in the nearest field in a Gauntlet – you could do it in a Gauntlet – and see where he was and come home. Well, the powers-that-be got to know about this and they said, if you do that once more you're off flying and you'll go back to your trade. I happened to be the duty pilot this day, there was no air traffic control, just one sergeant pilot, he used to sit in an office booking people in and out. And come half past four when everything stopped and I looked in my arrivals and departures, Taffy was missing. He'd gone somewhere to have lunch with somebody and he was missing. I thought, oh dear. Anyway, about five minutes later the phone rang and a familiar voice said, "That you, George?" I said, "Yeah, Taff?" "Yeah", he replied. "It's all right, I know where I am now. I'll be there in five minutes, ten minutes at the outside." Now their hangar was the nearest side to the leeward side of the aerodrome, the very first hangar at Duxford, and coming in from the east. And he said, "Tell the lads to keep the hangar doors open, I'll do a short landing and quickly turn it in. I'm in trouble anyway so try and keep it from them finding out. Keep the doors open, I'll turn right into the hangar, shut the doors and say nothing." I said, "OK."

'So I just went round the corner, and I said "Keep the doors open, he's on his way. As soon as he gets in he's coming straight into the hangar, shut them and mum's the word. OK?" Now the first fifty yards over the hedge, the grass was very long. Anyway, in comes Taffy and he does a very low approach on engine, doing a very short landing, and he lands in this long grass and into the hangar, shut the doors. Lovely. It takes him ten minutes before he comes into the office. I said, "Where have you been?" "Oh," he said, "I've just been looking at the carriage, I thought I hit something coming into land, but there's no damage to it."

'"Oh," I said, "oh my God." At half past four as I say everything stopped. The local farmer's sheep came in on to the aerodrome, and of course this long grass for the first fifty yards was ideal for them. I said, "It's the sheep." By this time they're on the aerodrome, so I said, "Let's go and look", and we found five dead sheep which he'd hit with his wheels as he came in. A huge flock, of course they never cut their grass, it was always sheep that did the cutting for you. So while we're still looking at these things, the bush telegraph got working and half a dozen families arrived with knives, choppers and everything and in no time there was nothing left of these things and the farmer never did find out. He never even looked for them. That was Taffy. We'd both have been court martialled if we'd been found out.'

Unwin remembers that pilots were soon fêted as heroes, and not just when they managed to supplement rationing provisions.

'There was shortage of this, shortage of that, shortage of everything – particularly beer, which is my favourite beverage, but you know there was never any shortage of beer to us. Whatever pub you went to, you go to the back door and ask for Nelly and there was always some beer for you. They always opened. You got an awful lot of perks that way. You were blue-eyed boys.'

Many of the pilots of 11 Group were of course based close to London and, for men like Gerald Stapleton, being released meant more than a pint in the local pub.

'The first thing you had to do in London was join a wine club. I joined Hoey's Wine Club. You get a card, and when you go to a nightclub, you present this card to one of the waiters, and he would go around to the liquor store and get what you ordered. He'd come back with a slip telling you how much it is, and then he'd take it back to the wine club and he'd get a commission on that, and that was you set for the night. If you wanted any more you could always get it. And we usually finished up at about one o'clock, not later.

'All the hotels were full up in London, and you could never get into a hotel. We didn't particularly want to because they were so expensive. So we went to a Turkish bath in Jermyn Street, and it had two vertical signs on it, "Russian Baths" and "Turkish Baths". They weren't allowed to put them on in the evenings because they were neon, but they used to put them on during the day and put them out when night fell. And it was the perfect sort of hangover cure, if you were the type who had hangovers.

'On one occasion, Oliver and Maxwell, we called them the "heavenly twins" because these two chaps were always together, the three of us went down to this Turkish bath. Afterwards, you have

> *'There was never any shortage of beer to us. Whatever pub you went to, you go to the back door and ask for Nelly and there was always some beer for you ... You got an awful lot of perks that way. You were blue-eyed boys.'*
>
> George Unwin

a massage on your cot, and we all had massages, but the masseur had left on Oliver's cot table part of the spirit rub. Now, you're lying there, naked, and he looks over the top, and there he sees Maxwell lying there naked, so he gets hold of the spirit rub and pours it over his more sensitive parts. And Maxwell gets up and hurtles down, with one thought on his mind, to get into the cold plunge. And he couldn't make it – there were wooden steps down, and they're wet, and then you get on to wet tiles. Now he's running flat out to get to this cold plunge, so he ran up and he couldn't stop, and he finished up with his back against these hot lag pipes. Now he's on his backside, and his hands were slipping, so we threw him in, because we followed him, Oliver and I. And then we got him out. The next day, about six hours later, we were flying.'

Stapleton bought himself a car in 1940 so that he could visit London more frequently.

'I had a car which I bought from Max Aitken, Lord Beaverbrook's son, who was at Biggin Hill when I was there, for £12 10s. It was a two-seater Ford V8, and it was camouflaged, and it had a piece of paper on the windscreen: "This vehicle has been camouflaged by the relevant Army authority to be driven on the roads of the United Kingdom". I didn't have to license it. I always remember that. And it had a dickey seat at the back.

'When London was being bombed, we'd drive in to see if we could help with anything. On one occasion, we'd got out of the car, where we could see a fireman couldn't hold his hose straight, because of the power of the water coming through it. There was a chap in a Rolls driving over the hosepipes. There were four of us, and we went over there, stopped him, and there were a lot of onlookers doing nothing – it was amazing. So we called them over, we turned his car over. For driving over the hosepipes.'

Unsurprisingly, these dashing young hero fighter pilots like Stapleton quickly attracted the attention of young ladies when they left their squadron bases.

'Girls came into it. At the nightclubs there were girls there, in parties. You'd never see one on their own, there'd be a group to pick out from. They're always there. The jitterbugging there was quite fantastic, because we were all pretty fit. And what became of the associations was that girls would give you their numbers, and say, "When you're next in town, give me a call." Oh yes, they were quite like that. Because these were all working girls, and they were out for a good time and we think they enjoyed it. But we were pretty canny in going to the Turkish baths where it was men only, because we knew what the next day would be. When you went on leave, that was a totally different matter, then you could get into an association, which wasn't difficult. And I met my first wife on leave, she was working in a shoe shop.'

So much for the pilots themselves; ground crew staff like Joe Roddis worked on the same airfields as the pilots but they didn't go to the same clubs. Despite the camaraderie that often did exist during the day, these two groups of men, both vital to the Battle of Britain, lived in separate worlds at night.

> 'We thought they could walk on water because they flew Spitfires. We'd have done anything for them.'
>
> Joe Roddis

'You couldn't get close to the pilots really. The first pilots, in the Battle of Britain, it was the early part of the war and nearly all the pilots had been university graduates, clever lads from really well-to-do families, and they'd not been brought up to mix with mechanics. I mean, when they went into the garage with their Bentleys they didn't talk to them, they said fill it up or blow the tyres up and that was it. There was no enmity. We thought they could walk on water because they flew Spitfires. We'd have done anything for them. And I suppose in a way we didn't want a first name. I would never, ever call an officer by his first name. Once you do that, discipline's gone. But I used to call every officer "sir" out of respect and if I knew his first name I wouldn't call him by it. But we got on with them in as much as I think they realised our worth as much as we realised theirs and in our opinion they were the most important thing on the squadron, the man that flew the aeroplane. But without our help they wouldn't have had one to fly, but it ended there. I mean we didn't go out drinking with them. Probably some squadrons did, I don't know. Bombers did, I think bombers were closer, but the first Spitfire squadrons no, there were pilots and ground crew and that's the way we liked it.'

The ground crew saw the pilots as heroes, just as the girls in the London clubs did, and treated them, especially the more senior officers, with respect, as Fred Roberts explains.

'We looked up to all the pilots. Some of the commissioned officer pilots were a bit stand-offish, you know, "I'm an officer, you're not," but there was only one or two of them. On the whole, yes, the pilots, we looked up to them. And we looked up more to the NCO pilots

because they understood this better, they had been through the ranks with us, previous to them becoming pilots.'

Peter Brothers (left) and a colleague at readiness, complete with silk scarf and 'Mae West' lifejacket

For Joe Roddis, this respect could be earned more by some pilots than others.

'Everybody knew Bob Doe was good, even Bob Doe knew he was good. He was always in the thick of it, somehow. Pilots were like that, some never saw the enemy, others couldn't shake them off, but the two pilots I think a lot of us had more respect for than anybody else were both sergeant pilots and they were Poles. They'd got out of Europe and there were quite a lot of Polish aircrew in this country and we were fortunate, and I mean fortunate, to get two sergeant pilots. Joe Klein, and Zurakowski. Now Zurakowski was on telly a few years ago talking about No 234 Squadron. He lived in London. Why I say we liked him, we really liked him. We couldn't get close to them, they couldn't speak much English, but they wouldn't expect you to do everything for them. They wanted to fasten their own parachute, not that they didn't trust us to fasten the straps, but why we respected them was that when nobody else would fly they wanted to.

'At Middle Wallop one day it was a pea souper, the birds were walking and over came a Jerry and we could hear it above this lot plotting the field and we didn't know whether he was going to just buzz off or drop something. These two Poles were out and into the cockpit screaming and shouting at the CO to let them go. "No, no, no", he told them and off he went back inside. But away and off they went into this fog, they hadn't gone ten yards before they've disappeared, but they got airborne, there were no runways, they knew there was nothing in front of them for at least half a mile except two hangars and they were airborne and they disappeared. The CO was biting lumps out of everything. And then we heard this Jerry come over, I mean they had a most distinctive sound, Jerrys. We heard him come over and immediately behind it two Spitfires and they were both firing at it, there were bullets everywhere, you know, and they shot it down. And when they landed were they in trouble, but that's why we liked them. They were there to do a job and nothing was going to stop them. The Poles were brilliant.'

> 'When they landed were they in trouble, but that's why we liked them. They were there to do a job and nothing was going to stop them. The Poles were brilliant.'
>
> Joe Roddis

The Poles on that occasion were lucky. Given the limited amount of training that many of the pilots had received, and the nature of the battle they were engaged it, it's no wonder that Gerald Stapleton remembers luck being a crucial factor in every pilot's fate.

'You thought it's never going to happen to you. That is what you live with. Because I think if you lived with anything else and you thought, "God, I'm frightened I'm going to do this", you couldn't live with it. I was lucky enough to get away with it. And that's absolute luck. If anybody tells you any different, they don't know what they're talking about. Why, for instance, did the cannon shell that came in between my two guns in the starboard wing of the Spitfire not go and hit the armour plate at my back? If it had, it would have shoved that armour plate forward and I would have been pinned up against the front of the cockpit, and I couldn't have got out. That's pure luck, and that's the only way I can describe it. With hindsight, it becomes more apparent that it was luck rather than skill. And being a live coward is better than being a dead hero, so you must learn to know when to run away and, when you're in a mêlée, fly away, when somebody's shooting at you, you take off, and that is that. The Germans had green tracer, and if you saw any green tracer coming past you, you were off. Off as quick as you could make it.'

With the constant demands and danger throughout the summer, it's no wonder that so many of the pilots prefer to look back at 1940 in terms of drinking beer at the back of pubs, attracting the girls, and going to London nightclubs. The prospect of going on the sorties that those young men went on is something that would terrify the vast majority of men. Fear, though, is something few pilots are happy to admit to. The pilots knew that if they suffered from fear, they'd never be able to do the job, and so even fear itself was feared. According to George Unwin, Bob Doe was highly unusual in admitting to suffering from fear.

'Bob Doe always said, "I was terrified". Now he might have been, I don't know, but I tell you, you can't go up there and fight for your life if you're terrified. You can't do anything if you're terrified, you can't even go gardening if you're terrified. You can't be terrified. Apprehensive, yes. I mean who wouldn't be? But on the other hand quietly confident. I think that's the expression. I was anyway and people like me were, I know they were. In fact if you missed a trip you were very angry – it sounds strange but in a way people of my experience thoroughly enjoyed it. It's a very serious thing, I know, but you wouldn't have missed a trip, not for the world.'

Tom Dalton-Morgan masked his fear by thinking of the heroic nature of the deeds he was undertaking.

'I felt that I was doing my job and I was doing it hopefully to the best of my ability. I don't think I felt any fear at any time. But what I did think quite consciously was that if I'm going to get killed in battle, good, good way to go, get killed in battle. That's what I thought about it, that's the way I thought about it, that's the way I think about it now, in retrospect.'

> *'Bob Doe always said, "I was terrified". Now he might have been, I don't know, but I tell you, you can't go up there and fight for your life if you're terrified. You can't do anything if you're terrified.'*
>
> George Unwin

Fear, though, was present, even if subconsciously, and even if the pilots tried neither to think about it nor talk about it. For Nigel Rose, fear manifested itself in his sleeping hours.

'I had two dreams that I remember, which used to occur not frequently but from time to time. One was shooting down an enemy plane and being considered quite a hero for doing so, I think there must have been a fairly easy Freudian explanation of that. The other one was opening a throttle, beginning to take off and going on and on and on and finally landing up in the far hedge, it wouldn't take off. So, I think, again, that must have been some unconscious fear, that the engine would cut out or not have enough power or something. I would wake up at that point and thank God it was a dream. Those two dreams I had after the war, too, those went on a bit.'

If drowning in the English Channel was particularly dreaded by the Luftwaffe flyers, fire was an ever-present fear for both them and Fighter Command's men. For George Unwin, it was a more terrifying prospect than drowning.

'I think being burnt was the worst – it was the one dread. Landing in the sea was a fear, too. We all carried dinghies. We always carried Mae West life jackets in the Spitfire and a dinghy eventually. But being burnt was the worst thing. I saw so many people burnt and in my squadron quite a few were burnt.'

Pilots and gunners of No 264 Squadron try to relax between sorties – but remaining on readiness

Before the war, it had been clear that aerial warfare would inevitably involve serious burns, and in the late 1930s the Emergency Medical Centre was set up, with a network of hospitals just outside London, to treat combatants who were so injured. Archibald McIndoe arrived in one of them, the Queen Victoria Cottage Hospital, in East Grinstead, Sussex, in September 1939, and created a specialist burns centre at the hospital. He was to treat hundreds of pilots who were victims of severe burning, pioneering reconstructive plastic surgery treatment. East Grinstead became known as the 'town that doesn't stare', so familiar were the residents with seeing severely burned patients – a number of whom formed the 'Guinea Pig Club'. While veterans were aware of McIndoe and his work, they were never encouraged to visit recuperating servicemen. For morale reasons, once pilots were in East Grinstead, they had entered a separate world.

As well as such unequivocal physical damage from warfare, the strain of fighting in the Battle of Britain also took its toll in another way; most pilots were in a permanent state of tiredness – though Peter Brothers reckons that 'exhaustion' is nearer the mark.

'I'll give you an example. One night, about half past three, four o'clock in the morning,

I was wakened by my batman to go on readiness, and he took the blackout screens down and said, had I slept through the bombing? And I said, "What bombing?" And he said, "Come and look out of the window," which I did. And there was a stick of bomb craters right across the lawn of the mess outside, I hadn't heard a thing, nor had I heard the anti-aircraft guns firing at the bomber, not a thing, I was absolutely out for the count. And, then, of course, you tried to make up sleep during the day, when you were on readiness – well, you played chess, you read the magazines and papers and that sort of thing, had a sleep and so on. But I think everyone got jolly tired.'

Nigel Rose certainly did.

'I think one did get in terms of sleep, rather tired, very tired sometimes. In my letters to my parents, which tend to remind me a little bit of what I was feeling at the time, I think I recall that there'd been perhaps four times I'd been out, and probably climbing up to fifteen, twenty thousand feet each time, and sometimes seeing nothing at all, you know. Occasionally seeing, a gaggle but losing touch, either because they went into cloud or somebody else was attacking them, some reason. But, nevertheless, the strain of flying, to intercept these things, was there and so, at the end of the day, you felt like a pint, really.'

> *I think being burnt was the worst – it was the one dread. Landing in the sea was a fear, too. … But being burnt was the worst thing.'*
>
> George Unwin

In the 1940s, pilots didn't generally discuss mental strain; having a pint and maintaining a stiff upper lip were the order of the day. Fatigue and stress-related illnesses were not widely considered. Those pilots who couldn't cope with the enormous demands being made of them were said, rather unsympathetically, to suffer from so-called 'LMF' – Lack of Moral Fibre. However, this condition was only fully recognised and treated later on during the war, when the Bomber Command missions over Germany were under way. Nigel Rose sees a difference here between the two kinds of pilot.

'During the Battle of Britain, on fighters, I don't think I ever heard of anybody getting into that situation, at all. I think that it was very much an up and down situation and I can't imagine anybody going to the CO and saying, "Look, I find this too worrying or frightening" or something, "and please send me out doing something else." I don't think anybody would want to take that sort of attitude, at all. I never met anybody. In Fighter Command, it was much less detectable. I think the circumstances in flying single-engined fighters were rather different from getting on board a large bomber with six or seven people, and having to go up over the North Sea for a couple of hours, going over the Dutch or Belgian coast, going at a target, bombing, probably night fighters up against you, both there and coming back. It must have been dreadfully wearing on the nerves for people on multi-engined bombers. So LMF did become recognisable and understandable, I suppose you could call it a sickness, in a way. But in fighters it was up and do your stuff and down.'

While few Battle of Britain pilots may have suffered from LMF, all of them had to deal

A Hurricane pilot, after being rescued from the English Channel, September 1940

with the harsh reality of comrades not returning from sorties. Men they'd spent hours with as part of a squadron, training together and going out on missions. Men who'd been friends as well as comrades, who'd been there for the beer and the women as well as the dogfights. This was too regular an incident for pilots like George Unwin to be able to dwell on. Whatever the terrible fatalities that might have befallen a squadron, there was still a job to be done, and still a line of Spitfires and Hurricanes that needed to be taken out to the front line.

'Well, of course, you do find it very difficult but somehow, and I've checked this with quite a few people, somehow you expected it. It hurt at the time but there were so many, you're losing so many at the time, that you just simply had to kind of say, well, hard luck, old boy, you've got it, you've bought it, you know. And that was that but as far as I'm concerned it never affected my flying.'

> 'Douglas Bader put it in a nutshell, "Nobody asked the buggers to come over here." That was his attitude.'
>
> George Unwin

There were times, though, when putting a brave face on it was not so easy. Unwin recalls how one of his colleagues, Flight Sergeant Harry Steere, was particularly disturbed after one mission.

'The first aircraft he shot down was a Messerschmitt. The Messerschmitt pilot sat on his petrol tank, which was a hard seat and when Harry hit the petrol tank, this thing burst into flames. The pilot half got out and was suffocated and fell back in and Harry got down on the ground and was sick as a dog telling this story to the intelligence officer. So it did affect you, I mean it had to affect you but you must not let it get you down.

I mean, all part of war. After all, Douglas Bader put it in a nutshell, "Nobody asked the buggers to come over here." That was his attitude.'

As Nigel Rose explains, it wasn't always immediately apparent that a squadron had suffered a fatality.

'When a sad thing happened, that somebody was killed and missing, there was practically always a delay. Somebody didn't turn up, you know, and you wondered what had happened. And it took some time to find what had happened to him, because he might have put down somewhere in a field or force-landed somewhere, because he'd been shot up, or he might have baled out over the sea, quite a lot were picked up, we had two or three people picked up out of the sea. And then sometimes, nothing was known, that was rather sad because probably he'd been shot down into the sea. And occasionally we found that they'd crashed on land and they were fairly quickly identified. Not always – some aircraft spun in and were only dug out years and years later. But in that case, I mean, if they didn't return, they were missing, presumed killed.

'We had one new wife, the famous case where she came and camped outside the airfield for a month after her husband was shot down and she never believed he wouldn't come back, but he didn't, sadly. His body was washed up and he was buried with military honours and so on. I think it comes back to things happening so fast that you didn't have an awful lot of time to mope. I mean, you did feel sad, particularly when your friends didn't come back, chaps you knew pretty well and had flown with, were close to, and so on. I mean, that was sad, but you didn't have an awful lot of time to sort of go into full-scale mourning over it. You were probably up on a flight, you know, thinking about other things.'

Hans-Ekkehard Bob readily admits that the loss of comrades did affect him.

'You cannot forget the human aspect of it all. There is no question that it is a sad state of affairs when people die or don't return or disappear, irrespective of whether it was someone close to you or not. It is always a sad state of affairs, and it makes you feel despondent. Of course you reflect that it could have happened to you too, but, as people say so aptly, "Life goes on", although of course immediately after it happens you don't think that, it comes to you later, when you have already almost forgotten about it. There were things that happened that were terrifying to witness, for example, when we were still flying with bombs on board, if there were any technical errors, and the bomb had been set to "live" and then exploded right there in the air, the plane would be ripped apart by the explosion. I mean, a situation like that is terrifying, if you witness that, it shakes you to the core. You can imagine it, you have a comrade or a friend flying alongside you, and then suddenly his plane dissolves into bits, a crazy situation. Those are situations that really get to you, it goes without saying, yes.'

> *'You cannot forget the human aspect of it all. There is no question that it is a sad state of affairs when people die or don't return or disappear, irrespective of whether it was someone close to you or not.'*
>
> Hans-Ekkehard Bob

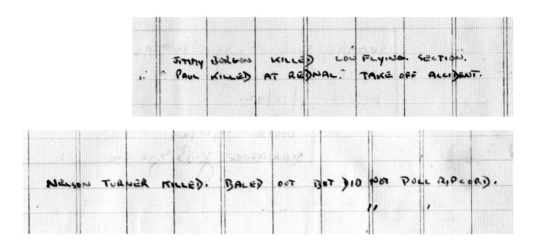

JIMMY BORGON KILLED LOW FLYING SECTION.
PAUL KILLED AT REDNAL. TAKE OFF ACCIDENT.

NELSON TURNER KILLED. BALED OUT BUT DID NOT PULL RIPCORD.

A pilot's logbook entries recording the death of friends and colleagues

Bob says that he didn't suffer from nightmares as a result of the battle, and believes that this is thanks to the nature of aerial combat.

'To have nightmares, you would have to have had some experiences involving a large number of dead people, where you had actually seen the dead people, but we ourselves didn't see any dead people, you see. People often say that aerial warfare is "clean" warfare, by which they mean that you don't see any corpses. It goes without saying that there is no such thing as "clean" war, but what is meant here is that when fighter pilots shoot down a plane, that plane is destroyed in the air or on the ground or wherever, and then it's all over and done with. You don't see much wreckage, and you see only to a limited extent human bodies or injured people.'

The ground crew staff, such as Joe Roddis, also had to come to terms with squadron fatalities, often of the pilots they'd worked most closely with, on the aircraft they'd been responsible for maintaining.

'There were pilots that just didn't come back. All the time, not just in the Battle of Britain – there was a war on. Invariably you knew what had happened because they'd be in threes. Very, very seldom would a bloke fly on his own, he'd be stupid if he did because you're watching each other's back all the time. But two would come back instead of three and we knew then we'd lost one and it wasn't until the pilots had landed and they said, yeah, he went down, we never saw him bale out, or we saw him go straight into the wood or straight into the ground, yeah, we lost quite a lot like that. I wouldn't say you got used to it, you never got used to it and it depended to a degree how familiar you were with the pilot. If it was a pilot that flew your aeroplane constantly and that was the one that went down that day, you would feel it. If he was off another flight – because the squadron was divided into two flights, A flight

> *'Two would come back instead of three and we knew then we'd lost one and it wasn't until the pilots had landed and they said, yeah, he went down, we never saw him bale out, or we saw him go straight into the wood or straight into the ground, yeah, we lost quite a lot like that.'*
>
> Joe Roddis

and B flight – you'd be sorry but that was the war, wasn't it, that's what it was about. Nobody went into mourning or anything like that, but of course there were people on the squadron who felt it, the Adjutant would have to write to his family or his wife or the CO and his mates. They'd feel it. To us we'd lost a pilot, we'd lost an aeroplane, get on with the job.'

As Fred Roberts recalls, these fatalities could not only be frequent, but also close to home.

'We lost a lot of experienced pilots. The first day of Dunkirk we lost three experienced pilots. The CO was shot down, we thought he had been killed, but he was taken prisoner of war. Watson, who was an experienced pilot – never found him. And Lyon was shot down, never came back to the squadron, he was injured badly, never came back to the squadron. And they were all pre-war experienced pilots. On another occasion, a group of us, along with twenty-year-old airmen, watched the plane coming in, and the pilot was younger than us, and his flaps didn't work, he'd been in action, his flaps didn't work. And when he landed,

> 'Our main concern was the pilot – we weren't bothered about the Spitfire, we wanted the pilot back. You could replace the Spitfire, they made 20,000, but pilots were very, very hard to come by.'
>
> Joe Roddis

he tipped up on his nose and overturned. And we couldn't do anything about it, we just stood there watching him burn to death, because the fire tender couldn't do much about it. And if you've seen ten or twelve twenty-year-old airmen crying, that's how we felt about pilots who didn't come back. The pilot was only eighteen.'

And by now it was pilots who mattered, more than the planes they flew. At the beginning of the war, the major concern for Fighter Command had been making enough aircraft available. Considerable effort had gone into improving production rates, and by June 1940 the results were beginning to show, something Lord Beaverbrook, appointed to the Air Ministry a month earlier, was quick to take credit for. In fact, it was due to the work of many people over a much longer period that Britain was able to produce more than twice as many fighters as Germany throughout the Battle of Britain. Germany failed to maximise its industrial potential, and the German war machine only reached a level of full production in 1944 when it was pretty much too late. So as the Battle of Britain progressed, the concern shifted from producing aircraft to replacing airmen. As Joe Roddis explains, pilots became quite simply more valuable than Spitfires in every sense.

'Our main concern was the pilot – we weren't bothered about the Spitfire, we wanted the pilot back. You could replace the Spitfire, they made 20,000, but pilots were very, very hard to come by, trained pilots, especially Spitfire fighter pilots. If you could bale out and get away with it, we couldn't care less about the Spitfire – we'd lost an aeroplane. Fair enough, it was only nuts and bolts and we'd got a man back to fly another and we'd always got another one, because we had eighteen, they were never all in the air at once. Not until Douglas Bader started his "Big Wing", then he wanted everything up that would fly.'

The demand for new pilots meant that training was continually being condensed and, as

George Unwin found, the newer pilots coming through to the squadrons as the summer progressed simply didn't have the necessary flying experience to face combat situations.

'In 1940 I'd been flying for about five years. I'd been flying Spits for two years and so there comes a stage when you know you can fly, after about three years you've got control of it, full control of it and I was in that very happy stage and of course it was the young fellas that came along that took the brunt of it and got most of the losses. I mean, a lot of the old people you talk to now were people who were in before the war. Peter Brothers for example and people like him. He was there by 1936. We had the experience. And the German pilots, the original German pilots, were very, very good, there's no doubt, but their aeroplane wasn't quite as good as the Spitfire – luckily.'

It was the squadrons in 11 Group in the south-east that were most in need of these replacement pilots coming through.

'At Duxford we were in 12 Group and we were billed the most southern aerodrome in 12 Group and we were never short of pilots. We were in the position of having several days when we could take these youngsters up ourselves and give them a bit of training that was far as we knew. So we were better off than Biggin Hill and Kenley. They just couldn't give them the time. With young pilots coming in, there was sheer lack of flying experience for the majority of them. I mean there's no way you can buy experience, you've just got to put in the time and that was their main problem.'

> 'It would be impossible to learn in ten hours what a combat pilot should do, automatically, when he is either going after an enemy aircraft or when an enemy aircraft is going after him. That was the problem that a lot of replacement pilots found themselves in.'
>
> Gerald Stapleton

Gerald Stapleton saw for himself the difference that reduced training time could make on a pilot's chances of survival.

'We did have replacements coming in, we lost seven pilots in the first week. And some of the pilots were experienced pilots, they were from Army Corps operation squadrons, that were disbanded after France. And these pilots were experienced pilots but not experienced in flying single-engined fighters. And that's one reason why we grew moustaches, to make ourselves look older, as they were older, and we youngsters would be telling them what to do. And they'd had this short conversion course from Lysanders, Army Corps Operation, to either the Hurricanes or Spitfires.'

A short conversion course could involve as little as ten hours in a Hurricane or a Spitfire, which, as Stapleton explains, was hardly adequate preparation for going into battle.

'It would be impossible to learn in ten hours what a combat pilot should do, automatically, when he is either going after an enemy aircraft or when an enemy aircraft is going after him. That was the problem that a lot of replacement pilots found themselves in. The lucky ones would have got out by parachute or crash-landed, the unlucky ones wouldn't be here any more. In ten hours, you can just learn how to fly the aeroplane, how to land it and how to take off. Taking off is easy, landing is trickier. And you haven't got the habit of flying in ten hours, in that particular aeroplane. To put your hand on all the controls that you have, without thinking about it. And with oxygen to remember, turn on your firing button – the number of people who press that button without turning it on, extraordinary, because you had a firing button on the control column, you had an on and off switch, and the first thing you did when there was anybody who said, "Tally ho!" the first thing you did was turn that button on. If you made a habit of that, then it was automatic. All things like that. And the more automatic you could get, the better your survival would be.'

Joe Roddis recalls that some of the replacement pilots towards the end of the summer didn't even have ten hours' experience in a Spitfire.

'Some of them would come with five or six hours' duration on Spitfires. I mean, let's face it, all they could do was take off and land and probably a few side slips and tight turns, a roll, a bit of formation flying, but they were thrown in at the deep end. And the experienced pilots would always try and put a new bloke with people who knew what they were doing, what they were on about, and they weren't told to look after them, that would be a slight on

> *'Let's face it, all they could do was take off and land and probably a few side slips and tight turns, a roll, a bit of formation flying, but they were thrown in at the deep end.'*
>
> Joe Roddis

the young pilot who probably himself thought I'm as good as any of these. I would. But they would keep an eye on them a bit more than normal or they'd say, "Get out the way, look behind you, dive, get up, do this, do that" – whatever language they used – but they weren't always quick enough and we did find, as time went on, during that period I'm talking about, that it was the pilots like Bob Doe that it was second nature to. His eyes were everywhere, he'd never stop looking, he'd eyes in the back of his head, that's why he lived so long and that's why he shot down so many. A young, a completely inexperienced youth – and they were only youths, some of them, they were only as old as we were – would think he was doing everything right, but a fighter pilot in action, when you think about it, he's got to be able to keep a hell of a lot of balls in the air at once, hasn't he? He's not only got to fly that damned aeroplane and watch his speed and watch his fuel gauge and watch this and watch that and watch what's happening outside and what's coming from above, what's coming from below, look in his rear mirror, what's behind – he's flummoxed, confused utterly, but it's only by doing all that that you could get experience if you live long enough. But some of the poor devils didn't and it was sad, really sad.'

While the onslaught continued, though, Fighter Command needed to send fighter pilots up and they simply had to hope that the boys could do the job, experienced or not. By September real breakthroughs were being made. It was becoming apparent that the Luftwaffe was falling far short of what they needed to achieve to win air supremacy over Britain.

Every battle has its tipping points, moments that in retrospect can be identified as decisive, and for the Battle of Britain there are principally three such points: 13 August, the so-called

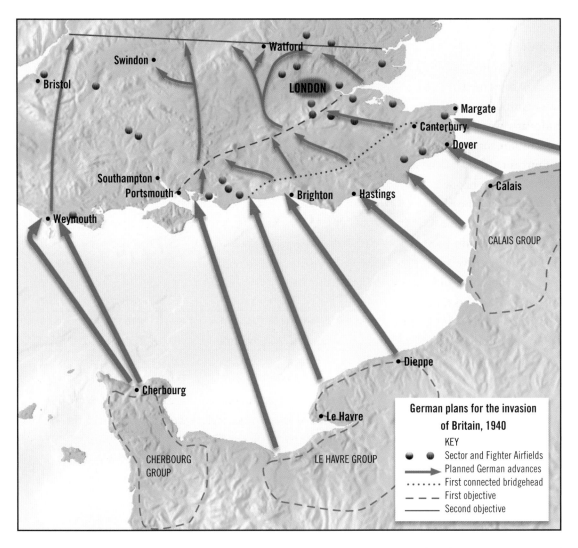

German plans for the invasion
of Britain, 1940
KEY
●● ● Sector and Fighter Airfields
→ Planned German advances
······· First connected bridgehead
— — — First objective
——— Second objective

'Eagle Day'; 18 August, dubbed the 'hardest day'; and 15 September, later commemorated as 'Battle of Britain Day'. Each of these days demonstrates how the Luftwaffe was simply failing to make the necessary progress for an invasion to become a plausible option. These days were of course embedded in a constant stream of others bulging with raids, sorties, death and combat, but in the passage of time these are the three that have most clearly risen out of the mêlée. They were the days of maximum effort from both sides, the days when it was all supposed to come together for the Luftwaffe, and which really tested Fighter Command. They were the days that were to prove – though no one quite knew it at the time – decisive, testing to destruction the respective strategies, pilots and technology employed by the two sides.

While these three particular dates have been so identified, there is controversy over the start and end dates of the Battle of Britain itself. The British and the Germans have, to this day, very different notions of just when, and over what period, it was fought. The British have always focused on two crucial dates, 10 July and 31 October, between which the Battle of Britain was fought and all but won. Of course, there had been aerial conflict before that start point, and the Blitz would carry on deep into 1941, but for the actual battle these have seemed like suitable bookends. Before 10 July, the attacks were neither sustained nor continuous enough to qualify as a full offensive; after 31 October the threat from the Luftwaffe was no longer critical – the Germans could inflict damage, and maybe have a serious impact on morale, but it was no longer plausible that they had the strength and resources to mount a full-scale invasion. German historians, meanwhile, have dismissed everything that happened before 8 August as being just a prelude to the battle, but have seen the entire Blitz bombing campaign up until May 1941 as part of the Battle of Britain. Whatever the calendar truth, it is possible to discern in the Battle of Britain a distinctive shape: a crescendo reaching a few ferocious spikes, before plateauing out, and finally dwindling as the war moved on to its global phase.

Following the initial raids over the Channel, in early July, the battle began to gain real momentum. It was on 10 July, a wet summer's day for most of the country, that Fighter Command's 11 Group detached whole squadrons instead of flights to forward airfields at first light. There was heavier enemy activity than usual, with radar spying around seventy German planes forming up in the Calais area, which later attacked a convoy escorted by six Hurricanes just off Dover. One ship was sunk, three Hurricanes shot down, and four Messerschmitt 109s shot down. Near Newhaven a train was hit and the driver killed; near Falmouth thirty people were killed, and ships, railways, power stations and an ordnance factory were all damaged. The RAF station at Martlesham Heath in Suffolk also suffered. There were further raids on Scotland, south-eastern and eastern England during the night. In all, on this first day of the battle proper, the RAF lost six aircraft, the Luftwaffe thirteen.

For the next month, this level of fighting continued, Fighter Command fending off German sorties during the day, Bomber Command missions heading across the Channel at night. But for the Luftwaffe this was still the warm-up. This was to be the period in which the Luftwaffe gained air supremacy over Britain. Their plan for August, as much as it can be described as a plan, would be the start of the actual German invasion offensive that would finish off what was left of the RAF, and Britain's independence with it. 'Adlertag', as the Germans called it ('Eagle Day') – the day Hitler had originally designated for the invasion of Britain – was to be the big curtain opener. It was planned as a deliberate attempt to escalate the probing, inconclusive nature of their earlier tussles by mobilising the whole of the Luftwaffe fleets now based in new and adapted bases across France and the Low Countries.

Things didn't bode well for 'Eagle' from the start. First off, the day itself was continually postponed, mainly because of actual or forecast bad weather. Eventually Goering settled on 13 August. Bad weather struck again, but this time Goering didn't choose to postpone, at least not the whole day. 'Eagle Day' would begin at 2 p.m., although in the event this message didn't get through in time, and some squadrons set out in the morning; the confusion that was inherent in 'Eagle' striking once again before it had even begun. When the moment finally arrived, the offensive was undoubtedly considerable, for Fighter Command the most severe test yet. Over came the raids attacking squadrons of Spitfires and Hurricanes. Airfields and radar stations were targeted in the hope of destroying Fighter Command's ability to fight back.

If it was Fighter Command's severest test to date, it was also their greatest victory. Despite the intensity of the raids, they lost just thirteen aircraft in combat and one on the ground. The RAF lost an additional forty-seven aircraft on the airfields that were bombed, but the damage to their airfields themselves was only temporary. All but three of the pilots involved survived. In the end, it was 'Eagle Day' more than any other that denied Goering the decisive outcome he so craved. It had been compromised before it had even begun, and it had taken several valuable hours to reorganise and remount the attack. The Luftwaffe was forced to regard this delay as a learning curve, that was all, it was a preparation for the next time. So much for the start of the invasion offensive.

The days following 'Adlertag' would see huge numbers of sorties. On 15 August, for example, the Luftwaffe launched more sorties than on any other day, more than two thousand in all. Once again, though, the RAF triumphed. The Luftwaffe destroyed thirty-four RAF fighters in combat, and two on the ground. This, though, was still not enough for an invasion to become imminent and, more crucially, the success came at a heavy price. The RAF destroyed seventy-five Luftwaffe machines. No wonder the Germans called the day 'Black Thursday'. It was also becoming clear that attacking British airfields was not having a significant impact on the RAF's fighting strength. The most serious impact on 15 August on Fighter Command's infrastructure was when three radar stations had their power supply cut. It had been restored by the evening. It was on this day that Goering suggested that the Luftwaffe stopped attacking radar stations, and also ordered his men not to raid airfields that had been attacked the previous day, assuming that it was a pointless exercise. This was a crucial strategic error, safeguarding 11 Group's infrastructure: the radar stations from that moment would be able to remain continually functional; and airfields were guaranteed enough time to recover from raids to continue operating.

'Eagle Day' and 15 August had, for the Luftwaffe, been an unmitigated disaster: the biggest missions yet, but virtually nothing to show for them. Still, the Germans retained their faith in the ability of their Air Force to deliver a decisive blow. German Field Marshal Kesselring nominated 18 August for the next big push against Fighter Command – a day of anticipated good weather. At the heart of the plan lay two coordinated attacks against what had been identified, rightly, as key airfields, each guarding access to London: Biggin Hill in Kent, and Kenley in Surrey. The intention was to tear the heart out of Fighter Command by rendering them both inoperable, destroying not only their facilities but as many of the planes that were based there as possible. This would be a plan that would test just how destructive a sortie day with more than a thousand aircraft could be, mixing and matching every combination of plane at Kesselring's disposal. Medium bombers, light bombers, dive bombers, escort

fighters would all be part of this mammoth offensive. They wouldn't just fly en masse, but in carefully staggered waves – at least, that was the plan. There would also be ferocious fighter cover for both raids, provided by Bf 109s and 110s, clearing a path ahead of the bombers, and mopping up whatever resistance the denuded RAF was capable of scrambling off the ground. As strategies go, this was nothing less than hammer and stiletto.

Pilots in a flight dispersal building waiting for the next scramble call

Biggin Hill would be taken out by a formation of around sixty Heinkel 111s, relying on the tried and tested method of simply unloading as many bombs as possible from altitude. Kenley would be attacked by a smaller but more accurate force, comprising Dornier 17s and the new, fast Junkers 88s. To compensate for their lower bomb capacity, they would be relying on different tactics, hitting Kenley with a lethal left–right combination of Ju 88s attacking with precision dive-bombing, to be followed five minutes later by the Dorniers sweeping in at rooftop level. What they lacked in punch, they would make up for in stealth and accuracy. Either way, it was anticipated that neither Kenley nor Biggin Hill would be playing much more of a role defending Britain once the dust had settled.

What the German controllers didn't know was that neither airfield had underground control rooms, those indispensable links in the defensive network. Instead, their work was carried out in flimsy brick buildings that were utterly vulnerable to bomb attack – actually far more valuable targets than the hangars and the runways. What a bonus that would be, if they too were to be destroyed. The day would be built around these, and other, carefully constructed tactics, each requiring consummate timing and navigational cunning to have any chance of real success. Exhaustive preparations had been undertaken, reconnaissance photographs were meticulously studied. Nothing was being left to chance. The British were to be overwhelmed by the sheer weight, but also the lethal precision, of Luftwaffe attacks.

Like 'Eagle Day', 18 August was a very deliberate attempt by the Germans to produce a decisive hammer blow that would in the course of a single day push the RAF back to the brink. By the end of hostilities that day, a perfect microcosm of the Battle of Britain had been played out – not that anyone would have been aware of it at the time. By this point, a fairly clear, though by no means definitive, picture of the RAF had started to emerge. The Germans were pretty sure what the major airfields were, where they were located, and their strategic importance. Perhaps there was confusion about what the larger goals might be, but in terms of tactics, the idea of aiming the sharp end of their hammer-blows at the fighter defences was clear enough.

Given that the 15 August was still the only occasion on which a thousand-strong sortie had been dispatched across the Channel in a day, nobody yet knew definitively just what damage could be unleashed. So 18 August would bring together the sum of what the Germans had learned, or thought they had learned, about their British adversaries over the previous weeks. The ground had been laid, Fighter Command softened, now would come the breakthrough moment that had, in earlier months, signalled the end of Poland, the end of the Low Countries, the end of France. They were confident this time of the success that had been all too elusive on 'Eagle Day'. German intelligence reports repeatedly told the Nazi hierarchy that the RAF was close to breaking point, that the British were down to their last handful of serviceable planes. Opposition would be light. They were convinced too that the airfields represented vulnerable, highly significant targets, that bombers would be able to pretty much destroy them, with decisive consequences for the defending forces now deprived of the wherewithal to mount any great aerial opposition. It also made sense to take the fight to the nerve centres of Fighter Command, and forget the early tactic of trying to draw the fighters up into a confrontation by attacking Channel convoys.

Often referred to as the 'hardest day' of the Battle of Britain, a detailed account of 18 August is an illuminating illustration of just what the pilots of Fighter Command had to face that summer. The day didn't start well for the Germans, though; hazy conditions over the south of England forced the initial takeoff to be aborted, and the force recalled. There would have to be a two-hour delay while the sun burnt off the mist. Eventually, visibility was deemed good enough and once again the formations of bombers and escorts prepared for the big assault. First up, the slower, lumbering Heinkels destined for Biggin Hill. So far, so good: sixty aircraft now all where they should be, and no problems either linking up with their fighter

escorts. The Kenley raid, however, got off to a shakier start; worse visibility around their bases had meant the Ju 88s were now behind the Do 17s, and not in front of them where they should have been. By lunchtime, the Bf 109s and 110s were off the ground, too, ready to overtake the slower bombers and carve a path for them through RAF defences. Kesselring now had his planned formations in place. It was a formidable force, comprising around 108 bombers and 150 fighters, flying on different but converging bearings, and at a variety of altitudes.

Members of No 501 Squadron flying in formation during the summer of 1940

This was the sort of attack that Dowding had been preparing for all those years, one that would tax every element of his elaborately prepared defensive network to breaking point: multiple raids, comprising multiple types of aircraft, in multiple types of attack. The first signs were good: at least one part of his Fighter Command plans were shown to be up to the task

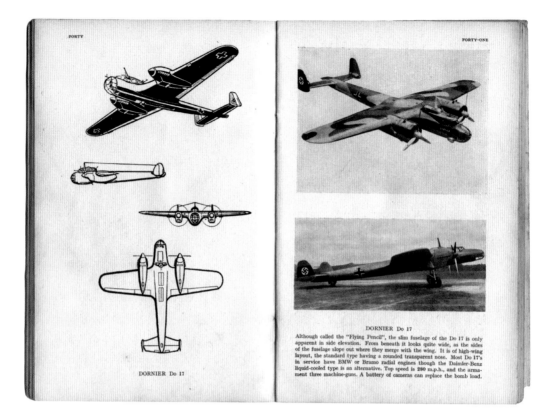

DORNIER Do 17

DORNIER Do 17

Although called the "Flying Pencil", the slim fuselage of the Do 17 is only apparent in side elevation. From beneath it looks quite wide, as the sides of the fuselage slope out where they merge with the wing. It is of high-wing layout, the standard type having a rounded transparent nose. Most Do 17's in service have BMW or Bramo radial engines though the Daimler-Benz liquid-cooled type is an alternative. Top speed is 280 m.p.h., and the armament three machine-guns. A battery of cameras can replace the bomb load.

A guide to spotting a Dornier Do 17 'flying pencil'

– radar. Another, however, was not. Fighter Command headquarters were by now fully aware that something big was on its way, and Dowding's command and control system kicked into action. Radar plots were taken, and the filter room was busy translating those into squadron orders. The problem came not from gathering the intelligence, but in the tactics used by the squadrons charged with taking on the incoming hostiles. One group of Hurricanes speeding to intercept would learn the hard way just how much better adapted to fighter tactics the Luftwaffe were, compared to Fighter Command. Everything prior to this point had worked like a dream; the scramble had been executed perfectly, the controller was 'vectoring' them to exactly the right place, as far as he was able. The trouble was that they were still operating that old RAF dogma, discussed in Chapter 3 – tight formation flying.

Meanwhile, a classic RAF riposte was in full swing. Five squadrons of Hurricanes and Spitfires were by now in the air, climbing as fast as possible to altitude, determined to cut the raids off, preferably before they got to drop their bombs. Twenty-three Spitfires and twenty-seven Hurricanes were getting ready to defend Biggin Hill and Kenley. That meant there were close to a hundred RAF fighters in position to take on the raids – an impressive turn-out, but it was only a ratio of two British planes to five German. Outnumbered, but still far in excess of what the Germans were expecting.

The first encounter was a disaster for Fighter Command, another grim reminder of how fast aerial combat had evolved since the early training manuals had been written. The Hurricanes, climbing, grouped together in the kind of tightly woven formation that had so impressed audiences at pre-war air shows, were about to discover just why the Bf 109 'bounce' was such an effective and terrifying tactic. Oberleutnant Gerhard Schoepfel, in command of a 'Staffel' of Bf 109s, caught sight of them, lined up below like ninepins. No wonder the Germans had nicknamed the British 'vic' formation the '*idiotenreihe*', or row of idiots.

The Hurricanes were oblivious, and Schoepfel pounced, diving from above. It took only two short bursts to account for the first pair of Hurricanes that crossed his sights; a third went down in flames soon after, a fourth after that. In that classic Battle of Britain way, a pilot's first and only intimation of being under attack was to have his plane knocked out from under him, shuddering at the hammer blows of German cannon fire, flames and smoke soon engulfing it. It had been a paragon of air combat: clinical, ruthless and devastating. Four Hurricanes had been dispatched in less than a couple of minutes. Again and again, Fighter Command fighter pilots would complain that this obsession with formation flying was suicidal, and the successful ones were the ones who quickly adapted newer, more fluid ways of flying, usually based, many were forced to concede, on the more successful Luftwaffe model.

The raiders were by now well on their way, preparing themselves for their fiery climax. Just after 1 p.m. the bombers were making landfall, now only forty miles away from their respective targets. The high-flying planes were reconciled to the fact their presence had long been detected by radar, but the wave-skimming Dorniers were hoping to evade being seen altogether. They were spotted, however, by naval vessels, and by the Observer Corps, which blew their chances of complete surprise. Within minutes, the plotters at Kenley were adding this new raid to the ominously swelling wave of incoming bombers. Unfortunately that was pretty much all they could do; the scrambled squadrons were at altitude, and couldn't be diverted. It was clear that the Dorniers were going to have pretty much a clear run at them. There was nothing for it but to ensure that every last aircraft on the ground at Kenley was scrambled immediately to get them to safety. The clock was ticking, everyone on the ground now knew they were minutes away from being attacked. And still the plotters had to stand by their tables, marking the progress of the raids that were converging directly upon them.

The approaching Do 17s, however, didn't have it all their own way. It had been planned that their final run would come on the heels of a devastating first blow delivered by dive-bombing Ju 88s. They were supposed to be flying into an airfield already crippled by bombs – but there was nothing. They had arrived first, and would have to attack Kenley without any cover. Nothing to do now, but fly in, punch hard, and get out. And then they were all over them, the German raiders fanned out, strafing the airfield and its defences before releasing their specially adapted bombs from as low as possible. There was plenty of return fire from the anti-aircraft guns, but not enough to prevent Kenley from being turned into an inferno; hangars evaporated in smoke and flames, buildings shaken and collapsed, ground personnel

The pilots of No 601 Squadron scramble to their Hurricanes during the Battle of Britain

buried by debris and rubble. This was what the Battle of Britain looked like from the ground.

Kesselring's strategy of bringing Britain to its knees by knocking out its airfields, decimating its fighters, was starting to look distinctly effective. But what, when the smoke cleared, had the bombers actually achieved? A hundred miles from home, and with every fighter squadron now fully alerted to their presence, the big test of Luftwaffe tactics was in fact still to come.

It was by now clear how much sense it had made trying to ensure the Do 17s came in low after the Ju 88s, and not before. One Dornier, lining up its final attack, was suddenly pilotless – a victim of an anti-aircraft machine gun round, the plane saved from ploughing into the ground by the quick-witted intervention of the navigator who seized the control column and took over control, all in a split-second. By now all semblance of a coherent formation had gone, and it was each plane for itself. Another Dornier then came close to becoming the victim of a new, rather Heath-Robinson piece of anti-aircraft technology, a combination of rockets, cables and parachutes designed to snag and bring to the ground exactly this kind of low-flying assailant. Only by virtue of having been caught in mid-turn did it succeed in shrugging off the cable, though not before suffering considerable damage.

Twenty-five thousand feet above them, things looked as though they were going the

Germans' way, too. Three more Hurricanes that had been patrolling, waiting for a chance to pounce on the bombers, were themselves victims of a Bf 109 ambush, mortally damaged, one ploughing straight into the ground at a nearby golf course. But the tables would turn, if only because taking the brunt of the 109s had allowed the other RAF fighters the chance to attack the lower bombers unmolested. Things got very busy, very quickly, ten thousand feet below, with Hurricanes from No 615 Squadron now flying straight into a large formation of Dorniers and their Bf 110 escorts.

If the 'vic' formation tactic had shown up the RAF to be wedded to outmoded ways of fighting in the air, then these attacking Hurricanes would prove that, in other respects, the RAF had thought long and hard about the art of shooting down bombers. Of all the ways of attacking a bomber, the head-on attack was at once the most effective, and far and away the most dangerous. Effective because of its utterly devastating psychological impact on pilots protected by nothing more than plexiglass; dangerous because of the combined velocity in excess of 400 mph required the sharpest of reflexes. It was the ultimate game of fighter 'chicken', and it claimed the life of the first pilot who tried it, who, with sickening inevitability, had mistimed his manoeuvre, and collided. But the lesson stood. Nothing broke up the bomber formations as effectively – at least that was the theory. Now they would find out.

The bomber attack now reached its critical phase, as Hurricanes had got into range and were firing their first shots. Exactly as anticipated, the effects were dramatic. Almost immediately one of the Dorniers was hit, losing control, forcing its occupants to escape by parachute – those still able to. Others were damaged but, just as crucially, the manoeuvre had forced the bombers to abandon their formation at just the moment they were finalising their bomb run. There was no time to reposition themselves for Kenley airfield, and they dropped their bombs on nearby alternative targets, or took them home again. Other Spitfires and Hurricanes were by now pouring into the area, attacking the escort 110s, quickly accounting for two of them – though one managed to escape by feigning being out of control, and then limping home when the coast was clear.

By this point, the force approaching Biggin Hill was preparing its final bomb run – sixty Heinkel 111s and their fighter shield of forty Bf 109s – mostly engaged with the one squadron of Hurricanes in a position to attack, and successfully keeping them away from the bombers. As RAF planes were close to the Germans, the order not to fire was given to the anti-aircraft batteries at Biggin Hill – which gave the Germans a clear approach, much to their astonishment. They all unloaded their full complement of bombs, carpeting the airfield with explosions. Both raids had now completed their work; now all they had to do was to get home, in the teeth of a fully mobilised Fighter Command. There were several damaged bombers that would offer straightforward targets, particularly as the fighter cover was beginning to run short of fuel. Now was the moment to really get stuck in. Park's controllers chose their moment to unleash the Spitfires and Hurricanes they had at their disposal in the skies above Margate and Canterbury, but increasing haze would make their job hard.

The haze wasn't enough to save the Bf 110s, though, which were now set upon by a number of Hurricanes from 56 Squadron. At least two were shot down after a furious exchange of fire. Fighter Command's job was now just to keep attacking what parts of the escaping stream of German aircraft they could find; various individual scraps flared up along their path; a struggling Dornier was finished off, and then a 110, though not before damaging its attacking Hurricane, whose pilot parachuted to safety. The haze made large-scale concerted attacks impossible; the best they could do was pounce on the aircraft that loomed out of the obscurity, and avoid the attentions of the 109s.

It was clear that the RAF was far from being the all but spent force the Luftwaffe pilots had been told it was. The Germans were escaping – but in desperate circumstances. Their planes were being damaged and shot down, and relief would come only on leaving British airspace, and the marauding defenders, behind. For many, of course, their saga wasn't over yet. Now the damage inflicted would start to tell as struggling engines began to shudder and fail, control panels fall apart, and still the sanctuary of their home bases in France were many, many miles away. For a proportion of them, all they were hoping for was any kind of landfall – a beach, a field, anything solid and flat on which to put down crippled aircraft. By mid-afternoon all the planes from this first wave of attacks that were still flyable had landed, one way or another. Time now to add up the cost of Kesselring's plans, to weigh up what had been achieved.

Of the nine Dorniers that had attacked Kenley at low level, four had been destroyed, two badly damaged, and the remaining three slightly damaged. None returned unscathed. Of their forty-strong crew, eight had been killed, five taken prisoner, three returned badly wounded, and seven had had to ditch into the Channel, now in a race against hypothermia waiting to be rescued. It had been a vital part of Kesselring's gamble that this low-flying raid would knock out Kenley without being hit back – and in this respect it had failed. They had been unlucky, of course, with bad weather fouling up their timings, and suffering the misfortune of being spotted earlier than they had hoped by naval vessels, but the real lesson to draw was just how robust Fighter Command defences had proved themselves. Not just in terms of the resoluteness of their fighter pilots but, just as crucially, in their capacity to marshal information over a very short timeframe and to be able to act decisively upon it. When you consider that both airfields were only forty miles or so from the coast – just a few minutes' flying time – it's undoubtedly impressive that fighters were still able to be alerted and mobilised in time to play a role in taking on the hit and run bombers. Not only had the RAF decimated the low-flying Dorniers, they had also destroyed nine other bombers, damaged ten, and destroyed twelve German fighters, damaging three more. Of course, this hadn't come without cost for the RAF. Fighter Command had lost seventeen fighters, with eight damaged, and a further eight destroyed on the ground. Four British pilots had been killed and seven wounded.

It had been Kesselring at his most cunning, mixing and matching types of raid, maximising the impact of the aircraft at his disposal – and if one part of the plan did seem to have come unstuck, well, not all was lost. The day of 18 August was still young – there were the raids he had planned for the afternoon yet to come, and perhaps the Luftwaffe would get its hammer blow after all.

The later raids differed from the first in one key respect: it would be the gull-winged Stukas, or Junkers 87s, that would be spearheading them, not the Dorniers and Heinkels used earlier in the morning. They belonged to Kesselring's colleague, Generalfeldmarschall Hugo Sperrle, a much less sophisticated military commander, but as keen as Kesselring to make his mark. He was in charge of Luftflotte 3, based to the south, across Normandy and Brittany, and like Kesselring to the north he had planned for 18 August to be one of the biggest raids yet attempted – involving a force of 4 'Gruppen' of Stukas, a total of 109 aircraft. These were the screaming dive-bombers that had proved so destructive in the opening salvoes of the war in Poland and France, though they had had their diving sirens removed before coming to their new bases. Their targets comprised smaller airfields and Fighter Command facilities, such as Gosport, Ford and Thorney Island, and a radar station at Poling near Littlehampton. As with the earlier raids, there would be full complements of Bf 109s and 110s offering escort protection, both close in, and further afield, sweeping ahead of them. By 2 p.m., they were aloft, in formation, and on their way to their targets, across eighty miles of Channel to the north.

Once again the early warning system proved its worth, with radar detection picking up the formations in good time to mobilise the local squadrons: Hurricanes and Spitfires from Tangmere, the airfield that Fighter Command thought would be the most likely target for the incoming raid, as well as from Westhampnett, Exeter and Middle Wallop. A total of sixty-eight fighters, half the number of fighters that were coming to meet them, and a quarter of the force of fighters and bombers combined, were all that could be scrambled in this area at that time.

The Stukas dropped their bombs in a completely different way from the other German bombers. Their purpose was accuracy – and terror – and they achieved both by being able to drop almost vertically out of the sky, releasing their bombs at the base of their awesome dives, before pulling away. From thirteen thousand feet, their descent, lasting around half a minute, would culminate at just under three thousand feet, at which point the bomb would be jettisoned, straight down the throat of the ground target. In the early days of the war this had proved an unbeatable tactic, especially against gun emplacements, armoured vehicles and buildings. It was planned they would achieve similar results over the south coast of England, knocking out key installations in the airfields and their allied radar stations.

That day, the first three formations of Stukas had attacked Ford and Poling, meeting only light resistance from ground fire. Very soon massive damage had been inflicted on both facilities, and many casualties. It was Poland and France all over again – only this time, there would be the RAF to deal with, a very different proposition from what they had encountered earlier in the war.

The makeshift building of flight dispersal at Duxford in the summer of 1940

Spitfires from No 501 Squadron had already drilled their way into the formations of escorting Bf 109s, destroying three in short order; now Hurricanes from No 43 and No 601 Squadrons would turn their attention on the Stukas about to launch their attacks on Thorney Island. This time, the Stukas would discover there was a price to pay for their lack of performance, though not before inflicting grievous damage on the third of the target airfields, which, like the others, was soon ablaze as the bombs struck home. Very quickly, first one, then a second, then a third Stuka was raked with fire and, spewing flames, oil and shards of fuselage, crashed into the ground. Though the rear gunner with only one machine gun was no match for the array of eight lining the front edge of the fighters attacking them, he could still pack a punch, especially at the short ranges at which these attacks took place. At least two of the attacking Hurricanes were thus beaten off, their pilots having to either crash-land or parachute to safety.

It was only a temporary reprieve. With the bombs gone, the Stukas faced their biggest ordeal, limping home, over a long, long stretch of English Channel, eighty miles of inhospitable water between them and the sanctuary of their bases. Their 109 escorts were still there, but none of the surviving dive-bomber crews were under any illusion about what faced them. Soon, a furious mêlée of Spitfires, Hurricanes, Stukas and 109s took shape over the south coast, down to as low as a hundred feet as the lumbering bombers took refuge in the only way they could, by flying slow and low, and praying their pursuers would overshoot. It certainly saved some of them, though with the air so packed with German planes the RAF were starting to make their shots count, as yet another Stuka cartwheeled into the water. Even those Stukas that remained in the air were taking hits – which almost invariably meant a dead rear gunner.

Luckily for the Stukas, the 109 escorts proved a much more formidable opponent, hitting four Spitfires of 602 Squadron in quick succession. Others were forced to bring their badly damaged planes back, any way they could. But the 109s didn't have it all their own way either; fighter ace Bob Doe, of No 234 Squadron accounted for one fleeing low over the water that had been caught attacking the barrage balloons that floated above Portsmouth.

In the end, the inferiority of the Stukas had helped level the fact that the RAF were so outnumbered. As the surviving Stukas began to cross the French coast, it was clear that they had been badly knocked up; several ditched along the coast, and even those that made it back to their airfields had wounded pilots and dead rear gunners. Many had reached home in ways little short of miraculous. Of the twenty-eight Stukas from Gruppe 1, ten had been shot down, one was damaged beyond repair, and four damaged more lightly. Seventeen men, including the formation commander, had been killed out of a force of fifty-six.

There was little consolation in the fact that the other three formations of Stukas had got off much more lightly, having suffered only minimal losses (they hadn't flown straight into the teeth of two entire Fighter Command squadrons). Although the others had suffered more acceptable levels of loss, it was impossible to avoid the conclusion that whatever damage they had inflicted on the airfields had been more than offset by the damage they themselves had suffered, something even the Luftwaffe couldn't afford to ignore. It was time to withdraw the Stuka from its front line duties against the British mainland and, indeed, it would play little further role in the Battle of Britain. It was an ominous first for the German armed forces – the enforced withdrawal of one of its most potent weapons, unable to make it on the battlefield.

It would be a day of varying tactics; after the low-flying Dorniers and the dive-bombing Stukas, the attacks that followed would revert to more familiar means – high-flying bombers. The Luftwaffe weren't finished yet. It was late afternoon, teatime, when once again the radar posts lit up – large formations gathering over the Pas de Calais. Their targets this time were the two big important airfields that hadn't been hit during the morning, Hornchurch and North Weald. Heading their way, a force of over a hundred Heinkels and Dorniers, with an escort cover of close on a hundred and fifty assorted Messerschmitts. Then 11 Group sprang into action, scrambling squadrons in waves; the first charged with hitting the incoming Germans as they crossed the coast, splitting the formations up, and leaving them for their colleagues behind them. Once again, a familiar pattern would take shape.

Hurricanes made contact with the swollen German formations, confirming what the radar operators had been calculating – this was big. One section would try to draw off the fighters, opening a path straight to the bombers for the others. Individual dogfights soon erupted, each a story of altitude, advantage won and lost, shots traded, and evasion achieved – or not. For the Hurricanes that broke through to the main formations, the challenge was to get close and fire decisive bursts at the vulnerable points – the bombers' cockpits and engines – without falling victim to their defensive fire. With the Battle of Britain now around six weeks old, it had almost become routine. For the damaged bombers, their choice was stark: bale out, crash-land (if the crew were wounded) or turn around and make for home.

By now the RAF fighters were low on fuel and ammunition. It was abundantly clear, as the surviving German formations carried on their way, that North Weald was their target. The next wave of intercepting squadrons was hastily scrambled. By now the Dorniers heading for Hornchurch were also being engaged by Hurricanes in their turn – though luckily for them, their defensive shield of Messerschmitt 109s was to prove robust enough to rebuff the Hurricanes. Two Polish pilots, once again proving what an extraordinary contribution the Poles would make to the air campaign, had each shot down a 109.

The cut and thrust of air combat carried on unabated; three Hurricanes were quickly shot down, each of their pilots parachuting to safety. But, for all their efforts, the RAF had succeeded in destroying only one Dornier, so it was a virtually intact formation that was now drawing closer and closer to its target, only to see the ground below them get shrouded in cloud at just the worst possible moment for the bomb-aimers. With Hitler's ban on bombing London and other civilian targets still in place, they had to turn back, still laden with bombs. For the fighters rapidly gaining on them as well as for some ground observers, it proved impossible to resist the alternative conclusion that the Germans were high-tailing it away because they were intimidated by the RAF's show of strength. Certainly that was how it was trumpeted the following day in the papers. But their refusal to endanger civilian lives didn't earn the Dorniers any respite from attack – quite the reverse. Thinking the bombers were fleeing, the Hurricanes and Spitfires pounced all the more energetically.

The 109s had by now returned to head the Hurricanes off, shooting down two almost immediately. More Hurricanes arrived, and they too wove their way through the mêlée, to get shots in at the bombers before finding themselves under attack from Luftwaffe fighters. Many of those involved would later recount what would become an almost classic combination of experiences. First a sky full of aircraft and tracer rounds, many avoiding collisions, as often as not with their own descent, by feet, even inches, only then to emerge into a sky completely bereft of any planes whatsoever. These furious engagements carried on relentlessly, each side trying to get some kind of purchase on the other.

Both sides suffered more damage on this day than on any other. The Luftwaffe destroyed thirty-four of Fighter Command's aircraft in combat and damaged thirty-nine, as well as destroying twenty-nine and damaging twenty-three on the ground. But the Luftwaffe lost sixty-nine aircraft in all, with thirty-one damaged. They had achieved some success against Fighter Command, but once again the price was too high, and once again the achievement fell far short of what was necessary.

Even for the Luftwaffe commanders, it was becoming only too apparent that they were not succeeding. They were beginning to see through their own side's propaganda. Their daily reports may have been called 'Erfolgsmeldung', literally a success report, but their losses were clearly mounting up. So the Luftwaffe switched to night raids, and it was on one of these early night raids that a bomb was dropped on London by mistake, the first civilian attack. In reply, the British bombed Berlin, and within a few days, the Luftwaffe were pursuing a new campaign of targeting cities and industrial sites, hoping to break the morale of the British public. It wasn't entirely clear at this stage whether a civilian bombing campaign would break morale or actually make it stronger. Churchill had already said that he didn't think it would work, and the experience of Guernica had suggested the same. For the Luftwaffe, though, they had to try new tactics.

This change of direction has often been described as decisive, the turning point in the Battle of Britain. It's a highly debatable issue but, given the lack of progress to date, it's unlikely that the Luftwaffe would have been in a position to launch an invasion by the middle of September even if they'd stuck to the strategy of 'Eagle Day'. Any invasion would need to be launched by 21 September, as after that date the changing tides would make the conditions unfavourable until the following year. However, the change of strategy by the Germans gave the RAF invaluable breathing space. In desperation, many squadrons had been forced off damaged airfields on to smaller airfields, and while Spitfires and Hurricanes could comfortably take off from grass runways, maintenance facilities were being increasingly stretched.

It was vital for 11 Group in the south-east to remain at the centre of the British war effort; any retreat would indicate the Germans making real headway; if 12 Group in the Midlands and North became the focus, it would effectively cede the Germans air superiority over their first part of Britain. Now, 11 Group's defences could be repaired, and the squadrons regrouped as they were spared the regular batterings by Luftwaffe bombers, giving the RAF a crucial chance to prepare for the next big assault. This came on 15 September. Not all pilots were in a fit state by now; the toll had been heavy, and many pilots like Nigel Rose were recovering from injuries:

> *'Personally, I wasn't in it, because I'd had this wound about four days before 15 September and was sitting on the ground, I think, watching what was going on.'*
>
> Nigel Rose

'Personally, I wasn't in it, because I'd had this wound about four days before 15 September and was sitting on the ground, I think, watching what was going on. I think I was helping the intelligence officer take in the reports from chaps coming back from their scraps, and so on.'

Bob Doe was also out of action on 15 September, like many pilots sent away from the front line of 11 Group with his Squadron to regroup.

'I was sunbathing in Cornwall. Not literally, in fact I was flying round a convoy off the end of Land's End. But what had happened was that my squadron, the Spitfire squadron I

An RAF officer examines the wreckage of a downed Dornier Do 17 'flying pencil'

entered the battle with, inside a month we were down to three pilots. So we were sent back down to Cornwall to acquire new pilots and retrain them. And I was only allowed to stay there about a week, but then I was posted back to a Hurricane squadron next door to Middle Wallop. But it's always been my habit to go to sleep when you're under any stress and so I was grabbing all the time I could. So I missed out on 15 September completely.'

Iain Hutchinson was also not due to fly on that day, but the lack of an aeroplane wasn't going to stop him.

'The 15th of September was a special day, in a way, because my aircraft was non-operational, and when the scramble was announced, I had no aircraft from my squadron available. So I ran to No 41 Squadron dispersal and managed to get into one of their aircraft, and took off, and flew as a pair, with one of their sergeant pilots. We were flying as a pair, and he was watching over on his side and I was watching over my side, and the next time I looked around, he'd gone and there was a Bf 109 in his place. I think the 109 actually shot him down, and he didn't go for me, but then I peeled off, and I can't remember what went on after that, but then I got hacked down, later on and lost his aircraft, the squadron aircraft for them, as well.'

This big day would show decisively how even the new Luftwaffe strategy had also failed for the Germans. It was this day that for the British, at least, represented the most significant turning point of the campaign, the biggest of all the big days, earning it the title 'Battle of Britain Day' ever since. As Nigel Rose says, 'The 15th of September is an everlasting day, and when we have our reunion at Bentley Priory now, it's always on the nearest Saturday to the 15th of September. Because it was a very big day, enormous raids came in on that day, and so enormous numbers of Germans were shot down and big claims were made by us.' The Germans tend not to confer on it any special status, certainly not as the day on which it was obvious that the Luftwaffe had been bested. For them it was just another day, but there is no disputing it: 15 September was in so many ways decisive. It deserves its status, and not just as a sop to Battle of Britain nostalgia. Unlike the previous 'big days', the arena for 15 September would be the skies over London. It would also be the day that would test that major new RAF strategy, touched on in Chapter 3, the 'Big Wing'.

> *'When the scramble was announced, I had no aircraft from my squadron available. So I ran to No 41 Squadron dispersal and managed to get into one of their aircraft.'*
>
> Iain Hutchinson

In the early days of the Battle of Britain, simply getting any planes into the right bit of sky at the right time had been challenge enough. Over those first few days, and weeks, though Fighter Command had been close to breaking point, Dowding's system had proved – just – capable of doing the job it had been designed for. It was a system that suited the charismatic commander of 11 Group, Keith Park, in particular.

The switch to bomber raids by the Luftwaffe over civilian and industrial targets had made 12 Group far more prominent in the battle as many of the targets were now in their range. The Luftwaffe were staggered to find as they ventured deeper into Britain that there were even more Spitfires and Hurricanes waiting to attack them. They'd been given the firm impression, after all, that the RAF had virtually been wiped out. So now the strategies of the commander of 12 Group, Trafford Leigh-Mallory, would get their chance. They were most enthusiastically endorsed by his star pilot, Douglas Bader. The Big Wing was a strategy that called for more than simply bringing together a series of small-scale ambushes. They wanted to deliver their own knock-out blow, involving assembling as many as half a dozen squadrons in the air over their respective bases and tackling the Germans in force, in a series of big, set-piece encounters. Instead of being picked off by Spitfires in handfuls, the Germans would be devastated by formations of scores of fighters. It made sense for 12 Group because, with their greater distance from the south-east front line, they (theoretically) would have the time to perform this complicated series of manoeuvres by which streams of fighters would take off, link up, and join forces to create the right size of attacking force. With Churchill's backing, 15 September would come to be the biggest test for the Big Wing.

For Billy Drake, the Big Wing was a waste of time on 15 September.

'We remembered when the Battle of Britain started. We remembered when the big days were going on when a lot was happening, but at the time we couldn't pinpoint the fact that that was "the" day that indicated that we were definitely in the ascendancy, that we were winning. It was all gradual and a definite crescendo of activity to indicate to us as – as pilots – that Fighter Command was doing their stuff and that our tactics and strategy were correct. For example, we immediately in 11 Group realised that these large formations that Douglas was starting up were a waste of time because they never appeared when they were wanted and we realised that there was some bad thinking that went on at that time.'

That day, 15 September, would be marked by screaming headlines on both sides, each proclaiming hundreds of victories scored over the other; 185 German planes destroyed, bugled the British headlines. In truth it was considerably less, fifty-six according to the most reliable of modern surveys. This was a large and significant number, though less than the figures reached on 15 and 18 August. The Luftwaffe had launched a staggering 1,261 sorties that day; 437 by bombers, 769 by fighters, the rest by twin-engined fighters and reconnaissance planes. Of those, just over 1,000 were flown in daylight. Extraordinarily, the Germans were lucky to lose only the 18 per cent of the bombers that they did. With unforecast headwinds of over 90 mph, one formation of Dorniers had reached London an hour late, too late for the escorts who had long since left to refuel. Worse for them, they flew right into the clutches of

> 'In 11 Group we realised that these large formations that Douglas was starting up were a waste of time because they never appeared when they were wanted.'
>
> Billy Drake

a staggering, and virtually unprecedented, formation of eleven squadrons of Fighter Command planes. It took every ounce of Luftwaffe skill and determination to get away with losses of 'only' one in five.

The heart of the day had taken the form of two daylight raids on London. The normal pattern was for there to be just one. But, in the spirit of endless tactical variation and experiment, today they had gambled on two. It had witnessed one of the battle's most extraordinary encounters – a Dornier rammed by a Hurricane, flown by one Sergeant Ray Holmes, who lost his own tailplane in the collision but miraculously survived, and indeed survived the war. Central London was treated to the terrifying sight, famously photographed, of the decapitated Dornier careering straight into Victoria Station.

The day also included further attacks on airfields. Luftwaffe pilot Ernie Wedding was involved in one such attack.

'We were briefed in the morning to fly sorties against airfields and each squadron was given a specific airfield. I was in what they called Luftflotte 2. We're flying into the sector of 11 Group on the airfields Manson, Brighton, West Malling, and other airfields near Folkestone and so on – Biggin Hill – they were all within Luftflotte 2 as targets. And one of them was North Weald and as it so happened I had to fly to North Weald. It was the first time that I

The distinctive Heinkel 111K, which had been one of the Luftwaffe's most successful planes during the Spanish Civil War

attacked the airfield. Before that I had factories, railway crossings and Channel duty, shipping. And then I was allowed to go on a low-level raid right because the airfield raids were low-level. You came in high and you dropped and you had mostly the heaviest bomb you were carrying for that would be fifty kilograms, hundred-pounders, and you had a lot of machine gun ammunition, more than usual. Normally on a Heinkel 111 you had 750 rounds per gun, but on that day you had 1500 rounds per gun. So you could do damage with the machine guns. As we got to North Weald we turned the runway over. The runway was out of use. All right, that wouldn't have made any difference to the fighters, they could take off on grass, but heavier aircraft couldn't use the runway for quite some time.'

Peter Brothers was also on the front line on the day.

'The 15th of September was a rather busy day. According to my log book, I shot down a Junkers 88 which caught fire and also shot down a Dornier 17. The Dornier 17 became a nuisance, because he put a lot of bullet holes into my aircraft, and severed one of the aileron cables. And I never thought I'd have the guts to bale out of an aircraft, it's a long way down. But I was half-way out before I could stop myself and realised I still had a bit of control over the aircraft, and so I sat back down in the cockpit

> *'Normally on a Heinkel 111 you had 750 rounds per gun, but on that day you had 1500 rounds per gun. So you could do damage with the machine guns. As we got to North Weald we turned the runway over.'*
>
> Ernie Wedding

Peter Brothers' logbook from 15 September 1940. He has drawn the swastikas reversed to show that the German planes were destroyed

again and I managed to successfully get it back to Biggin Hill. I'd come from Martlesham but I landed at Biggin Hill because I knew it, and it was the nearest airfield, and there they mended it for me.

'The pilot of the Junkers 88 came to see me after the war, in July 1981. And he said, "You shot my engine." And I said, "Yes, it was burning rather nicely, wasn't it?" And he said, "And you killed my gunner and my navigator, and I jumped out", and his daughter who was with him said, "Very wise, Papa." And he was great fun. And we had a lot of drink and chat together. But it was a busy day, two aircraft that day. And it was the day that they claimed – or the press claimed – 185 enemy aircraft destroyed, which I think turned out to be about 56 or something but, of course, there was a lot of confusion and so on.'

On the larger scale, it was a vindication of RAF tactics, old and new. The command and control structure had once again proved resoundingly successful. Hardly a single RAF sortie had flown without encountering Luftwaffe formations, the great majority being pointed the way by their controllers. It was the most powerful vindication imaginable of Dowding's system. Out of fifty-one squadrons of Hurricanes and Spitfires scrambled, all but one successfully engaged the Luftwaffe. These were previously unheard-of rates of detection. And Bader and 12 Group had been given the perfect opportunity to test out the Big Wing, five squadrons converging on an unescorted formation of bombers; they even had to queue up, and wait for the last of the 11 Group fighters to finish their attack. Then it was their turn: an endless cavalcade of attacking fighters. Later in the day, they would get a second chance to put the idea through its paces, though this time, a curtain of escorting Luftwaffe fighters broke them up, dissipating the effect.

In retrospect, it is clear that actually the Big Wing critics had been right; a law of diminishing returns was coming into effect. Too many aircraft, too little airspace. The inevitable result, confusion and muddle. And fewer Luftwaffe aircraft destroyed than would most likely have been the case had they attacked in the way Park had perfected, one squadron

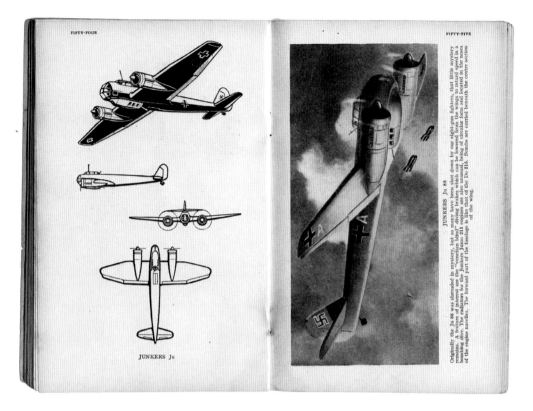

Diagrams published to help amateur observers spot a Junkers 88

at a time. Not all the attacks on 15 September came from Big Wings, though. George Unwin made a lone attack on two German planes.

'I think I did two or three trips that day. September was a hell of a month anyway, of course – we were in the "Big Wing" then. It started operating on the 7th of September and from then on life was very easy. The 15th of September was a very busy day, I'll always remember that. On the second trip we did, there was a lot of cloud around on that particular day and I got lost and separated from the rest of them like most of us did. The Germans flew in twos, and I was lucky enough towards the end of the patrol to see a couple of these chaps heading rapidly for home, and they never saw me and I was right behind them, and so I knew that, his number two being with him, there could be no other German around so they were both sitting ducks. I just went up behind them and shot the first one down, the leader, and the other one, for some unknown reason, never took any evasive action at all, he must have been very young, inexperienced and so I shot him down and they both went into the Channel just off Deal.'

Allan Wright was also flying solo on 15 September, but for different reasons.

'That just happened to be the first time that I'd done what they called a "Jim Crowe", where a Spitfire was sent up from the south coast and his job was to have an actual eye report on the enemy who was coming. It wasn't your job to attack them, it was to report on them. You would be one of the first people to see the enemy forming up in battle, no question.

A German pilot with head wounds being brought ashore after being picked up in the Channel

You would be the first to actually see them, they'd be seen on radar but that's not the same thing. I happened to be the first one given that job. I was attacked by the two 109s who were leading the formation so I wasn't able to stay there any longer to give any further information. What happened after that, I don't know. It was going to be in rotation, anyway, so I wouldn't be asked to do it again. It was very unpopular, because you always want to fight with your mates, you wouldn't want to have to do this solo job.'

There is one respect in which the Big Wing tactic did triumph: the blow it struck on the already faltering German morale. They had got used to seeing Spitfires and Hurricanes when all their intelligence briefings had reassured them the RAF was a spent force. So far, though, they had only been in small groups, never in a formation almost as large as their own. This was the aspect that most struck home on 15 September for the Germans. Not only that, but it was seen twice in one day. It hadn't been a fluke, or some massive last-ditch blowout either. This was an unmistakable sign of just what depth of numbers the RAF still had, and with what extraordinary confidence they were prepared to mobilise those numbers.

The significance of 'Battle of Britain Day' goes well beyond tallies and conflicting statistics. The day earns its blue ribbon status because this was the moment Hitler realised that the RAF were never going to be defeated, at least not in the time-frame necessary for any kind of autumn invasion, if that was his ambition – and if it wasn't, the insurmountable challenge that the RAF represented was none the less all too clear. It had been a slap in the face to a German High Command still gloating on the basis of the reports their intelligence services were eagerly feeding it. If they had started the Battle of Britain grossly underestimating RAF strength, then, as the conflict continued, that gap between the real figure and the one doing the rounds in Berlin corridors of power grew wider and wider. The RAF was supposed to be inches from complete collapse; instead, it had managed to send wave after wave of fighters into the air, meeting all the major raids head on. The whole point of the double raid on London had been to divide and conquer, to ensure that at least one of the raids would find the RAF licking its wounds on the ground. By 15 September, it was only too apparent that this was far from what had actually happened. Not only was the RAF very clearly not on its last legs, as they had been repeatedly led to believe, but it was stronger (even if numerically in terms of planes, rather than in terms of experienced pilots) than it had been when the conflict had started over two months ago, in early July.

'I never thought I'd have the guts to bale out of an aircraft, it's a long way down. But I was half-way out before I could stop myself and realised I still had a bit of control over the aircraft, and so I sat back down in the cockpit again and I managed to get it back to Biggin Hill.'

Peter Brothers

This was the day that marked the end of the big daylight raids, and pretty much quashed, for the time being at least, the threat of invasion. Whatever Goering might have now thought, the decision was taken out of his hands; the invasion wasn't going to happen any time soon – 17 September is generally regarded as the moment that the invasion plan fell from view. Now all the effort devoted to bombing was utterly divorced from any plan to invade; 12 October saw it officially 'postponed'. The invasion barges and other accoutrements of naval equipment were pulled away from the French Channel ports. By the beginning of December, even Hitler now conceded that the Luftwaffe had been unable to defeat the RAF.

The Battle of Britain was as good as over. The raids continued, but over the next few weeks they petered out. The Luftwaffe found itself enduring ever greater losses of bombers, many of them left unprotected as the Bf 109 fighters could only get as far as London to protect them, having enough fuel for just twenty minutes' flying over Britain. They were forced to switch to night raids, but the RAF was in any case developing increasingly effective night fighter equipment with Airborne Intercept ('AI') radar fitted on to planes for the first time. With Operation Sealion, the invasion plan, postponed, Hitler's thoughts turned to Russia.

The pilots of Fighter Command had done their job and prevented the Luftwaffe from gaining air supremacy over Britain. For the first time in Europe, Nazi power had been checked.

Spitfire School Aerobatic Airshow

Twenty-two year old private pilot Dave Mallon has now reached the final part of his nine-hour advanced Spitfire training course. Following in the footsteps of the Fighter Boys who flew Spitfires and Hurricanes in the summer of 1940, he has learnt the basics of Spitfire flying and is now ready to go onto aerobatic training.

Dave is once again being instructed by Peter Kynsey, pilot in charge of the Fighter Collection at Duxford, who has already taken him through formation flying. Back in the briefing room, Peter explains the principles of aerobatics.

'Aerobatic flying is quite important in combat. You are going to be flying the aeroplane quite close to its limits, going at high speed and low speed, flying at very unusual altitudes, upside down one moment, right way up the next.'

This part of the training isn't just for show. For combat flying, aerobatic skills were vital, allowing pilots to be able to intercept the enemy effectively, to get out of danger quickly, and most importantly to take the enemy by surprise in an ambush situation. As Brendan O'Brien had warned the pilots during their Tiger Moth training, 'It's the one you don't see that you gets you.' Time and again in 1940, it had been the surprise attacks that had been the most successful for both sides.

Peter Kynsey is keen to make sure that Dave has the chance to experience a variety of aerobatic moves.

'Aerobatic flying gets you used to that kind of thing, and you have to be thinking very fast, so it's a good experience for getting you used to the kind of manoeuvring you'd be doing in combat.'

So once again, on the runway at Duxford, the roar of the Merlin engine is heard as Dave and Peter get back into the dual-seater Spitfire.

They take off, and a few minutes later, Dave is performing some basic aerobatic manoeuvres under Peter's instruction. He's doing well, setting the controls for a simply roll. 'I've got a reference point,' he tells Peter, remembering what he was told in the briefing room.

The roll is a success. 'Very good,' says an impressed instructor. 'No problem at all'.

Next, Dave is to perform a more complicated roll. This time, Dave's inexperience shows through, and while certainly not disastrous, by Dave's own admission, the roll's not perfect. Peter is sympathetic though.

'It's more difficult when there's a bad horizon, isn't it. Quite tricky. Let's try another one, and we'll just be a bit more gentle on the pitch.'

Dave, eager as ever, gets ready to have another go at the manoeuvre. 'Ok, so we'll accelerate to 250 knots,' he explains as he gets into position. Peter offers one final bit of advice.

'If we're over-exerting, and you feel yourself being light in the seat, put on a tiny bit of back pressure.'

This time, Dave does a full roll, and it works. Peter encourages him through the process, 'Put a bit of back pressure on', and Dave looks satisfied that he's mastered another move. Once again, Peter is pleased with his pupil. 'There we are,' he says as the roll comes to an end. 'We didn't stop the engine, so that's pretty good.' Many veterans recall engines cutting out during aerobatic manoeuvres during the Battle of Britain which could lead to a dramatic reduction in speed, dangerous when the enemy was on your tail.

Dave has reached the last day of his training. Having mastered the Spitfire's controls, experienced formation flying, and learnt some basic aerobatic manoeuvres, it's time to show off what he's learnt. So in the last hour of his course, Dave and Peter put on an aerobatic display over Duxford Aerodrome, the place where so many Battle of Britain pilots were based during 1940. And who better to judge his efforts than Air Commodore Peter Brothers, one of the most successful pilots during the battle. As well as the distinguished veteran, Dave's other instructors Carolyn Grace and Brendan O'Brien are also there to watch.

Peter, Carolyn and Brendan concentrate fully on events overhead as Dave and Peter Kynsey perform their first roll. 'Oh yes, very nice' says Peter Brothers approvingly, no doubt the memories of his own Spitfire flying experiences flooding back.

Brendan, who took Dave, along with three other pilots, through his paces in a Tiger Moth, is keen to find out how representative this is of the aerobatics the Fighter Boys learnt.

'Is that a useful combat manoeuvre, or is it just fun?' he asks Peter. 'Could be useful, oh yes,' the veteran replies, although he's far too transfixed on the display above to really answer the question.

Up in the Spitfire, Dave is having the time of his life, and the aerobatics are going well. 'Very good,' congratulates Peter after another successful roll. 'How was that for you?' An exhilarated Dave answers simply 'Magical. Absolutely magical.'

Dave Mallon and Peter Kynney
during their aerobatic display
for Battle of Britain veteran
Peter Brothers

By now, Dave is keen to stretch himself to the limits of his training. 'Shall we do a loop now?' he asks Peter. Also enthused, Peter is happy to comply, 'OK, loop it is'.

Dave is meticulous before performing the loop to check all his controls carefully, and seeks reassurance from Peter. His careful preparation pays off, and the loop impresses Peter Brothers on the ground.

Brendan is also entranced by the display. 'Wonderful sound, isn't it' he says. 'Oh yes, a lovely noise' replies Peter. Carolyn is also delighted to see her Spitfire taking to the skies, 'Rather special, isn't it?'

As the display draws to a close, Brendan is still curious about Peter's own flying experiences. 'Did you do victory rolls when you came back to your home base?' he asks. 'Oh yes, we did initially,' comes the reply.

The display over, Dave Mallon lands the Spitfire back on the runway at Duxford for the last time. He's had an incredible experience over the past few weeks, a chance to fly a Spitfire, a chance that few others will share. 'Well Pete, that was amazing,' he says to his instructor, more than satisfied. 'Thank you very much.'

After Dave has opened the cockpit hood, Battle of Britain veteran Peter Brothers is the first to come over to the Spitfire to congratulate the young pilot on his display. Carolyn introduces the two pilots. 'Elegant little show,' says the veteran, in his typically understated way. 'You enjoyed it?' he asks Dave, although the question is hardly necessary. Dave's facial expressions are betraying his emotions all too clearly, 'Oh yes, like nothing else. Unbelievable, wonderful.'

So, Dave completes his Spitfire flying course. He's

had a total of twelve hours flying in a Spitfire, more than some of 'the Few' in 1940. It's Brendan who asks the question which everyone watching has on their mind. 'How do you think you'd have survived if it was for real?'

Dave considers the question carefully for a moment. 'I honestly think I'd fly the aircraft. It wouldn't be a problem,' he says, a note of assurance in his voice. 'I'd give it my very best shot. As long as none of those 109s spotted me!'

Over lunch, Dave has the opportunity to ask Peter Brothers in detail about his combat experiences. Having flown in a Spitfire himself, he has a virtually unique perspective compared to any other modern day pilot, and is fascinated by Peter's recollections of the Battle of Britain.

After lunch, there's one last treat in store. More than sixty years after he flew with No 32 and No 257 Squadrons in this epic battle, Air Commodore Peter Brothers climbs into the Spitfire himself once more. With Carolyn Grace at the controls, Peter can once again experience the sensation of flying in this most ladylike of planes.

'You're flying my aeroplane. I'm greatly honoured, sir' Carolyn tells him proudly.

'It feels just like it used to feel' replies Peter. He may once have flown Spitfires during Britain's darkest hour, facing enemy fire on a regular basis, but this time the flight is purely for pleasure. As the Spitfire performs a gentle roll, Peter has a good look around the Spitfire cockpit, and there is no doubt of the unqualified pleasure this noble veteran can finally have, flying proudly in a Supermarine Spitfire.

Dave Mallon under instruction
from Peter Kynney during his
advanced training course

CHAPTER FIVE

THE TRIUMPH OF THE FEW

'We won because we were fighting on home soil and that is quite an advantage. And we had no intention of letting them come in. We had something to fight for. They probably didn't have anything to fight for. But we did. We were fighting for our homes.'

Bob Doe

The aerial conflict that shattered English skies in the summer of 1940 was almost instantly canonised. An Air Ministry booklet published the very next year gave it, formally, the name it has kept ever since: 'The Battle of Britain', boosting morale and helping to establish the legend of the victory of the few against the many. Never mind that the battle was, and in fact still is, as maddeningly fluid in terms of its chronology as it is ambivalent in its outcome. Its grip on the historical imagination, with such potent and iconic elements, grew stronger in the years after the war, and was expressed cinematically in the 1969 movie, the eponymous *Battle of Britain*. With its star-studded cast of British stalwarts, headed by Laurence Olivier as Hugh Dowding and Trevor Howard as Keith Park, it paid brave lip-service to some of the less attractive aspects of the battle: the fact that many pilots died, and died horribly; and that Fighter Command leadership was riven by conflict. Yet it couldn't help but be a praise song to the noble RAF, creating a picture of an utterly exhilarating triumph against all the (rather inflated) odds.

13th September, 1940

THE WAR

No. **47**

3D WEEKLY

Incorporating WAR PICTORIAL

SPITFIRES SAVE PARACHUTING PILOT FROM THE "BLIGHTERS"

When an R.A.F. sergeant pilot landed by parachute from his blazing Hurricane during an air battle over Kent on September 2 he told how he had been machine-gunned by Nazi planes on the way down: "The dirty blighters had a crack at me as I jumped out." Two Spitfire pilots came to his rescue, circling round him to keep the Germans away during his 20,000-foot drop. His watch had been shot from his wrist. This was the third case in a few days of German aircraft machine-gunning R.A.F. men who baled out.

Previous page: cover of an issue of *The War Weekly* – the success of Spitfires was valuable for British war propaganda

In a cynical, or perhaps simply analytical, age, revisionism makes its way into even the most hallowed of icons, which must not be allowed to stand unexamined. In the years that followed, necessary attempts were made to cool the Battle of Britain jingoism a little, to remind its excitable advocates that in fact the numbers tally was pretty close, that it had been a bitter battle of attrition and that, in the end, all that happened was a German withdrawal and redeployment to the East, rather than some kind of Trafalgar-style climax.

So how close, in the end, was the outcome? Was it a battle that Britain won or one that the Germans lost? And just how decisive was the Battle of Britain? Did it really change the course of the war? For German veteran Hans-Ekkehard Bob, it's not even clear that Britain did enjoy victory as such.

> *'I do not consider that Germany lost the Battle of Britain. I think that the end result was neutral. Nobody won.'*
>
> Hans-Ekkehard Bob

'I do not consider that Germany lost the Battle of Britain. I think that the end result was neutral. Nobody won. We didn't manage there in Great Britain to maintain our air superiority. In 1940 we had certainly had air superiority at one stage, only it wasn't noticed. And the British Air Force admits that there were days when they didn't have a single fighter aircraft that was capable of flying a mission, but Germany or the German side hadn't realised this or noticed it. That is why, in my opinion, giving every due recognition to both sides – to the bravery on both sides and to the strategic possibilities which existed – one could not speak of a victory, unless you want to say that because the Germans did not carry out a landing in England, or did not want to carry one out – which is something that one could argue about, *why* this landing was not carried out (some people say that Hitler had a soft spot for England, that he was an admirer of England and that he didn't want to humiliate the English and so on – there are several different variants as to why it didn't happen), but taking everything into account, it is my opinion that in that battle there were neither victors nor vanquished. Only losers – we all lost. England lost and Germany lost. England lost its vast dominions, its world supremacy, and Germany lost – but what? Its dignity, its national identity. Looking at it from the point of view of the time, both lost, neither won.'

While Bob makes a valuable point about the long-term outcomes for both sides, this would be too modest an assessment for the events of 1940. However close the outcome, there was a clear outcome. Whatever the invasion strategy might have been, the Luftwaffe were at least out to achieve aerial supremacy over Britain, and in this they failed. For the first time since the outbreak of the war, the tide of Nazi conquests had been held at bay; Britain had not fallen in the way that Norway, Denmark, Holland, Belgium, Luxembourg and France had. Britain had been left in June 1940 to fight on alone, and by October had proved it was still there for the fight. The Nazis couldn't, after all, do as they pleased. The Wehrmacht never would march through London as it had through Paris, Warsaw and Amsterdam. So, for British veteran Bob Doe, it was a result that truly counts as one of history's decisive moments.

'I think to realise why the Battle of Britain was important, you've got to see what the Germans planned to do when they got here, as they were going to. Had we not won the Battle of Britain they would undoubtedly have crossed the Channel and invaded us. And we had no defences at all. We'd left all of our armoury and guns in France when we came out at Dunkirk. We had no defence, we had lots of men with rifles and that's all we had. And that would be useless against tanks, wouldn't it? So they would have invaded us. The fact they didn't invade us was because they couldn't cross the Channel until they had complete air supremacy over the Channel. Which they never achieved.'

There was of course still a long struggle ahead, but the boys of Fighter Command had at least ensured that the struggle could continue. Something of extraordinary historical significance really did take place, and for the Germans it was a disturbing revelation, as Christopher Foxley-Norris would hear.

'After the war, von Rundstedt was Commander-in-Chief of the German Army, and I knew him quite well. He was being interviewed, and they had asked what he thought was the turning point of the war, was it Stalingrad or Kiev, or something like that. Oh no, he said it was the Battle of Britain. And they said, "Well, that's rather an odd statement to come from an Army officer." He said, "Ah, that was the first time we realised we could be beaten, and we were beaten, and we didn't like it."'

The Battle of Britain is often presented as a close-run thing, as a virtually hopeless RAF fighting against almost impossible odds. It may well have felt like that at the time, but with hindsight we can see that the Luftwaffe never in fact had a serious chance of achieving aerial supremacy. The first indication of this comes from the cold statistics, the 'scores' of the two sides. The aerial assault on Britain had cost the Luftwaffe 1887 aircraft; resisting that assault had cost Fighter Command 1023. The overwhelming majority of German losses had been at the hands of Fighter Command, representing an overall kill-rate of 1.8:1. The margin of victory was not in fact narrow; the Luftwaffe had never come close to making an invasion of Britain, if that was what was intended, a realistic prospect. Fighter Command's victory had been decisive. Not only had the RAF survived the Battle of Britain, they had even ended it in a stronger position, with more pilots available; on 6 July, four days before the battle began, Fighter Command's operational strength had been 1259 pilots; by 2 November that figure was 1794 pilots, an astonishing increase of 40 per cent. Of course, many of the new pilots were ill trained and would have been vulnerable in the extreme had they gone into combat, but that was at least as much of a problem for the Luftwaffe. The narrow lead the RAF had in terms of pilots at the start had, by the end, become a chasm. The Luftwaffe had 1126 pilots available in July, but by September this had fallen to 990. Not only does this show the impact of

> *'Had we not won the Battle of Britain they would undoubtedly have crossed the Channel and invaded us. And we had no defences at all. We'd left all of our armoury and guns in France when we came out at Dunkirk.'*
>
> Bob Doe

Hugh Dowding and Douglas Bader, centre, at a Battle of Britain reunion in 1945

pilots shot down, being taken prisoner, or falling into the Channel on their way home as their planes ran out of fuel, it also reflects the Luftwaffe's failure to keep up pilot replacement rates. A further factor is that many of the German losses came from multi-crewed bombers. In all, the Luftwaffe lost 2698 pilots, the RAF just 544.

As these figures indicate, the RAF was not actually as close to breaking point as it appeared. More importantly, the Luftwaffe not only couldn't match the RAF's strength, but it was ever further away from winning supremacy. Taking a few more hits, and keeping a few more pilots, wouldn't have been enough; the Germans would have needed to destroy Fighter Command to the point where they couldn't fight back, so that Messerschmitts could fly over Britain unhindered by Spitfires and Hurricanes. The Luftwaffe itself needed to suffer a low hit rate so it would be strong enough to support Operation Sealion, the actual invasion. This was more of a dream scenario by October than it had been in June. Despite all the attacks on airfields, Fighter Command had continued to fight back. The Luftwaffe's efforts had been concentrated most heavily over the south-east of England, where 11 Group had borne the considerable brunt of the offensive. Even here, though, air supremacy remained a distant target for Goering's men. That had been the big shock of 15 September: when 11 Group had taken squadrons off the front line to rest and regroup, they'd been able to replace them with squadrons from 10, 12 and 13 Groups; German pilots discovered to their horror that the RAF didn't even have all their fighting strength in 11 Group.

So, bald statistics aside, what was it that was counting against the Luftwaffe from the outset? What happened to all that early German bluster that had Goering promising Hitler the prize of British capitulation in weeks? The answer is a fatal disparity between the rhetoric and the reality. The German high command suffered time and again from delusions about how strong they were, and how weak they believed the enemy to be. Hitler had proved himself a genius at confounding the consequences of these gaps in everything he had done in the past; truly the triumph of the will. Why should attacking Britain, poor, broken-backed Britain, be any different? In this instance, Hitler found himself up against an opponent capable of making that gap pay.

It didn't help the German cause that they were relying on over-confident intelligence, that was incapable of ever getting a true grasp of just how many British fighters were being built, and so they never did acquire an accurate indication of what Fighter Command's operational strength actually was. Their informants were making the familiar mistake of simply subtracting believed RAF losses from a static figure, their best estimate of fighter numbers. That figure was too low to begin with, and was never corrected to incorporate the many hundreds of new planes coming out of the factories to replace those destroyed. The Germans fatally miscalculated British fighter production, usually by as much as 50 per cent. A report in July by Oberst Beppo Schmid, who ran the 5th Abteilung intelligence-gathering operation, for example, claimed that the British aircraft industry was producing around 250 front-line fighters a month. The true figure in July was actually 496. It was one of a number of miscalculations arising from inaccurate intelligence, and it was a crucial one. It would only be in the middle of September that the German command would fully realise the shortfall in their achievement deriving from the RAF's replacement rate.

> *'He was being interviewed, and they had asked what he thought was the turning point of the war, was it Stalingrad or Kiev, or something like that. Oh no, he said it was the Battle of Britain. And they said, "Well, that's rather an odd statement to come from an Army officer." He said, "Ah, that was the first time we realised we could be beaten, and we were beaten, and we didn't like it."'*
>
> Christopher Foxley-Norris

Nor did the Germans recognise just how effective the repair services were, the speed and efficiency with which damaged fighters were being salvaged and repaired, or, if too badly mauled, then stripped of components for use in new fighters. Not only did this systematic miscalculation depress the German aircrews, who were repeatedly told that the RAF was down to its last fifty fighters, and would wryly comment, day in, day out, that here come those last fifty – again. It made a complete nonsense of the larger strategic aims. To invade or not to invade? Nobody ever quite knew; the Germans were racked by uncertainties just as historians have been ever since. Strategy was directed by Hitler, as commander-in-chief, working with Generals Keitel and Jodl as well as the heads of the three services. Jodl, in particular, had various ideas about what attacking Britain might involve, what kind of targets, but no thought-out battle plan. The high command left the door open for the invasion option, without ever absolutely committing to it. It became one of those eventualities the Germans prepared for, up to a point, without ever really nailing the details. Finally, even Hitler could tell Goering was spouting hot air, and quietly shelved invasion plans so he could carry on with the invasion he really cared about, that of the Soviet Union.

That air power was itself still relatively new and untested didn't make defining the Luftwaffe's strategic aims any easier. Nobody had ever subjugated a whole nation with nothing but aircraft before. Destroyed towns, yes, but not whole countries. The string of European conquests in the earlier part of 1940 had been achieved with Blitzkrieg, which combined air power with armies on the ground. In taking on Britain, the Luftwaffe had been left for the first time on its own, with no tanks to back up the lightning strikes. The most obvious casualty of this was the Junkers 87 'Stuka' dive-bomber, which had been the star of Blitzkrieg, complete with its deafening siren, the first indication of the approaching army. In the summer of 1940, though, the Stuka faced a determined and modern fighter defence for the first time, and it failed the challenge of being the main attack rather than just announcing it. It was easy prey for Spitfires and Hurricanes if it got separated from its fighter escorts and was quickly withdrawn.

Kesselring, and to a lesser extent Sperrle, did the best they could to work out a strategy to suit this new moated enemy. Kesselring in particular got as close as anyone to devising what might have been an irresistible combination of tactics – but, at key moments, priorities would shift. First it was coastal convoys, then radar stations, then the airfields, and finally just London and other large cities. Later armchair analysts can now point to what the result might have been had the Germans concentrated harder and longer on, say, fighter bases, or, more crucially, the operations rooms and the radar masts. Given how close to breaking point Fighter Command was, they may well be right; a more sustained attack on the infrastructure of Fighter Command might have dramatically reversed the fortunes of the two sides. The Luftwaffe didn't concentrate on any of the strategies for long enough, though, and so they never found out for themselves.

That confusion started at the top and worked its way throughout the Luftwaffe. Both Goering and Hitler still hoped they could remove Britain from their Continental war with some kind of diplomacy, leaving it high and dry to be dealt with later. There was the fact, too, that the sheer velocity of their conquest of France had caught even the Germans unprepared for what lay next. But the Luftwaffe was facing graver disadvantages than these.

For one thing, so intoxicating is the story of Britain's race against time, the drama of Dowding's brilliant exploitation of apparent German hesitation, that it is easy to forget that the Luftwaffe also faced an uphill struggle to prepare itself for war. It, too, had been using every last minute building up its numbers of both planes and pilots. It is also easy to overlook the fact that the invasion of France hadn't been achieved without cost, that the Luftwaffe had prevailed but had lost hundreds of planes and precious crews: 1428 aircraft destroyed, and a further 488 damaged, as well as many pilots killed. The RAF had only lost 959 aircraft. The overrunning of Poland, Norway, and the other European countries had also, while being quick and decisive, had an impact on the Luftwaffe's strength. It's hard to believe, but Goering's great Luftwaffe was down by a quarter of its strength before the Battle of Britain even began. No wonder they weren't in an overwhelming hurry to start flying over the English Channel.

When the battle did start, the confusions, and the lack of proper intelligence, continued to hamper the German effort. Poor intelligence lured Luftflotte 5 to launch attacks on the North from Scandinavia, expecting little resistance; they were wrong, and were mauled, effectively meaning Luftflotte 5 never again played a role in the Battle of Britain. The German command also completely overestimated the effectiveness of bombing, both in terms of the debilitating effect that damage would have on the British war effort, and in terms of the impact on public morale. They underestimated the importance of the radar system, taking a long time to wake up to its power, not because they were blind to the technology but because for them it had been something to use at sea, not in the air. They did try to disrupt it, by attacking the vulnerable masts, but not as resolutely as they might. Kesselring, at least, did learn to adapt his tactics to take radar into account, by endlessly varying his attacking formations, and by trying whenever possible to fool the radar into prematurely committing planes to raids that would prove to be feints. Later, when it was acknowledged how important radar was, they made a number of errors about the actual infrastructure, thinking them impossible to disable (they weren't), and invested little effort in the technology of jamming.

> *'Our bomber formations were flying too spread out, contravening their instructions, they were supposed to fly in close proximity. But this is obvious: if you want to bring together a lot of planes – and there were thousands of them then – at a specific point, you have to gather there, you use fuel, the whole thing pulls apart.'*
>
> Hans-Ekkehard Bob

However, the Luftwaffe's failings went beyond underestimating British capabilities. Like the British, the Germans would discover that not all their aircraft were up to the job, and even of those that were, they weren't always allowed to use the most advantageous tactics. It wasn't just the Stuka that found itself outmatched. Before the war, it hadn't been the Bf 109 that had put most fear in the hearts of RAF observers, but its bigger brother, the twin-engined Bf 110, or 'Zerstøerer' (Destroyer), capable of carrying bombs and matching a single-engined fighter's performance. In the end, while the Bf 110 did excel as an attack bomber (mounting a series of utterly devastating low-level raids, particularly against radar stations), the role it was mostly given, fighter escort, found it wanting. The Bf 110 was ultimately too slow and clumsy, and from the very earliest days of the battle would resort to the tactic of simply flying in circles, each plane guarding the one behind it. Of course, the RAF had problems with some of its aircraft, too, the Fairey Battle and the Blenheim proving in 1940 to be obsolete to the point of being death-traps for their pilots. At this level of performance, second best was

An iconic Battle of Britain image: a squadron relaxes on the grass in front of a Spitfire

simply nowhere near good enough. The Fairey Battle and Blenheim were never supposed to be the linchpins of the RAF, though; it was always going to be the Spitfires and Hurricanes that really took on the attack. The Stuka and Bf 110, had, on the other hand, been expected to be decisive weapons for the 'Eagle' offensive. The fearsome Bf 109, which undoubtedly in the right hands was utterly the Spitfire's equal, was in turn fighting the enormous disadvantage of its limited fuel capacity, restricting its time in combat to minutes only. That was only made worse by Goering's command that they abandon their high-altitude free chase (for which the Bf 109 was unmatched) and replace it with flying alongside the bombers, hobbling back and forth in their hopeless task, speed and altitude forfeited to offer comfort to the beleaguered bombers.

Hans-Ekkehard Bob points out the futility of Goering's policy.

'Our bomber formations were flying too spread out, contravening their instructions, they were supposed to fly in close proximity. But this is obvious: if you want to bring together a lot of planes – and there were thousands of them then – at a specific point, you have to gather there, you use fuel, the whole thing pulls apart. And then they were headed West, towards England, meaning the bomber formations were spread out so far that we were unable to protect them. Goering ordered us to adapt to the bombers' speed and we were supposed to fly alongside them. This meant throwing away the fighters' advantage. The whole point of a fighter's advantage is the fact that it's fast. And now we were ordered to give up our speed and to fly alongside the bombers. In doing so we were totally inferior. In this situation, when the English arrived and were flying towards us from high altitudes and at great speed, we didn't have the slightest chance. This meant that we incurred heavy losses.'

The Luftwaffe's bombers, too, were, finally, too small, too vulnerable, to deliver the much-promised Armageddon over southern England. The late 1930s had seen Goering playing a numbers game, abandoning development of the big four-engined bomber in favour of smaller, two-engined Heinkels and Dorniers. That helped swell the numbers being produced, but at the cost of their destructive potential. As the Allies were to learn later, the sorry truth was that crude urban bombing was the preserve of the four-engined heavies, and the Germans didn't have any. The Germans, too, had been cavalier about other aspects of aerial technology that the British had embraced, radio being an obvious example. It didn't help that bombers and fighters couldn't talk to one another – they used different frequencies – which made coordinating their formations all but impossible. Its adoption by fighters was achieved too little, too late, with many Luftwaffe pilots still happy to communicate as they had done over Spain, by hand gestures and dipping wings. There was a point to this: radios were heavy, they took up valuable space in an already cramped cockpit and they were notoriously unreliable. But the British used them to great effect, and the Luftwaffe would be left to follow suit.

When attacking Britain, the Luftwaffe had started with the strategy of choosing what they hoped were the most crucial targets, the airfields and radar stations of Fighter Command. Motivated not just by (an all too brief) reluctance to bomb civilian targets, but by the intention of crippling Fighter Command, it would work only if they succeeded in identifying what those targets actually were. The larger airfields were easy enough, but it was the second-string facilities that caused greater confusion. All too often, valuable planes and aircrew would be lost attacking targets of little strategic significance. In the era of grass airfields, and plane numbers rarely rising above tens, it was all too easy to confuse low-grade airfields with those of Fighter Command. There was also the question of just how you attack an airfield anyway. In France, and later in the Soviet Union, there had been rows of assembled aircraft all lined up waiting to be hosed by attacking gunfire, but in Britain advance radar warning was usually adequate to ensure the bulk of operational planes were in the air by the time of the attack. That left a number of airfield buildings, ranging from hangars to the vital operations rooms and, of course, the runways. But short of destroying those operations rooms, or the buried telephone lines they relied upon, the damage done – though spectacular – was rarely permanent. Grass runways could be repaired, hangars replaced. Among modern

> '*The whole point of a fighter's advantage is the fact that it's fast. And now we were ordered to give up our speed and to fly alongside the bombers. In doing so we were totally inferior … when the English arrived and were flying towards us from high altitudes and at great speed, we didn't have the slightest chance. This meant that we incurred heavy losses.*'
>
> Hans-Ekkehard Bob

air forces, the job of destroying airfields remains one of the hardest to achieve, calling on a range of very specific, very destructive ordnance. In 1940, it was hard to see what you could do except dig enormous divots. Time after time, airfields appeared to have suffered large-scale destruction only to be in working order again by the next day.

For Keith Park, of course, whose airfields they were, things had seemed disastrous, but Dowding was less concerned.

'I agree with the Air Officer Commanding 11 Group [Park] that the damage done by air attack to aerodromes has been serious, and that it was beginning at one time to affect materially the efficiency of our fighter operations. Nevertheless, I must point out …The thirteen aerodromes in the Group underwent a total of over forty attacks in three weeks, but Manston and Lympne were the only two that were unfit for day flying for more than a few hours. That although the scale of the attack certainly exceeded our capacity of the works organisation existing at the outset, this was rapidly strengthened, and I do not wish to express any dissatisfaction with the measures taken to effect this improvement.'

What the Luftwaffe was learning – just as the Royal Navy Harriers would forty years later in the Falklands conflict, and the RAF a decade after that in the Gulf War – was that airfields are just about impossible to destroy from the air. Although the shift away from Fighter Command towards the civilian population of London struck many as the Luftwaffe's most grievous strategic error, allowing Fighter Command respite at a point of near collapse, it's far from clear that this was true. What it demonstrated to Hitler was that neither of his main methods of subjugating Britain would work. Britain was not going to be coerced out of the war; and so invasion – even the reckless Hitler realised – was lunacy incarnate. The airfields hadn't been destroyed. Neither had the RAF, whose fighters had simply not been knocked out of the sky in the numbers necessary – in the way that had happened in Poland, and would later happen in the USSR. And as devastating as the Blitz had been in its first two months, it, too, had failed to deliver the promised capitulation. The bombing of British cities continued until May 1941, but the Luftwaffe was forced to retreat into the night, and the hope that civilian bombing on its own might take Britain out of the war had disappeared.

So what had those pilots actually achieved? At one level it looked simply that their greatest feat had been to survive. With survival had come the first major setback the Germans had yet experienced, and with that, even the slimmest possibility that the British might yet have an active role in this war. The Battle of Britain goes further than this, though. It wasn't just that the Luftwaffe lost – by any objective criteria it was a campaign that the RAF won – it's that, in the end, it was a British 'win'. The nature of the victory is one worth pondering. Not the traditional story of indomitable English amateurism taking on the grim might of the German war machine – but precisely the opposite.

RAF success started with Hugh Dowding. Unlike Goering, he had a clear and definite plan, from which all his strategic and later tactical decisions would arise. And he stuck to it. In the end it proved to be an extraordinarily good plan. Before the war, he had even drafted for the

Air Ministry a forecast of what a major air attack would look like, and in most of its details it proved remarkably prescient, evidence of a keen intelligence actively engaged with the reality of defending Britain from air attack.

Dowding had the technology, too, with which to ensure Fighter Command was up to the task. He had been instrumental in the specifications from which both the Spitfire and the Hurricane had emerged. They in turn had been conceived, designed, built and then mass-produced thanks to the brilliant interventions of other key figures, particularly Reginald Mitchell and his team at Supermarine, and Sydney Camm and his team at Hawker. Both planes leapt into the sky powered by one of the great engines in air history, Rolls-Royce's Merlin. It may have lacked some of the Bf 109's refinement, but its contribution to Fighter Command success is undeniable. It was Ralph Sorley who had ensured the new powerful fighter had the minimum armaments required for the dirty work of shooting down Luftwaffe planes, the eight machine guns that had provoked such scepticism when first mooted. And Dowding had the eyes and ears of RDF, or radar, thanks not just to the technical prowess of Robert Watson-Watt, but his and his team's ability to translate the phenomenon of radio waves into a fully operational early warning system.

'The thirteen aerodromes in the Group underwent a total of over forty attacks in three weeks, but Manston and Lympne were the only two that were unfit for day flying for more than a few hours.'

Hugh Dowding

Dowding was lucky in another way. Above him was Prime Minister Winston Churchill, whose faith in Fighter Command gave him the courage to lead his call for national defiance of the Nazi threat. The Battle of Britain belonged to Churchill as surely as the stagnant nightmare of Operation Barbarossa, the Wehrmacht's great Russian offensive that would be launched in 1941, would belong to Hitler. Below Dowding were his Group Commanders, of whom surely the most significant was Keith Park. It was Park who grasped the organisation Dowding had helped create, and turned it into a battle-winning weapon. It was Park who for five solid months steered the British tactics, day by day, hour by hour. But more than that, it was Park who never lost touch with the realities of his pilots' lives, who communicated with them, and understood them in a way that is always the hallmark of the greatest commanders, certainly in a way that Dowding never could. The figure in his white flying suit, emerging from his personal Hurricane, named 'OK 1', on his many and regular visits to his front-line airfields, remains one of the most vivid and inspiring of the Battle of Britain.

Dowding and Park's plan worked. So, too, did the infrastructure it had required. But it was in the air, where, as the Americans say, metal meets flesh, that all this would have counted for naught if the pilots hadn't been able to take on the Luftwaffe. They did it with flying skill, those lucky enough to have had sufficient training to have gained it. And with courage – those with enough resolve to overcome every self-preserving instinct screaming at them to get the hell away. Not everyone could manage this, which is hardly surprising. Few of us could do it now. But enough could, despite the extraordinarily high chances that they would be killed. The stories of the young and inexperienced taking off having had their low chances explicitly spelled out to them, only to fall at the first hurdle, picked off by hardened Luftwaffe veterans, are impossibly moving to read.

None of the strategic foresight and planning would have made any difference if the men at the sharp end of all of this hadn't themselves been so good. Finally, any evaluation of the Battle of Britain has to face up to those three thousand men who comprised the pilot body of Fighter Command, behind whom stood the rest of the RAF and its associated forces. Churchill was in no doubt of the nature of their achievement, neither was the nation – indeed, the whole of the free world. For the Germans at this point, it probably hadn't quite sunk in. At the start of 1941, after all, they had few reasons for pessimism. At best, Britain had won itself a reprieve, a stay of execution, but this wouldn't, surely, last for ever. It's only from the perspective of 1945 that the significance of the Battle of Britain truly registers, the precondition for virtually everything that happened later.

All those pilots who flew, overcame their fear, engaged the enemy formations, against such apparent odds, did everything Churchill and Dowding had expected of them. They had turned numerical and psychological disadvantage into a resounding result. They did it because enough of them learned to shoot, and to shoot close enough to bring the Luftwaffe planes down. From the early days of four hundred-yard 'Hail Marys' – pressing the trigger and simply spraying the sky in the hope of a hit – all the way to hundred-yard attacks, head-on attacks and all the other grim tactics of aerial warfare in the era of the metal monoplane. Again, it wasn't a universal skill: the great majority of Battle of Britain pilots either shot down nothing or little more than one or two 'probables'. It didn't matter, because their job was to provide the cover required by that tiny minority who did have what it took, the 5 per cent of pilots who in an air war account for nearly half the 'kills' on the scorecard. That 5 per cent of Fighter Command that Britain did have – pilots like 'Sailor' Malan and Bob Stanford Tuck, as well as those like Bob Doe and Peter Brothers whose testimony features in this book – proved themselves among the most outstanding air combat pilots of any air force. They led, organised, and executed their combat tactics with an unnerving mix of cold-blooded attention to detail and hot-blooded instinct, an ability to fly and fight in a way that can never be taught. Their successes radiated through their squadrons and out into Fighter Command, proof that it was possible, that resistance wasn't futile. The Luftwaffe learnt it, too. The RAF was no pushover; even when, as was inevitable, they inflicted their own losses, and still the Spitfires and Hurricanes rose to meet them.

It is in the nature of air warfare that the point of it is to shoot down aircraft. It's strange that a battle whose hallmarks are blurred confusion and a riot of conflicting events all taking place in the blink of an eye, whose central experience was so often the nightmare of mutilation and death, should in the end yield something so clinical and precise as a scorecard. But the Battle of Britain did just that and, as we have seen, it's a scorecard that shows the RAF to have trumped their opposition.

In essence, Britain won the Battle of Britain because Fighter Command had enough pilots who learned how to fly not just planes, but two of the world's finest fighters, the Hawker Hurricane and the Supermarine Spitfire. They then translated those skills, the twists,

Hawker Hurricanes as seen from the cockpit of a Fairey Battle

turns, dives, the manipulation of hands and eyes, the intuitive grasp of the plane's outer limits, into a weapon capable of taking everything that one of the world's most threatening powers could throw at it, and prevailing when, all around them, everything else had capitulated. The Hurricanes and Spitfires of Fighter Command succeeded where the armed forces of much of Europe had failed – they held back the Nazi tide. It was a journey that had started on the grassy fields of pre-war runways, not just in Britain but across Europe, and across the Commonwealth. A journey that picked up momentum through the gruelling stresses of training and endless evaluation, and which culminated in the skies over southern England.

All of these reasons do not add up, however, to saying that the Luftwaffe were fighting an unwinnable and futile battle. Far from it. It is still all too clear what the result of destroying Fighter Command would have been – the removal of Britain from the war, either by invasion or, more likely, by some kind of time-winning armistice. It didn't come to that because, in the end, the Germans didn't have a sure enough blueprint of what to use their Luftwaffe for;

their errors were strategic. So, while the Luftwaffe never came near in one sense because the damage they inflicted never accumulated into something significant, had the tactical mistakes been rectified it really could have been a different matter.

The German pilots didn't lack courage or conviction; they were just as determined as their British counterparts. Perhaps they lacked the utter iron resolve of those defending their own homeland (and would discover the difference themselves, later on in the war). It was an observation frequently made that at the crucial moment, where an RAF fighter would have carried on regardless, a Bf 109 pilot would break for home, to fight another day. Bob Doe certainly believes that the inherently defensive nature of the RAF's job was a significant factor: 'We won because we were fighting on home soil and that is quite an advantage. And we had no intention of letting them come in. We had something to fight for. They probably didn't have anything to fight for. But we did. We were fighting for our homes. And that's a telling point.'

The German pilots did believe, though, that they had something to fight for. There was no doubt that in their bomber and fighter pilots, the Luftwaffe had a force utterly committed to the job demanded of them. Their morale took a beating as the Battle of Britain went from days, to weeks, to months, but it never collapsed. Hans-Ekkehard Bob is clear that the Luftwaffe pilots believed in what they were fighting for as much as their RAF counterparts.

> *'We were driven by the idea of defending Germany, of doing what we could for Germany, so we were clearly motivated. We thought that we had somehow to rectify a situation in which we were the ones under attack.'*
>
> Hans-Ekkehard Bob

'Basically you had a very different attitude then to the one that people have now. We were driven by the idea of defending Germany, of doing what we could for Germany, so we were clearly motivated. We thought that we had somehow to rectify a situation in which we were the ones under attack. Because according to the information we had received, the Poles in the Polish Corridor, where a lot of Germans still lived, were harassing the Germans, and we had to fight against this. So we were motivated, we fought, we did what we could. It is difficult to understand now, because people simply cannot reconstruct or understand what it was like then.'

Bob argues that the motivation of young Germans to redress grievances they felt had been inflicted on their homeland was strong.

'We did not fight for Hitler, nor for anyone else, we fought for Germany. As young men, we felt that, because of the circumstances after the First World War, with the so-called Versailles diktat so hampered by the Allies, we were simply unable to put up with this. We Germans felt ourselves to be hugely disadvantaged, after the conditions of the Versailles diktat were implemented here, there was famine, there was unemployment, we had 30 per cent unemployment, and you had unemployed people receiving five Reichsmarks a week, an unemployed person with a family, five Reichsmarks a week! We simply could not put up with a situation of this kind any longer. And it was this that gave rise to Hitler, and it was Hitler who said: "We won't stand for this any more!" Had it been someone else, he would have acted likewise, we simply could not put up with it any more.'

Ernie Wedding, another Luftwaffe veteran, also believes that the outcome of the Battle of Britain is nothing to do with any kind of pilot superiority.

'The German fighter pilots were just as good as the British pilots. They were not any better or any worse. And they had the same attitude as British fighter pilots, to knock the enemy out of the sky and to protect their own formations. And I think, as has shown later on with exchange pilots through NATO, actually I've heard that RAF pilots said they'd rather fly with German pilots than with any other nations.'

Nor was the superiority of the British planes to explain the result. There is no question of the fate that would have befallen Britain had fighters as good as the Hurricane, and certainly the Spitfire, not been available in 1940. What they gave was parity in the sky – both in numbers and in quality. But while they both offered state-of-the-art performance (or a good approximation to it in the case of the Hurricane), it was perfectly clear that opposing advantages merely cancelled each other out. In the end, what Camm and Mitchell guaranteed the RAF was that the outcome would hinge not on technological obsolescence, but on what air combat had always hinged on: the skills of the pilot, and the tactical advantages of height and position he had created for himself. Given the speed of technological development in both Britain and in Germany, that was achievement enough; it would have been simply inconceivable for either side to produce a plane that on its own could have proved decisive.

> *'As young men, we felt that, because of the circumstances after the First World War, with the so-called Versailles diktat so hampered by the Allies, we were simply unable to put up with this.'*
>
> Hans-Ekkehard Bob

The RAF did, admittedly, have the advantage of being able to get its pilots back in the air in remarkable time, often driven by the pilot's own resolve to carry on the fight as quickly as possible. Every parachuting British pilot would, unless injured, be flying again soon, sometimes the very same day. Every parachuting German, on the other hand, was on a one-way ticket to a prisoner of war camp. If you take the casualty statistics of the Battle of Britain, it is quickly and chasteningly obvious how soon Fighter Command would have folded up had those pilots who were shot down not been able to get back up into the air. Read the memoirs of virtually any fighter pilots, and you're struck by just how often, and how inevitably, they were forced to bale out. It was more than an occupational hazard – it was an occupational certainty. Some did it more than once. If each of those occasions had meant the permanent removal of that man from the battle, there is no doubt the outcome would have been completely different.

To describe the RAF's victory as decisive is not to say that it was inevitable, or in any sense to undermine their sense of achievement. The RAF's superiority over the Luftwaffe in 1940 came not from an inherent numerical advantage, but from the tactical ways in which the two air forces were used. A couple of months could have made an enormous difference for Fighter Command. The RAF had needed every last second of time given it by the hesitating Luftwaffe to build its numbers up to something close to the critical mass required. Had the

Peter Brothers served with No 32 and No 257 Squadrons and was awarded the DFC on 13 September 1940

assault begun in May rather than July, the RAF wouldn't have been ready. The Luftwaffe may well not have had the great strategic overall plan they needed, but they weren't stupid. They knew the RAF was the key to Britain's defence, and they went after it with everything they had. They even took Dowding's brilliantly prepared defensive force to the very limits of their breaking point, and they did it by putting numbers and lives where their mouths were. They attacked the RAF every way they knew how, attacking its planes, its airfields, wearing it down not just in one-to-one fighter combat, but by sheer weight of numbers, by day and by night. The tactics may have been half-baked, but the execution wasn't. Nothing short of a reply utterly commensurate in rigour, resolve, cool-headed organisation and unbreakable courage in the air would have sufficed. A weakness in any one of these would have been enough; the dam would have been breached, and one way or another, Britain, too, would have slipped into the darkness – a quisling state or a fully Nazi one would have made no difference.

In 1940, though, everything came together for the RAF. This was victory for Britain. Victory won by pilots such as Peter Brothers.

'Had we lost, been invaded, forgetting the problems the population would have had, one way or another, we would have been in a horrible situation, Germany controlling the whole of Europe, no stepping stones for help from America. Werner von Braun, whom I met in Germany at the end of the war, designed the V-1 and V-2 rockets and, after the war, joined the Americans, and he was the chap who put a man on the Moon. Now, can you imagine, after the war, when we'd lost, von Braun would have still been with the Germans, designing long-range rockets to hit New York. And I have no doubt – I think what the Germans are likely to have done, was to say to the Japanese, "Well, you keep the West Coast busy, and we will move into the Argentine, where we have so many friends, and assemble our forces and move up, not fighting our way through Brazil or anything, they'll no doubt greet us as friends, and straight up – up into America." And I think the Americans would have had a very tough time fending off the Japanese and the Germans, and with the whole of Europe's munitions behind them, and so on. So, to me, that battle was the important point, and it was the turning point of the war. People talk about El Alamein as being the great land victory, well, it was, I don't denigrate it in any way, but there wouldn't have been an El Alamein if we'd lost the Battle of Britain. And it's as simple as that. So it really ranks with the Armada and whatever you like, Agincourt and so on, the victories of the few against the many.'

What's clear is not only that the RAF won, but that they won by some margin. At a terrible cost, certainly, but the outcome was conclusive, as Ernie Wedding, in contrast to his comrade Hans-Ekkehard Bob, concedes.

'The Battle of Britain, from our side it was a complete waste of time. Because they fell into the trap that Churchill set. For the RAF it was a victory. It was a complete loss to the German Air Force, it was a victory for the RAF. It was the last onslaught on the 15 September where we lost a hell of a lot of aircraft. The claims made where later on they had to be rectified, they were not quite as heavy as the RAF made out, but this happens all the time on both sides. But I think it was a feather in the cap to the RAF and especially to the high command of the RAF, to Dowding and to Churchill to some extent because they didn't lose their nerve. See, whereas our high command changed their tactics, which were completely wrong. They should have stuck to the tactics they started with and then the picture would have looked different. But that is my impression of the Battle of Britain.'

More than sixty years after that remarkable summer of 1940, the events still resonate in the memories of those who took part in them. For some, like Geoff Wellum, the experience seems to lack a reality.

'We'd never known of another air battle like it. Quite honestly. That was sustained. It seems unreal. And until the sixtieth anniversary year, I put it all behind me, fairly successfully. I didn't like to talk about it. But it's drawn out in the last three or four years, I suppose. And things that I thought were in the little brain cell I've got at the back came out and yes, I started to dream again and see it again and I can see it now. I can see a hundred and fifty plus. I can see a Bf 109 that got on my tail one day. I got away from him,

> '*There wouldn't have been an El Alamein if we'd lost the Battle of Britain. And it's as simple as that. So it really ranks with the Armada and whatever you like, Agincourt and so on, the victories of the few against the many.*'
>
> Peter Brothers

because I saw him just in time. But he was so close I could see the paint that peeled off the leading edge of his wing. So he must have been within twenty or thirty yards of me. Yeah, I can remember that. You cannot go through an experience as a nineteen-year-old, which I was, and not have a tremendous impression on you for the rest of your life. But it seems unreal.'

When Wellum went back to Duxford and saw a Spitfire again, it brought back a lot of memories.

'Full of ghosts. Friendly ghosts. But full of ghosts, those aeroplanes were. I got quite emotional, actually. I was supposed to be working in a tent, but I hear the Merlin start up and I'm going to have a look at this. And they plummeted off, you know, just like a scramble really. I was back, sixty years ago. Yeah. Plummeting off into the … full of my ghosts, my old mates.'

For Ernie Wedding, the fact that he took part in the Battle is also hard to accept as real.

'You saw the bomber formation, you saw the fighters that were accompanying you. You saw the black and the white clouds coming up, anti-aircraft fire and you saw the Spitfires and Hurricanes trying to knock you out of the sky. Then when you dropped your bombs you saw the smoke coming up, people running around … turning over, set on fire. It was just, how should I say, like a B-movie, it seemed to be unreal. It was real all right because we participated in it, so I myself, I thought – not first but later on – what a waste of lives, money and time. Just go out there and drop bombs on a factory, killing people, for what? I didn't have a grudge against the people. They hadn't done anything to me. But I was sent out to do something to them that they didn't like. Later on, as I came here to England and I talked to a lot of ex-servicemen, they had the same opinion what I had. Why? It's just because politicians, they're starting the war, we've got to fight it. They're finishing the war and then they make even a bigger mess of it than it was before. And each war hasn't achieved anything except brought more misery to people and the revenge tactic comes into it. In a war … old men sending young men to die, and I hope that we never have another war like we had from '39 to '45. But the world is always spoiling for it. Who has the bigger stick?'

> 'In a war… old men sending young men to die, and I hope that we never have another war like we had from '39 to '45. But the world is always spoiling for it. Who has the bigger stick?'
>
> Ernie Wedding

For some of the pilots, the late joiners, the last-minute replacements, the Battle of Britain could be measured in hours. Sadly, for many, too, it was a battle that ended in hours. For the 2373 pilots who survived the Battle of Britain, though, there were still nearly 5 years of the Second World War to fight. Another 791 would lose their lives during those years. There was little time to stand back and reflect on what had happened in 1940. For men like Nigel Rose, the Battle of Britain was only one part of their war.

'I can't remember anybody saying, on the squadron, "Now, this is going to be called the Battle of Britain and it's a sort of nodal point in the war", or any other sort of thinking, "Well, this is something special", at all, it just seemed to be the job in hand that we were doing, along with the Navy trying to bring the convoys across the Atlantic, and the Army, well, they'd just got out of Dunkirk but they were preparing to go back and do their stuff. But, it's curious, I think we were just concerned with doing what we were supposed to do, as much as possible. And some did it better than others.'

For John Sykes, the end of the Battle of Britain meant that it was time to leave the RAF and return to the Navy.

'We were made sort of redundant after about two or three months, I think it was. I think we were retired out of the Air Force, they just said we weren't any longer required. It struck me, you know, going home reporting to a naval establishment, funny they should just kick us out like that. I can't remember anybody saying nice to see you, thank you very much for coming or anything like that. It was just we went home, we'd done what we were meant to do and that was it. After rejoining the Navy, we got formed up and we went flying. I think I went down to Southampton where Cunnliffe Owens had a Spitfire factory, and we were flying Fulmars. I formed up No 807 Squadron at a place called Worthy Down, just north of Southampton. It never seriously occurred to me until much later on in life that we had ever done anything terribly important. There was nothing much going on, no funny posters and no flag waving or anything like that.'

For the Spitfire, too, there was the rest of the war to fight. Supermarine continued to develop the plane, coming up with twenty new models of Spitfire beyond the two that had been used in the Battle of Britain. The Mark V was put in service in February 1941, designed with improved high-altitude performance functions in case the RAF had to refight the Battle of Britain. Later, the Mark V would be fitted with a carburettor air intake filter system to allow it to go into action in the dusty conditions of Egypt, Libya and Malta. The Mark VIII was produced from November 1942 and was used in large numbers in the Mediterranean and Far Eastern theatres of war. The Mark IX was urgently brought into service in August 1942 as the Luftwaffe launched the Focke-Wulf 190 on a new bombing offensive against Britain. The Mark XIV became operational by June 1944 for the next German bombing offensive on London using flying bombers. While none of these Spitfires would be part of an iconic piece of history in the way that the Marks I and II were, they were part of the Spitfire's ongoing contribution to Britain's war effort.

The strain of having fought in the Battle of Britain had taken its toll on many of the pilots. George Unwin was lucky to suffer from only a minor irritation – if a significant one.

'When the war finished I was at central gunnery school, Squadron Commander up at Leckingfield, and of course we had a hell of a party, and then there was some kind of relief. Not disappointment, but we'd had enough, you know, you were rather glad it was over and you could go back to living a normal life and so on and so forth. And that's how I felt. I think most people did because, after all, nearly six years we'd been at it and the strain, which you didn't know, which affected me in one way. I got a tremendous itch round my beard. Wherever my beard grew, itch. No rash, nothing. I could hardly sleep with it and I went to every medical officer in every station I went to. I had every kind of coloured ointment, even black, to rub on it. None of it worked. And then they restarted the Auxiliary Air Force and I was given a prize plum job, No 608 Squadron, North Riding of Yorkshire, to restart up at Thornaby near Stockton. And in the process of enlisting people, ground crew and air crew, an old doctor came along and he said he used to be the doctor before the war when he was weekend flying, and could he join? I said yes, even though there was no vacancy, and he had full use of the mess and facilities.

'I was having a drink with him one evening and I kept scratching, and he said, "What's the matter with you, what do you keep doing that for?" I said, "I don't know but I've had it for two or three years now." And he said, "I've got a great friend of mine who's a dermatologist specialist and neurologist in Leeds, would you go and see him?" I said, "Yes, I'll do anything to get rid of this." He said, "Don't tell him who you are." So I went along, in civvies. This dear old fella sat me down, he said, "Give me your hand", and he just held my hand and we chatted about this – not about the war or anything, he just sat. Then he said, "You've had a rough time, haven't you?" I said, "No, no, I haven't had a rough time, I had a wonderful time." He said, "You've been flying all through the war." I said, "Yeah." "What on?" I told him. He said, "Nothing to worry about, your nerves are completely shot away and they're worn out. They'll recover. Don't ever put ointment on your face, it's not suitable for it." My local doctor would give me all kinds of ointment. But he was dead right, after about six, nine months it all went. But I didn't realise this. Well, this is the kind of effect it can have on you.'

Despite the undoubted strain, though, many veterans look back on their experiences of 1940 fondly, like flight mechanic Joe Roddis.

'My family, from the fact that I wasn't at home and by the tone of my letters, thought I was having the time of my life, and I was. I don't know what my mother thought. She probably didn't like the idea of having four sons all in the war. One in the Far East on aircraft carriers, another one on the big ships, *Prince of Wales* and *King George V*. Another one in the Air Force, and me. They used to make a hell of a fuss of you when you went on leave, it used to get embarrassing. The lads that you'd gone out with before joining the Air Force to the local dance hall or the pictures, or you'd started having the odd drink, unbeknown to your dad, and they'd got jobs that kept them out of the forces, they used to look at you a bit queer, but you didn't get on very well with them, you used to think, you know, if I'm there why aren't you? It was a bit silly, that. But all in all, going on leave was good. You met your family, you met your old friends, but the time to go back could never come quick enough for me. Because you were more at home. You were closer to the chaps that you were doing that with every day than you were with people that you saw once or twice a year.'

> '*They were the happiest days of my life. I'd do them all over again if I could and do the same thing.*'
>
> Joe Roddis

In fact, for Roddis, the end of his time with the RAF was something of an anticlimax.

'It seemed very mundane, very dull. I mean when I came out of the Air Force I was on a superb job and I didn't really want to come out but that was selfishness because my wife had brought up two kids and moved about and kept different homes and things, but I was getting all the fun and she was getting all the work. And when I came out initially I thought, oh, I didn't like this one bit, especially working at Royce's where nearly everybody there had had a job that kept them out the forces, they didn't know what you were talking about. When my daughter put an advert in the paper one day saying would anybody who knew my father, Joe Roddis on No 485 New Zealand Squadron, please contact me, somebody did and it was a new lease of life for me. I met blokes that I'd been with and served with right from the invasion long before that. I met pilots from New Zealand again and talked to them and shared memories. It was a whole new lease of life and I could introduce my wife to them all in this country and it changed our life quite a lot, to get back into the Air Force side of things again. I had a good life, I had a good time at Royce's, don't get me wrong, but the excitement had gone.'

Roddis was seventeen when he joined the RAF, and he stayed until he was forty-four.

'When I came out, I was a young bloke, but the spice had gone out of it really. It was all right going fishing and going to Donnington and watching Barry Sheen tear himself to bits and going to air displays, that was the best times and Farnborough, I used to love that. Or going to air displays and meeting people. Ah, but no, they were the happiest days of my life. I'd do them all over again if I could and do the same thing. I was happier as an airman first- and second-class flight mechanic on No 234 Squadron than ever I would have been if I'd have had stripes on me arm. I didn't want responsibility. I'd got enough with an aeroplane, I was happy. If I'd been promoted I wouldn't have had an aeroplane. I wouldn't have had that job I had looking after one aeroplane. I'd have just have been shuffling blokes about and telling them what to do and what not to do. That wasn't my way.'

The fighter pilots of the Battle of Britain are modest about what they achieved, talking about the events of the summer of 1940 as just doing the job they were given. Nigel Rose is typical in this respect: 'One certainly went in and had a stab and did one's best. I wouldn't say that I was particularly brilliant. I hope I frightened more people than frightened me and I hope I damaged some, too, and I might have shot down one or two. I claimed two and a half or something like that. I would like to feel I was brave enough, at any rate, to stick with it.'

Iain Hutchinson is also modest about what Fighter Command achieved in 1940, but he does have a real sense of pride looking back: 'I couldn't classify the battle as being horrible. It was intense, it was a great strain. But I felt really fortunate to be able to take part in it, because I realise how important it was. And I was really proud, if you like, to be able to be there and do something about it, instead of being on the sidelines. And I've felt the same way about it ever since.'

> *'If I was asked what was owed to the pilots who won the Battle of Britain, I would say all they've ever asked is to be remembered. That's all.'*
>
> Bob Doe

Bob Doe also looks back with pride: 'If I was asked what was owed to the pilots who won the Battle of Britain, I would say all they've ever asked is to be remembered. That's all. They don't want thanks, they just want you to remember that we won this battle. Not necessarily for you, it was for the country. And we're very proud that we did.'

By retracing the path taken by these young pilots all those years ago, we have remembered, and honoured, their extraordinary achievement. The mastery of the most sophisticated flying machines the world had ever seen. The danger they faced on a daily basis for four months. The relentless sorties, often from airbases under attack. Without the skill and courage of the RAF's pilots in the summer of 1940, we would all be living in a very, very different world.

Bibliography

The Battle of Britain, Air Ministry, 1941

The Burning Blue: A New History Of The Battle Of Britain, edited by Paul Addison and Jeremy A Crang, Pimlico, 2000

Fighter Boys: Saving Britain, Patrick Bishop, Harper Collins, 2003

The Dark Valley: A Panorama of the 1930s, Piers Brendon, Jonathan Cape, 2000

Winston Churchill: A Brief Life, Piers Brendon, Pimlico, 2001

Spitfire Summer by Malcolm Brown, Carlton Books, 2001

The Most Dangerous Enemy, Stephen Bungay, Aurum Press, 2000

Finest Hour, Tim Clayton and Phil Craig, Hodder and Stoughton, 1999

Fighter, Len Deighton, Grafton, 1987

Bob Doe: Fighter Pilot, Bob Doe, Spellmount, 1991

Billy Drake: Fighter Leader, Billy Drake and Christopher Shores, Grub Street, 2002

Spitfire Into Battle, W G G Duncan Smith, John Murray, 2002

Lighter Shade of Blue: Lighthearted Memoirs of an Air Marshall, Sir Christopher Foxley-Norris, I Allan, 1978

Sigh For A Merlin: Testing The Spitfire, Alex Henshaw, Air Data Publications, 1996

The Last Enemy, Richard Hillary, Pimlico, 1997

Harvest of Messerschmitts: The Chronicle of a Village at War, Dennis Knight, Wingham Press, 1990

Radar: A Wartime Miracle, Colin Latham and Anne Stobbs, Sutton, 1996

Gun Button to Fire, Tom Neil, William Kimber, 1987

The Battle of Britain: The Myth and the Reality, Richard Overy, WW Norton, 2001

Goering: The Iron Man, Richard Overy, Routledge, 1987

Why The Allies Won: Explaining Victory in World War II, Richard Overy, Pimlico, 1996

The Road to War, Richard Overy and Andrew Wheatcroft, Penguin, 2000

1940 – Myth and Reality, Clive Ponting, Hamish Hamilton, 1990

The Battle of Britain, Matthew Parker, Headline, 2000

The Spitfire Story, Alfred Price, Silverdale Books, 2002

Spitfire Mark I / II Aces 1939-41, Alfred Price, Osprey, 1996

Battle Of Britain Day, Alfred Price, Greenhill, 1990

The Hardest Day, Alfred Price, Cassell, 1998

Eminent Churchillians, Andrew Roberts, Phoenix, 1995

Stapme: The Biography of Squadron Leader Basil Gerald Stapleton, David Ross, Grub Street, 2002

Bader's Duxford Fighters: The Big Wing Controversy, Dilip Sarkar, Ramrod, 1997

Battle of Britain, Dilip Sarkar, Ramrod, 2001

Fighter Pilot, Dilip Sarkar, Ramrod, 2001

2nd TAF Spitfire: Story of Spitfire ML407, Hugh Smallwood, Solo Enterprises, 1995

The Battle of Britain, Richard Townshend Bickers, Salamander Books, 1997

Index

Credits

p18 © Hulton-Deutsch Collection/CORBIS; p23 courtesy of James Spence; p25 *War Weekly* material courtesy of Ronald Hulbert © Newnes Publishing; p27 courtesy of James Spence; p31 courtesy of The Imperial War Museum; p32 *War Weekly* material courtesy of Ronald Hulbert © Newnes Publishing; p44 courtesy of The Imperial War Museum; p49, 50, 53, 59 *War Weekly* material courtesy of Ronald Hulbert © Newnes Publishing; p67 *In Flight* material courtesy of Ronald Hulbert; p73, 75 courtesy of The Imperial War Museum; p78-9 German and Italian Aircraft material courtesy of Ronald Hulbert; p85, 90, 98-9, 101 courtesy of The Imperial War Museum; p104 German and Italian Aircraft material courtesy of Ronald Hulbert; p109, 112 courtesy of June Marriott; p115 *War Weekly* material courtesy of Ronald Hulbert © Newnes Publishing; p118 courtesy of June Marriott; p124 *War Weekly* material courtesy Ronald Hulbert © Newnes Publishing; all other images courtesy of Rdf Media.

The publishers would like to thank all those who lent material for use in this book. Efforts have been made to trace copyright holders. Should there be any omissions, the publishers will be pleased to give full credit in subsequent reprints and editions.

Acknowledgements

The most striking thing about reading this book, and watching the series it accompanies, is hearing from the veterans about the extraordinary events they were part of in 1940. Our thanks must go firstly to all those who contributed to the book and the series, recalling so vividly their part in the Battle of Britain. These include many of the surviving pilots: Cyril Bamberger, Peter Brothers, Tom Dalton-Morgan, Bob Doe, Billy Drake, Iain Hutchinson, Ludvik Martel, Tom Neil, Nigel Rose, Gerald Stapleton, John Sykes, George Unwin, Edward Wells, Geoff Wellum, Sir Archie Winskill and Allan Wright. We were also lucky to be able to talk to Sir Christopher Foxley-Norris, who sadly died in September 2003, and his wife, Lady Joan Foxley-Norris. Ernie French, John Milne, Fred Roberts and Joe Roddis gave fascinating accounts of their work in the ground crews, and Sir Edward Fennessy on the development of radar. Hans-Ekkehard Bob and Ernie Wedding put forward the valuable perspective of the Luftwaffe pilot.

While the recollections of the veterans are undoubtedly special in themselves, it was thanks to Carolyn Grace that we were able to put modern pilots into a Spitfire, recapturing what was so special about this aircraft. Anna Walker and the Tiger Club kindly set up the Tiger Moth training programme, while Brendan O'Brien and Peter Kynsey provided excellent pilot training in addition to Carolyn's. Christian Baker, Dave Mallon, John Sweet and Ben Westoby-Brooks all participated enthusiastically in the quest to recreate the sensation of flying Spitfires in the summer of 1940.

Behind the scenes, we are grateful to a wide variety of experts who gave an invaluable historical perspective on the events of the Battle of Britain. Stephen Bungay gave us a particularly extensive and enlightening interview, while Dr John Ackroyd, Piers Brendon, Dr Edgar Jones, Professor Richard Overy, Chris Shores and Chris Wren all made fascinating insights on specific aspects of the history. A large number of people at the RAF, Ministry of Defence, Imperial War Museum in London, the Imperial War Museum at Duxford and the RAF Museum at Hendon have provided logistical and factual help for the book and series, and we are grateful for the willingness of all concerned to make the project happen.

The book itself has only been possible thanks to Channel 4 Books at Macmillan. Emma Marriott and Annie Schafheitle have been supportive and encouraging editors, while our sub-editor, Christine King, made numerous insightful suggestions on the draft text, and often went beyond the call of duty to keep us to our schedule. Dan Newman worked incredibly quickly, and with much inspiration, to turn the text into such a striking book. We are very grateful to the many veterans who kindly lent us their photographs, as well as Jack Pritchard who took many of the photos of the modern-day reconstructions of a Spitfire flight.

The book itself wouldn't have been possible without the series, and so we are heavily indebted to Hamish Mykura and his colleagues at Channel 4 for backing this project from the outset. At RDF Media, Christopher Sykes and Nick Watts not only made a television series but found time to offer much support for the book. Diana Francis has given us considerable practical and moral help and encouragement throughout the writing process. Tamara Bodenham, Richard Higson, Antonia Bolingbroke-Kent, Tom Edwards, Joseph Maxwell and Hattie Pugh were all crucial to the series being made, and have, sometimes unwittingly, also contributed much to the book as well.